Planning without Facts

Planning without Facts

LESSONS IN RESOURCE ALLOCATION

FROM NIGERIA'S DEVELOPMENT

By

Wolfgang F. Stolper

*With an Input-Output Analysis
of the Nigerian Economy, 1959–60
By Nicholas G. Carter*

Harvard University Press
Cambridge, Massachusetts
1966

TO MY WIFE

Written under the auspices of the Center for International Affairs, Harvard University

Created in 1958, the Center for International Affairs fosters advanced study of basic world problems by scholars from various disciplines and senior officials from many countries. The research at the Center focuses on economic, political, and social development, the management of force in the modern world, and the evolving positions of Western Europe and the Communist bloc. The research programs are supervised by Professors Robert R. Bowie (Director of the Center), Hollis B. Chenery, Rupert Emerson, Samuel P. Huntington, Alex Inkeles, Henry A. Kissinger, Edward S. Mason, Thomas C. Schelling, and Raymond Vernon.

This volume is one of several resulting from a broad investigation—directed by Professor Mason and generously supported by the Ford Foundation—into the relative roles of business and government in the process of economic development.

Contents

Tables

TABLES FOR INPUT-OUTPUT APPENDIX

Figures

Foreword

By Chief S. O. Adebo

Ambassador and Permanent Representative of Nigeria at the United Nations and Commissioner-General for Economic Affairs

When Dr. Stolper asked me, a non-economist, to write a foreword to this book, I warned him that my effort was unlikely to be much use to either author or reader since there were sure to be passages in the book which would be beyond the comprehension of a layman. His reply was that he would regard his effort a failure if a person like myself, for reasons of incomprehensibility, failed to appreciate the arguments and conclusions that he was putting forward, for he was not writing a book for the expert alone but one that he hoped that both the expert and the intelligent layman would read and understand.

This hope has been given expression in Dr. Stolper's introduction to the book. I also think, after reading the final copy myself, that it is a reasonable hope. If I can gain a fair understanding at first reading, I am sure anybody can. I shall of course have to go through once again to be able to absorb all the salient points made in this valuable compilation, but that is because the book contains so much "meat" that a second and even a third reading would be justified; it is not because of any lack of clarity arising from the use of professional jargon.

And yet there is no lack of professional jargon in this book— enough I hope to satisfy the expert reader. There is the customary invocation of the great names, Keynes, Schumpeter, and the like, and the theories they propounded. The author is to be commended for following this tradition of his profession without compromising the readability of his book.

Dr. Stolper has chosen an intriguing and therefore attractive title, *Planning without Facts,* a not inappropriate choice since the contents of this book are largely the result of experience gained in helping to prepare a development programme for a country lacking the statistical and other basic information normally required for that exercise. But the author has been concerned to show, not only that one sometimes has to make do with little or no facts because they are not available, but also that some planners seem disposed to make use of material of dubious reliability "to give a gloss of learnedness to economic foolishness."

Other striking points made by Dr. Stolper include the following:

(a) A development programme should aim at maximising short-term growth rates; hence, projects which "pay off" in the immediate future are on the whole to be preferred to those which begin to do so only in a distant future.

(b) Most external economies that are truly relevant are quantifiable; those that are not do not deserve to be allowed to affect the issue as to whether a project is or is not worth embarking upon.

(c) "'Economic' or 'social' profitability, calculated so as to allow for interactions in the economy and for proper pricing, is the only operational criterion for determining the size and composition of an investment program."

(d) "Before redistribution can take place there must be something to be redistributed."

(e) The peasant farmer is not a fool; he will not adopt a so-called modern method of production in the absence of clear proof that it will pay, nor will he accept an incentive that is not convertible into "real goods."

(f) "In health, push as many resources as you can into preventive medicine."

(g) A developing country desperately short of trained teachers would be unwise to promote an elementary education programme postulated upon a teacher-student ratio that even wealthy countries find it impossible to maintain.

(h) Beware of facile arguments for the subsidising of projects.

(i) "It seems better to aim for minimum targets that can be fulfilled or surpassed than for maximum targets that cannot be met."

I have reproduced the points in rather arbitrary order, without any suggestion of relative importance. Indeed, I would myself regard all as equally valuable for the promotion of realism in economic planning.

There are one or two of the points made by Dr. Stolper (within and outside of those reproduced above) that I would not personally have put in the exact words that he used. For instance, it seems to me to be going too far to say that profitability honestly calculated is the *only* investment criterion. Indeed, the author, after suggesting that it was, proceeded, a sentence or two later, to point out that the payment of subsidies may be justifiable in certain circumstances. Political considerations of a legitimate kind can hardly, in certain cases, be ruled out, a point which is stressed by the author himself in a subsequent section of the book. It would therefore have been safer, if only to avoid misunderstanding arising from quotations out of context, to say that profitability honestly calculated is "a most important" investment criterion. One might add after "criterion," for greater effect, "and one that cannot be ignored or played down with impunity."

Subject to the above general reservation, so far as a person like myself is concerned, Dr. Stolper is preaching to the converted. Much of what he advises coincides with what some of us who have been official advisers to governments in developing countries have preached for years, but which perhaps we have not been able to put across with such clarity and force as he has done. He himself realises that some readers may feel that in regard to some of his positions he has unduly stressed the obvious. He has, in my view, successfully disposed of such a criticism by pointing out that some principles which seem obvious to some people are nevertheless so consistently played down, if not completely ignored, that they require to be strongly restated and emphasized —"one does not kill an ox with a surgeon's knife."

Dr. Stolper would not possess the reputation he does if he were a producer of volumes merely restating or emphasising acknowledged positions. *Planning without Facts* contains original thinking and provocative challenge to planning theories and practices which I am sure he himself would be only too glad to see commented upon by members of his profession and others concerned with the preparation and execution of development programmes for developing countries.

Naturally I am happy to note his statement that some at least of his criticisms of the Nigerian planning effort "are known to the Nigerian planners and they are undertaking the necessary steps to correct the situation."

Dr. Stolper has rendered the planning world a valuable service in producing *Planning without Facts*. I hope that all persons interested in the subject will pay him the compliment of reading the book. They will, I feel sure, find it an interesting and a rewarding experience.

June 1965

Author's Preface

The manuscript of this book was finished long before the military coups in Nigeria and Ghana, which, in Dr. Johnson's words, surprised but did not astonish me. As a result of the Nigerian coup of January 1966, I added two footnotes in Chapter II (notes 2 and 7) and rewrote one sentence on page 28. The upheaval induced no other changes, for this is not a book on politics, nor on the politics of development. Nor is it primarily about Nigeria. It is a book on the economics of development, with Nigeria providing a particularly interesting case in point. Of course, political problems have not been sidestepped where they were directly relevant to the economics under discussion, and the final chapter, which in retrospect turns out to be much more than a burst of rhetoric, touches briefly on the politics involved.

There remains the pleasant task of thanking at least some of the many people to whom I am indebted.

My interest in economic development started in 1946 when, with Dr. Chiang Hsieh, I wrote for the International Labour Organization a committee report on economic development in Southeast Asia, which appeared anonymously in New Delhi in 1947.[1] The next opportunity came when Professor Max Millikan invited me to join him and Arnold Rivkin in an African project at M.I.T. Although no publication resulted from this, it led to a continuing urge to go to Nigeria. When, in 1960, the Ford Foundation asked me to go under their auspices to Nigeria as Head of the Economic Planning Unit in the Federal Ministry of Economic Development in Lagos, I seized the opportunity.[2] The Department of

1. *Problems of Social Policy and Industrialization in South East Asia* (New Delhi: Committee Report of the Regional Member Conference of Asian Member States of the International Labour Organization, 1947).

2. Because of my past official position, it is unfortunately necessary to

Economics of the University of Michigan most generously gave
me the extended leave required for this adventure in my advanced education.

In Nigeria, I received excellent briefing and guidance from the
Permanent Secretaries in the Ministries of Economic Development and Finance. I should like to think that they reciprocate the
feelings of friendship and affection I have for them and that they
will accept this acknowledgment as an expression of my gratitude. It was my very good fortune to serve (in chronological
order) under three highly competent civil servants: Charles W.
Thompson, now Bursar of Birmingham University; E. G. Lewis,
now with the British High Commission in Karachi; and Godfrey
Lardner, now with the Economic Commission for Africa in Addis
Ababa. I am proud to think that they trusted me as a friend as
well as an economist. I know that my own effectiveness, such as
it was, was greatly enhanced by the very intimate personal and
working relationship that existed with all of them. I also feel a
debt of gratitude to my Minister, the Honorable Waziri Ibrahim,
Federal Minister of Economic Development, who willingly discussed with me not only matters that came up in the regular
course of business but frequently also the background and economic problems not directly related to the making of the Plan.

In the Federal government, I wish to acknowledge especially
five civil servants with whom I had much contact and from whom
I learned a great deal: Mr. B. J. Daramola, then Permanent Sec-
retary of Commerce and Industry; Mr. R. A. Clarke, Permanent
Secretary of Finance, now with the International Bank for Re-
construction and Development (IBRD); Mr. Roy Fenton, then
Governor of the Central Bank; Mr. John Garba, now with the
IBRD; and Mr. Alison A. Ayida, who has become Mr. Lardner's

---

make the usual disclaimer and state that all views expressed in this book are
my own and not necessarily those of the Government of Nigeria, or of any
one of its officials, or of any one of my colleagues, or for that matter of my
friends who read the manuscript.

successor in the Federal Ministry of Economic Development. I wish to mention also Dr. Narayan Prasad, Economic Adviser to the Prime Minister, who taught me much despite frequent and fundamental differences on policy.

Of course, I wish to thank my colleagues and staff of the Economic Planning Unit: Professor Lyle M. Hansen, now with the IBRD, and Mr. Peter B. Clark, now at U.C.L.A., both of whom were sent to Nigeria with me under the auspices of the Ford Foundation; Dr. Ebenezer Iwuagwu and Mr. Sam Akande of the staff of the Economic Planning Unit, and particularly Mr. Cheido Obineche whose death in an accident robbed Nigeria of a promising civil servant. They all worked very hard under difficult conditions. I hope that they feel it was all worthwhile.

Nigeria is a big country, and it is impossible to learn about it in Lagos alone. My colleagues in the Regional Governments and universities helped dispel my ignorance in our frequent contacts. In the Northern Region, I should like to mention specifically Alhaji Ali Akilu, Permanent Secretary of Economic Development; Mr. Talib, Permanent Secretary of Finance; Mr. Peter Gibbs, at the time Deputy Permanent Secretary of Finance in charge of Planning; Mr. Bernhard Jansen, Ford Foundation economist; and Mr. Wally Price and Mr. John Goss, principal and chief agricultural officers of Bornu Province respectively. In the Eastern Region, my particular thanks go to Dr. Pius Okigbo, then Permanent Secretary of Planning and Adviser of the Premier of Eastern Nigeria, and later Economic Adviser of the Prime Minister of the Federal Republic and Nigerian Ambassador to the Common Market; Dr. Frank Moore, Economic Adviser supplied under the auspices of the Ford Foundation; Mr. Ray Coatswith and Mr. Philip Barton, then Permanent Secretaries of Agriculture and Finance, respectively; and Mr. Sam Oti, now Permanent Secretary of Planning.

In the Western Region, there is first and foremost Chief Simeon Adebo, then Chief of the Civil Service and now Ambassador and

Permanent Representative of Nigeria at the United Nations and Commissioner-General for Economic Affairs. Also extremely helpful were Chief Isaac Dina, former Permanent Secretary of Finance and the distinguished co-author of *Nigerian Cocoa Farmers*;[3] and Mr. Andrew Wilson and Mr. S. Chukujekwe, respectively Permanent Secretary and Senior Assistant Secretary in the Ministry of Planning of the Western Region, and now Principal Secretary and Permanent Secretary of the Ministry of Economic Development in the Midwest Government.

Ibadan is the seat of the (Federal) University and of the (regional) University of Ife. I think gratefully of the discussions both in Ibadan and Lagos with Dr. H. M. A. Onitiri (now director of the Nigerian Institute of Social and Economic Research); Dr. Sam Aluko, now Professor at the University of Nigeria at Nsukka; Dr. H. A. Oluwasanmi and Dr. O. Olakanpo, as well as Mr. Charles Brown and the other members of the Department of Economics and of the Nigerian Institute of Social and Economic Research.

In London, Mr. J. C. A. Faure of Unilever and Sir Eric Tansley of the Nigeria Produce Marketing Board, both now retired, gave me freely of their time to introduce me to the intricacies of the commodity markets for groundnuts, oils and fats, and cocoa.

When the first draft of the manuscript was finished a number of friends read it critically and were willing to spend considerable time discussing parts or the whole with me. I hope that the book as it has finally emerged will please them, for on the whole I took their advice. Mr. David Bensusan-Butt of the Australian National University, Canberra; Mrs. Polly Hill Humphreys, then of the University of Ghana and Cambridge, now a Research Associate of the Center for Research on Economic Development at the University of Michigan, and associated also with the Nigerian

3. R. Galletti, K. D. S. Baldwin, and I. O. Dina, *Nigerian Cocoa Farmers: An Economic Survey of Yoruba Cocoa-Farming Families* (London: Oxford University Press for the Nigeria Cocoa Marketing Board, 1956).

Institute of Social and Economic Research and Clare Hall, Cambridge, England; Professor Torsten Gårdlund of the University of Lund, Sweden; Dr. Ojetunji Aboyade of the University of Ibadan; Dr. Jerome C. Wells, now on leave from the University of Pittsburgh, and on a joint appointment with the Center for Research on Economic Development, University of Michigan, and the Nigerian Institute of Social and Economic Research, Ibadan; Dr. Alasdair MacBean, now with the Ministry of Economic Cooperation in London; and of course Professor Edward S. Mason of Harvard—these knowledgeable readers went through the manuscript with a fine-tooth comb. I accepted virtually all their criticisms, and I am deeply grateful for the act of friendship which their review of my manuscript constituted. In addition, individual chapters have profited by intensive discussion, partly by correspondence, with S. Chakravarty, now Professor of Economics at the University of New Delhi; Professor Louis Lefeber, now of Stanford University; Professors Max Millikan and P. N. Rosenstein-Rodan at M.I.T.; Professor Montague Yudelman, now at the University of Michigan; Dr. Archibald Callaway at the University of Ife; Dr. Frank Moore; Mr. Champion Ward and Mr. Frank Sutton of the Ford Foundation; Mr. Hiroshi Kitamura of ECAFE, Bangkok; and Mr. David Carney of Freetown, Sierra Leone. Finally, the excellent advice of an anonymous reader has been responsible for changes in the structure of the book and occasionally in emphasis.

Many others too numerous to mention have had a part in my education about Nigeria. I strongly feel it proper in addition to acknowledge my intellectual debt to Walras, Schumpeter, Leontief, Samuelson, Chenery, Tinbergen—I refer to his work on the theory of economic policy rather than specifically to his *Design for Development*—Meade, Hirschman, and Chakravarty. I have been consciously and unconsciously affected by their ideas as I went about my tasks as a government official and as a writer.

There are four other persons whom I wish to mention more

specifically. Ojetunji Aboyade, as Lecturer in Economics at the University of Ibadan, offered help and friendship. He became my successor as head of the Economic Planning Unit. He and his wife, Bimpe, visited Ann Arbor where he taught for a year. In constant discussions I learned a great deal from him about his beloved country. With his arguments he induced me to change many a formulation, though some disagreements on some not very basic points remain.

Only Mr. J. Donald Kingsley, who was the Resident Representative of the Ford Foundation in Lagos, can possibly know how much his quiet understanding helped to maintain my morale in difficult moments. Never interfering, always understanding, he was a pillar of strength.

Professor Edward S. Mason made it possible for me to write the first draft of the book in the stimulating surroundings of the Center for International Affairs at Harvard University. For thirty years he has been a good and trusted friend and mentor. It was the best possible introduction in Nigeria and elsewhere to be identified as a "Mason boy." I am only expressing what dozens of other friends and students feel, and I feel good that I at last have the opportunity to say it publicly.

Finally, there is my wife, who patiently held the fort at home while I was off in Nigeria, who helped with her interest, understanding, and love, and who was ever willing to type and retype the manuscript. I dedicate this book to her.

Wolfgang F. Stolper

Center for Research on Economic Development
University of Michigan
Ann Arbor, Michigan

Planning without Facts

I

Planning without Facts

A. THE PURPOSE OF THIS BOOK

I T is the primary purpose of this book to discuss systematically how one might deal with actual problems of development planning when time and information are limited. The bias of the book is operational. There is no attempt to present a new theory of economic development. But the book is nevertheless theoretical. The operational slant requires certain procedures, and it makes others inadvisable.

All good modern theory is operational in the sense that the concepts used are potentially quantifiable, the relations postulated potentially measurable, and the parameters required potentially observable. The practicing development economist must, however, find approaches in which he uses actually and not merely potentially measurable and quantifiable magnitudes. It follows that even operational theories may be quite useless if in fact it becomes impossible to produce a reasonable quantitative estimate at the time when a decision has to be made. Thus, per capita income is an operational concept in the sense that it is potentially measurable. Yet a development economist often cannot wait until population or income data are sufficiently full and accurate to be useful to him, and a theory in which such data become crucial policy variables does not help him very much.

Similarly, it is logically satisfactory to assume a target income ten or twenty years hence and to determine an optimum path to

1

reach this target. But, at the same time, it is inherent in any actual situation that no one can conceivably know in any detail how the future will look. As a theoretical construct the approach from the future to the present is invaluable. As a policy prescription, however, it must be translated into a program that starts with the present and plans from the present forward into the future.

The approach followed in this book is, therefore, shaped by the need for being specifically, and not only generally, operational. I do not question for one moment the usefulness of general theories. Clearly, I rely on dynamic general equilibrium theory as the major guide to action. The point of the book, however, is to discuss how such general theory can be translated into a feasible action program. Devising such a program requires simultaneously considerable theoretical subtlety—which is notably lacking in some aggregative models—and a willingness to take risky policy decisions which comes dangerously close to the implementation of snap judgments.

The making of snap judgments is inescapable in any actual situation. Some can be avoided by recognizing them as unnecessary. Some can be postponed because it is not really essential that they be made today rather than tomorrow. Some are better postponed because the potential losses from being wrong clearly outweigh any possible gains from being right. But others simply must be made.

The central problem of development is how to mobilize and allocate resources for growth. This mobilization and allocation may involve the creation of institutions and of a political consensus. It involves economic policies and specific action by government and the private sector. But all the actions and policies must take place in a specific context. Different economies do not differ so much in the central nature of the problem as in the fact that the equations describing them and the parameters characterizing their reactions differ.

Professor Jan Tinbergen has pointed out that policy and theory are logically mirror images of each other.[1] All the parameters that from the theoretical standpoint are among the "givens" become the target variables for the policy maker, and all the equations and factors assumed to be variable from the standpoint of pure theory become the data of the policy maker.

To apply this insight, however, means adapting it to the specific situation of a particular country that has decided to develop. The problem for the development economist—be he a planner or adviser, or simply a scholar interested in understanding the process of economic development—is to combine in the solution of a particular problem everything he has learned as an economist, sociologist, anthropologist, and simply as an educated sensitive person; to exercise imagination, patience, tact, and rationality in the proportions which the particular problem requires.

From the standpoint of pure theory it is necessary to make assumptions and to trace through their consequences. But the development planner cannot assume his facts: he must find them as best he can. In the search for facts the fields of scholarship related to his are essential to him. Experience may be useful, too—provided it does not get in the way of learning. For every problem that is similar in one place to the problems found elsewhere, there are dozens that are different and that require different ingredients for their solution. Breadth of experience is a much overrated commodity. The application to Country B of lessons learned in Country A may be as much a source of error as of wisdom. There is no substitute for a direct study of the peculiarities of Country B.

Much of development theory proceeds—properly so—on such

1. Jan Tinbergen, *On the Theory of Economic Policy*, Contributions to Economic Analysis, no. 1 (Amsterdam: North Holland Co., 1952); Tinbergen, *Centralization and Decentralization in Economic Policy*, Contributions to Economic Analysis, no. 6 (Amsterdam: North Holland Co., 1954).

assumptions as that the future is known and that the existing
starting point is well defined. The practitioner, by contrast, very
quickly finds himself afloat in a sea of uncertainties. Should not
his confusion and lack of basic data in an actual situation have
some influence, not only on the decisions that must be made (or
perhaps can be postponed), but on the theoretical approach to
development itself?

It has in any case influenced the order of this book. The re-
mainder of this chapter deals with two major aspects that appear
to distinguish the problems of development in Africa south of the
Sahara from the problems found elsewhere: the lack of hard
facts in crucial fields and the absence of a population problem.[2]
The next chapter sets out the characteristics of the Nigerian situation. Its purpose is to explain how a particular situation affects
and limits decisions. Nigeria is, of course, simply a case in point,
albeit a particularly interesting one. Other countries might have
done as well. But I am most familiar with Nigeria, and the Nigerian experience is the foundation of the study.[3]

Chapter III outlines the general approach to development
problems which follows from a situation in which the future
is clouded and the present insufficiently known. The approach
may be characterized as optimizing as one goes along; as viewing
the long run essentially as a sequence of short runs; and as incorporating into present decisions only as much of the future as
is reasonably known. Following from these problems of timing
and information, Chapter IV discusses the uses of aggregative

2. This is possibly too conservative a statement. Many parts of Asia also
do not suffer from a Malthusian problem, and the uncertainties about basic
data are inherent in any situation. Nevertheless, I leave the statement to
indicate that it is certainly true for the part of the world that is most
familiar to me.

3. Since participating in Nigeria's development effort, I have had further
experience in Malta, Liberia, and Tunisia, and I have had detailed talks with
planners and development economists in Egypt, Iran, India, Pakistan, and
elsewhere. These experiences and discussions induce me to believe not only
that Nigeria is an excellent case in point but also that the problems discussed and the solutions advocated are more universal.

data. The main point here is that, to be meaningful, aggregative data must be linked to disaggregated facts and that the major use of an aggregative model lies in its providing a consistency check. The long Chapter V deals with the translation of the general view into specific investment criteria. The argument there is that the only valid investment criterion is economic profitability; that this criterion is general, that it can be interpreted as the solution of a general equilibrium system, that it is the only operational criterion, and that other investment criteria are either invalid, non-operational, or implicit in economic profitability. The term "profitability" has offended many people who would have accepted all the arguments if only such words as "social productivity" had been used. Yet I prefer to let "economic profitability" stand, if only to make quite plain that profits and losses are different, and because, in the reality which I know, "social" considerations are all too often used to justify manifest economic nonsense.

It is inherent in the approach followed in this book that it is not possible or desirable to separate a purely theoretical argument from factual information, however scanty. Thus there is method in the madness of jumping back and forth between theoretical arguments and the actual Nigerian situation. In mathematics it is sufficient to disprove a theorem if a single instance can be found contradicting it. Yet in economics we continue to make such assumptions as that workers don't save and capitalists don't eat, in the face of conspicuous consumption by the rich and gradual accumulation of farm properties by the poor.[4] If

4. An interesting case, contradicting the general assumption that savings increase as the income distribution changes in favor of the rich, is provided by the experience of the Federal Republic of Germany: the share of total wages and salaries in total income has increased to an unprecedented 64 percent; yet private savings by wage earners have risen rapidly. As Professor Kindleberger put it: "With income redistribution nothing happens because wage earners behave like capitalists." Charles P. Kindleberger, "Germany's Persistent Balance-of-Payments Disequilibrium," in Richard E. Caves, Harry G. Johnson, and Peter B. Kenen (eds.), *Trade, Growth, and the Balance of*

a theoretical argument is thrown out as irrelevant to the facts, the result is not *ad hoc* theorizing but a more viable approach. This is the burden of Chapters III through V.

Chapters VI and VII take up the fiscal and economic policies which are the link between the nation and the world market and between government and the private sector. Here, too, factual and theoretical discussions will be intermixed. Finally, a brief Chapter VIII on the relation between economics and politics concludes the book. The purpose of this last chapter is to indicate that a heavy emphasis on economics should not and need not make the planner insensitive to social and political conditions. But an equally important point is that dividing what happens in a country into economic and non-economic aspects of life may be useless; for it is unlikely that non-economic ends can be achieved without economic means.

B. LACK OF FACTS

"Lack of facts" suggests to a planner first of all lack of statistics. And indeed, statistics, especially in underdeveloped countries, are neither plentiful nor easily interpreted. No economist can do without them; he will make use of all the statistics he can get his hands on, and he will, of course, organize the collection of more and better statistics. At the same time, it is dangerous to take statistics which are the end result of detailed investigations too seriously, to derive policy conclusions from them without a careful study of the underlying detail, and to make policy prescriptions on the basis of international comparisons. There will be occasion to discuss the ambiguity of the terms "investment" and even "national product" in circumstances in which a very large part of production does not go through the market nexus.

Payments: Essays in Honor of Gottfried Haberler on the Occasion of His 65th Birthday (Amsterdam and Chicago: North Holland Co. and Rand McNally & Co., 1965), p. 242.

It cannot be repeated too often that economic development refers to a specific country in specific circumstances of time and place, and policy prescriptions must spring from the recognition of the historic uniqueness.

These remarks are neither anti-statistical nor anti-theoretical. Theory is, after all, only a method of organizing facts, of asking relevant questions, of analyzing a situation. The "lack of facts" to which this book refers cannot be remedied by organizing the collection of more and better statistics. The basic problem is that all too often it is quite unclear precisely what question should be asked; sometimes the question is asked wrongly; and it is by no means certain that answers always exist.

Suppose that national-income data from a certain country indicate that investment was x percent of gross national product (GNP). This is an interpretable statement, provided one is clear how income and investment were actually measured, since an operational concept is defined by the manner in which it is measured. The statement is interpretable because x percent of GNP is the sum of the money values of factories built, machinery purchased, houses erected, railway lines laid, generating equipment installed, and so forth.

Few people would quarrel, say, with the view that it is desirable to raise the investment ratio in this particular country to $x + y$ percent. But what is the meaning of such a statement without any specification as to how that can be done? Suppose overall statistical analysis indicates that a steel mill might be economical. But there are hundreds of methods of making iron and hundreds of types of iron and steel products. To put up a steel plant inevitably entails deciding exactly what will be produced there. That in turn depends on what the available iron ores can be used for and how much is available at what cost. If the ores have properties that make them unusable in orthodox iron-making and steel-making facilities, it is no use to expect orthodox mills to produce the iron and steel. Perhaps nothing can be done with iron produced by other methods, as seems to have been the case with the ill-fated backyard blast furnaces of China. Or will science devise methods of using the available ores? Unless answers to such questions are found, and indeed unless the right questions are asked, it is fatuous to expect planners to raise investment ratios.

Similarly, few people would quarrel with the notion that agriculture in such and such a country should be modernized and transformed. Yet this cannot be simply done by "investing" more in agriculture, by buying tractors and fertilizers, for example. We know that plants need certain nutritional elements, but we do not always know without substantial and time-consuming experimentation which fertilizers will do what. Perhaps, as with oil palms, they will only feed the economically non-usable parts of the plant. It has taken years of careful experimentation to find a fertilizer application that increases the oil yield from palms rather than making the trees grow taller, forming harder, thicker kernels, or causing too many male blossoms to appear. We do not know enough about soil qualities and composition. We often do not know of crop rotations that work and are economically or socially feasible. In the tropical rain forest, heavy tractors may destroy the light soil. The creation of organic matter is difficult because of the heat and speed of bacterial action, and no feasible crop rotation has been found that does not involve grass as a cover crop. But with the tse-tse fly, cattle have a difficult time, grass as a cover crop is unknown, and its introduction difficult. In many cases research results arrived at in advanced countries are relevant to the problems of an underdeveloped country, and of course fruitful research has been undertaken in many of the former colonies. It is therefore possible to overstate the case. Yet knowledge of tropical soils, of tropical agriculture and forestry is only in its infancy.

Examples can be multiplied almost *ad libitum*. Polly Hill has given an account of the number of years it took and the frustrations that had to be overcome before cocoa was firmly established in Ghana.[5] The Farm Settlements which in the Southern Nigerian Regions are counted on to "revolutionize" agriculture still rely essentially on the old standbys of cocoa and oil palm, supplemented by the old food staples of yam and cassawa, though also with the newer rice and poultry.[6] In Lake Chad fisheries, economic methods of constructing a simple fishing boat and of preserving the catch in a manner acceptable to the population have yet to be found.

All of the foregoing examples relate to scientific data proper. But knowledge is also lacking in the domain of the social sciences. What kind of education should a child have before he comes into the labor market? How precisely does land tenure work? Is it true that in Africa, in West Africa, in the specific area with which the planner is concerned, land-holding patterns are an impediment to development?[7] How can the patterns be changed, if necessary, with a minimum of destruction and so as to get development on a positive path? It is easy enough to destroy, just as it is easy to waste capital and skilled labor. It is exceedingly difficult to create and to set things moving on the path to self-sustaining growth.

The basic problem which the development economist faces is precisely this kind of ignorance, which goes far beyond a mere lack of statistics. Some of the information he can get only by experimentation on the spot. For other information he must turn to his fellow social scientists. The economist has a right to ask them how a society works, to help him gauge the effect a measure will have. For there is always the danger that a proposed measure

5. Polly Hill, *The Migrant Cocoa Farmers of Southern Ghana: A Study in Rural Capitalism* (Cambridge: Cambridge University Press, 1963).

6. For a detailed economic analysis of the Farm Settlements, see Jerome Wells, "An Appraisal of Agricultural Investments in the 1962–68 Nigerian Development Program," unpublished Ph.D. dissertation, University of Michigan, 1964.

7. Hill, in *Migrant Cocoa Farmers*, shows conclusively that the land-tenure system has not been an impediment to modernization in Ghana.

will not produce the intended effect and may even be detrimental.

But if the economist has a right to expect help from his fellow scholars, he has also a duty to learn from the situation, a duty which he cannot escape. He should, for example, be expected to resist attempts to raise investment ratios when in fact there exists no known way of investing the funds productively. In a general approach to development planning (and development theory) the lack of factual knowledge seems to have a number of important implications.

First, it is obvious that acquiring the necessary knowledge should have the highest priority. This itself presents difficulties. The accretion of knowledge has been a slow process of trial and error, of false starts and lucky guesses.[8] The truth is obvious only in retrospect. Because the acquisition of the necessary knowledge takes time, it is extremely dangerous to pander to the idea that development can be a quick and painless process.[9] C. P. Snow

8. Deciding what is slow is a matter of taste. I should have thought that to bring about significant changes within one generation was achieving a fast pace. Yet I have been called a defeatist or worse for making such a proposition. In another case Mr. Thomas Balogh and I agreed that a certain change would take 20 to 25 years. He referred to this as accelerated development, I as a slow process.

9. The *Federal Government Development Programme, 1962–68: First Progress Report*, Sessional Paper no. 3 of 1964 (Lagos), explains that "the major factors responsible for the poor performance in the primary production sector include:

"(i) many of the projects are connected with research in one form or the other and their implementation required a considerably longer time than one year. Adequate preparation and organizational changes necessary for such implementation are necessarily time consuming. There was also an acute shortage of junior technical staff experienced in research work;

"(ii) the adequate preparation and proper evaluation of certain projects such as the Lagos Fishing Terminal and landing facilities, are so complicated that they could not be started in the period under review;

"(iii) the inadequate executive capacity particularly of professional and middle grade technical staff required for implementing the major projects . . ." (pp. 9-10).

The analysis shows the care taken in the preparation of actual projects in the Nigerian plan, and it is a credit to the responsible authorities. It is quoted to indicate how irrelevant much aggregative planning is and how irresponsible talk of accelerated development can be.

may be correct in suggesting that modern science and technology have made world-wide developments both possible and inevitable. At the same time, the scarcity of resources is real, and the obstacles to the application of science and technology in different environments are great. They are not merely social or psychological. Science and technology and the process of accretion of knowledge have their own built-in limitations to overcome as well as the obstacles put in the way of accretion by ignorance, social customs, and inertia.

Second, the development planner or the development theorist has to come to terms with his starting situation. The planners' decisions have to be made within a framework of known facts, legal and social surroundings, and executive abilities. The development theorist is faced with a situation in which it is irrelevant to assume that the development planner has a full array of alternatives before him and that he can choose the one which will get him most efficiently to a future goal that has been clearly defined. It is inherent in the situation that no such full array can exist and that the future cannot be precisely defined. Just as only part of the present is known, only part of the future can be apparent. Obviously, there is nothing wrong with theorists' assuming that some social welfare function is known, but it is noteworthy that for theoretical purposes such a function need not be further defined. When it comes to executing policy, however, concrete definitions must be found. To make use of the theoretical insights of the Leontiefs, Tinbergens, Chakravartys, Lewises, and Chenerys, operational concepts have to be devised without a detailed knowledge of the distant future.

Third, it is essential to recognize the time it takes to test in reality the knowledge acquired or thought to be acquired. How often can the failure of so many large-scale agricultural projects, the high cost of most industrial projects, be traced to the impatience with the length of time it inevitably takes to accumulate the necessary knowledge? There is considerable evidence that time was not taken to accumulate data on rainfall, to experiment with the use of particular fertilizers in particular soils, the use of irrigation, the size of fields, the effects of transplanting, and so on. There is evidence that projects are started without being thought through. There is evidence that projects that start small and feel their way by experiment grow faster, become bigger, and create more income and employment than projects that start too big from the beginning.

Fourth, the very lack of detailed knowledge requires that decision making be decentralized and delegated. This conclusion seems to run counter to accepted doctrine. It is often stated as a firm fact that only centralized political control and detailed central planning and execution can achieve the breakthrough needed for development. It is assumed that the facts are known. Absence of administrative and entrepreneurial talent is stated to be a reason for centralization and state control. Yet this is a questionable proposition. Until China became Communist, centralized planned economies had emerged in the modern world only in relatively advanced economies—some of them, such as East Germany or Czechoslovakia, highly advanced. All of them have found it necessary to decentralize, to use the price mechanism more extensively, to give the man on the spot more power of decision. It is no accident that when the methods of centralization are tried in a place like Guinea they have failed (and it is to the great credit of Sekou Touré that he has not hesitated to reverse policies which have not worked). Failures in other places have thus far been hidden by the ability to draw on past achievements and previously accumulated foreign reserves.

Despite the political examples, the argument is not political or ideological but has to do with efficiency. A charismatic leader at the head of a dynamic state organization may impart to a country the energy absent from a lethargic private sector. But arousing latent talent is one thing, and substituting for it is another. It is a fallacy to suppose that government can take the place of entrepreneurship. It is people who run government, usually the same kind of people who can run anything else. They may differ in temperament and motivation but not in general training or ability. The government may start and own an enterprise. The case to be made is not one for free private enterprise but for the greater efficiency of decentralized execution, whether in a socialist state or not.

Because of lack of facts, only the man on the spot can make the best possible decision in detail. He knows the soil he has to deal with; he can adjust to the vagaries of the weather; he knows what problems of labor he runs into. Perhaps he lacks the necessary imagination, and fails. But that may be equally true of the man at the center, with the additional handicap that he does not know local circumstances. Planning, coordination, and general direction can come from the center; execution cannot.

There is, of course, another side to the coin. In advanced countries, the market mechanism provides an excellent signaling mechanism, holding the individual parts together, a mechanism which may not work perfectly but which works and which can be manipulated by monetary and fiscal policies and more direct interventions. It is quite true that such a well-developed market frequently does not yet exist in underdeveloped countries. But what are the realistic alternatives? Surely not to discard what little guidance *is* available. Rather it is of prime importance to create such a market, to start an enterprise that will monetize increasing portions of the economy, to create the incentives that will draw additional resources, human and physical, into the economic nexus, incentives that work at all levels. Only by decentralization can low skills find their niche in the productive process. Central control is not likely to create a place for them. It is more likely to inhibit their emergence.

The lack of executive capacity and of knowledge in usable form requires that indirect methods of development be used to the utmost: incentives, policies, development of markets, of money markets, of tax policy, of training, and so forth. This can be done as much with government ownership as with private ownership, with individual property rights as with tribal and traditional property rights. The call for government to do things is frequently not so much a political decision—however politicians may dress it up in their speeches—as it is evidence of a serious lack of imagination and a serious misunderstanding of what an economy is and how it works. All of this is true even if government did not tend toward monopoly and restriction of production when expansion is what is required, subsidies when profits are called for. It is a waste of resources to use scarce administrative talent when less qualified people could do the job, to use specific means for a specific job when general policies could reach many more people and utilize more resources more effectively.

Fifth and finally, the lack of facts imposes the manner in which development planning can proceed. This point has already been mentioned, and since the purpose of this book is to describe how certain problems have been attacked, in the hope that the proposed solution will be useful to other planners, there is no need to write at length about it in the present chapter. The plan for a country cannot be a rigid blueprint. Although particular projects and policies lie at the heart of planning, they must be coordinated as far as possible. A plan ought to give an intellectual framework within which decisions can be made continuously. It ought to allow the repercussions of actions and policies to be evaluated as far as is necessary in practice.

The underlying intellectual framework of the book is dynamic general equilibrium economics in the form of input-output analysis. Yet it would be impossible and indeed dangerous, for planning purposes, to draw up input-output tables and then proceed mechanically. The data do not exist, for one thing. Even a 20×20 table is hardly detailed enough to be operational. Therefore, what one hopes to do is to link projects to each other as

far as possible, provide alternatives, resist *ad hoc* pricing, and
make every attempt to trace repercussions until further secondary effects seem to be of little importance.

More important is a distrust of all aggregations. It is easy
enough to produce optimistic projections and make things come
out right. But the real function of an aggregative framework is
to allow one to test the consistency of individual decisions. Only
if individual decisions can be linked to each other and to the
aggregations are the aggregations a legitimate tool of planning.

A plan ought to allow for central direction and control and
decentralized execution as the only manner in which new decisions can be evaluated, brought to the attention of the planners,
and approved or disapproved. It ought, if possible, to be so arranged that it can be continuously revised upward, while downward revisions are avoided. It ought to be such that new facts
can be brought to light and can be made to lead to new decisions. It ought at any moment to utilize all existing relevant information while minimizing dependence on facts that should be
known but are not. It ought to make maximum use of existing
resources while leading to continuously increased resource availability and an almost automatic upward revision of goals. In all
of this, it ought to steer clear of meaningless aggregations and
detailed prescription that have no empirical basis.

The foregoing discussion indicates that the title of the book
is not an exaggeration. To be sure, the book contains numerous
statistics and miscellaneous information. To be sure, the factual
information available for Nigeria is, if anything, better than for
many an African country. Yet, when decisions on new investment
or on increasing the rate of investments are made, the planner
suddenly finds himself in a near vacuum. When new taxes are
to be imposed, there is ignorance of likely reactions. When a
school curriculum for a developing country is to be designed, it
is next to impossible to get beyond generalities with no opera-

tional content. The truth is that a wealth of statistics can hide a void of facts; having some statistics may at times be better than having none, but even this is not invariably so.

It goes without saying that one cannot make policy without politics and that politics quite naturally has priority. Economics and economic development are only means to an end. One can hardly get as enthusiastic about the free market or a central five-year plan as about a late Beethoven quartet or a Bach fugue. It may well be that economic development has not, in fact, the high priority in the thinking and aspirations of the people or even of the leaders of underdeveloped countries as these leaders pretend. It is reasonable that in new countries, the creation of nationhood and the firm establishment of political stability should have and probably does have much higher priority. The economist can accept all that. But there is good and bad politics, politics that does and politics that does not achieve its ends. It is the thesis of this book that good economics and good development can make a significant contribution to political ends; that bad economics will backfire; and that, under the circumstances found in Africa, decentralization of economic decision making is not merely politically desirable but is essential to the success of political aspirations.

C. ABSENCE OF POPULATION PRESSURE

Africa south of the Sahara does not as a rule know the Malthusian problem that plagues many parts of North Africa and of Asia. The density of population—as far as we know—is relatively low, and land is still available for extensive use by traditional methods.

Yet even this generalization is suspect. We have very little knowledge of the size, the age composition, and the movement of population, to say nothing of other economic variables. The 1960 census of Ghana brought surprises. The 1962 census of

Nigeria that was expected, at a cost of more than a million pounds, to give accurate information on essential population variables had to be repeated. Yet even if it turns out that Nigeria has a population of 55 million instead of the 36 million usually assumed or that its annual rate of population growth is greater than the average of 2 to 2½ percent usually assumed—facts that will be established only when the planned post-census sample survey is concluded—still Nigeria will not have the population problem of India or China.

In some areas (Eastern Nigeria, for example), possible signs of population pressure appear: reduction in the number of years of letting land lie fallow, soil erosion, silting up of rivers, and the like. There are also migrations. But these phenomena may have very different explanations. If there is no population pressure, land can be abused—America provides sufficient examples of such abuse. It can therefore be misleading to speak of the "good adaptation" of traditional agricultural practices.

Similarly, migration may be a sign of overpopulation. But it need not be. Polly Hill has shown that the cocoa industry of southern Ghana was the creation of migrant farmers purchasing unused land and developing it. It was the work not of the poorest farmers but of incipient capitalists.[10] Migration, soil erosion, or for that matter even the problem of so-called school leavers are not proof of a Malthusian problem, nor do they necessarily point to inefficient agriculture. They are indications of social change.

A potential Malthusian population problem arises when a very high birth rate and a very high death rate combine to keep population initially at a more or less stable level. Once an outside influence reduces the death rate, the rate of population increase immediately soars.[11] Unless a savings and investment effort is

10. Hill, *Migrant Cocoa Farmers.*
11. The term "outside influence" is used to suggest that death rates are easily and quickly influenced by means which do not work through the social fabric, such as public health measures. Reductions in birth rates— unless new methods are found—require, on the other hand, changes in social

very big, it will simply serve to maintain a larger population at
the same low level of existence, at worst with much the same
age distribution and hence potential explosiveness.

Malthusian crowdedness does not at present menace Africa
south of the Sahara. The population structure undoubtedly has
the potential explosiveness just sketched, and this carries important implications for the development planner; but it is still
possible for population to hive off so that the population increase
can be absorbed without a fall in the standard of living and
without any particular savings or investment effort. The existing
methods of agricultural production do not require excessive
amounts of capital for land clearance and planting, though they
do require terribly hard work. The fertility of tropical African
soils is often more apparent than real, but increased population
can find its outlet in the increased use of additional land, and
income might even increase along the way. Thus Polly Hill
has shown that increased cocoa prices in Ghana have led to
increased land acquisition of previously idle land, and in fact
much capital formation made possible through higher palm-oil
and cocoa prices has taken the form of land acquisition for cocoa
plantings. Hla Myint has pointed out similar facts for Malaya
and Burma.[12] This is not the picture of the Malthusian population problem. If anything, the theoretical problem is "development with unlimited supplies of land"—a variation, with a bow
to its famous author, of W. A. Lewis' well-known title.[13]

---

attitudes. Hence it is easy to create a Malthusian problem and difficult to
combat it.

12. H. Myint, "The Gains from International Trade and the Backward
Countries," *Review of Economic Studies*, XXII (1954–1955), 129-142. See
also Hill, *Migrant Cocoa Farmers,* as cited above, and Polly Hill, "The
Migrant Cocoa Farmers of South Ghana," *Africa*, XXXI (July 1961), 209-
230. My one-sentence summary is of course a caricature of Miss Hill's important argument, which is subtle and detailed.

13. W. A. Lewis, "Economic Development with Unlimited Supplies of
Labour," *The Manchester School*, 1954, reprinted in A. N. Agarwala and
S. P. Singh (eds.), *The Economics of Underdevelopment* (Bombay: Oxford

Such excess population as exists can easily be absorbed by relatively minor migrations. Sufficient land is available within the same political boundary—e.g., in the Calabar area of Nigeria's Eastern Region—and less often within the same tribal area. There are obstacles to such migrations, as there are obstacles to improvements in techniques or to reductions in the birth rate. Ignorance, lack of communication, inertia, and tribal and local antagonisms all cause hardships and hinder the effective use of land, but all of these can be handled with or without population policies that are intended to affect birth and death rates. Such policies may, of course, be advisable nevertheless.

The presence of an explosive population situation is at times equated with the presence of redundant labor and disguised unemployment. Yet the fact that land is as yet not scarce indicates that the two are not the same. It is fairly clear that in African circumstances the development problem cannot be described as a simple case of redundant labor and disguised unemployment. Nor is there a simple "Keynesian" problem of unemployed resources that could be easily solved by an increase in aggregate demand, deficit spending, and other inflationary policies. The basic problem seems to be, not a surplus of labor and a shortage of demand, but low productivity and lack of complementary factors.[14]

The facts which would make the "Keynesian" analysis applicable can, of course, be *assumed* to exist. It is questionable, however, whether they actually do exist in Nigeria or are general in Africa or perhaps even in large parts of Asia. The so-

University Press, 1958). This book was reprinted as a Galaxy Books paperback in 1963 by Oxford University Press, New York.

14. This emphatically does not mean that there is no room for expansionary monetary policies. The problem is discussed in Chapter VI. Even where labor is redundant the only way of increasing employment is to make available additional complementary factors. See the brilliant analysis of R. S. Eckaus, "The Factor-Proportions Problem in Underdeveloped Areas," *American Economic Review*, XLV (September 1955), 539-565, reprinted in *The Economics of Underdevelopment*, cited in preceding note.

called school-leaver problem in Nigeria is sometimes adduced as evidence of a problem of disguised unemployment.[15] Coming to town at the age of about twelve years (no one can be sure in the absence of proper birth registration) to seek jobs which are not there, while avoiding jobs in the country, Nigerian school leavers are no more qualified for skilled or even semi-skilled jobs than their counterparts in the United States. Their expectations are unrealistic. While there is excess labor in the towns, shortages are reported in the country, where older people find it difficult to hire labor to harvest cocoa or palm kernels at falling prices.[16] The reason that school leavers cannot be employed in the towns at existing wage rates is that the jobs they could do, even with increased demand, would lose money and could be made economic only by *ad hoc* measures involving guaranteed prices and subsidies as well as scarce complementary factors for which alternative uses are preferable. They could go back to the farms and work at lower wages. They could be further trained. Simply increasing demand, however, will not add to net output; it will cause balance-of-payments problems and lead to a waste of other complementary resources which are at least as scarce as skilled labor. The problem, to repeat, is not one of insufficient demand; it is a matter of insufficient complementary factors and low productivity.

The absence of the Malthusian problem suggests that in Ni-

15. For an excellent discussion of this vexing problem, which is of increasing political and economic importance, see Archibald C. Callaway, "School Leavers and the Developing Economy of Nigeria," in Nigerian Institute of Social and Economic Research, *Conference Proceedings* (Ibadan: The Caxton Press [West Africa], 1960), pp. 60-72. The problem appears to be much older than I realized. Miss Hill has pointed out to me that "an 1889 report on economic agriculture in the Gold Coast referred to it in contemporary terms."

16. As with the school-leaver problem, it is by no means clear what the extent of any shortages is or how their emergence is to be interpreted. The shortages may result from temporary peak demands. They may instead result from the fact that wages are not sufficiently attractive to induce farmers into wage employment and away from their own subsistence production.

geria and throughout West Africa it would be inappropriate to use for planning purposes a shadow or accounting price of zero for labor. Planning models assuming unlimited supplies of labor are likely to be misleading. The justification for assuming a zero shadow price of labor in Asia is that its marginal product is presumed to be zero or even negative, while for social and political reasons the average product and wage cannot fall to or below zero. But when there is no excess supply of labor in this sense, when there is always enough land to permit labor to produce some positive output of food and shelter within subsistence production, the proper price for labor may be below the legal minimum for government and major businesses, but it is not zero. And though the minimum wage paid by government certainly has a habit of pervading the economy, much as the American steel price does, it essentially affects only a small portion of the economy and does not penetrate far into the agricultural sector.[17]

The absence of the Malthusian problem makes it illegitimate to neglect the so-called subsistence sector and to assume that any increase in output by "modern" methods is a net addition to total product. Anthropologists and sociologists tell us that frequently the most active members of a community leave the village to find employment elsewhere. The village may deteriorate as a result, or it may benefit from the capital flows from the migration. The economic implications seem quite clear. The increase in output of the "modern" sector is purchased by a decreased output in the "subsistence" sector. Yet "modern" production needs a high amount of capital and other complementary factors as compared to "subsistence" production.

It may well be, therefore, that a high priority should be given

17. Since labor has to eat, it is probably unwise to use a zero price for labor even when it is redundant. The logic of shadow or accounting prices is unassailable. Calculating and applying them is something else again, as discussed later, especially in Chapters III-V.

to investment in the subsistence sector, which thereby is changed and becomes increasingly integrated into the money economy (an example might be a feeder road). If there were true excess population, that is, truly idle people on the land who eat but do not produce, their removal from the village would be unequivocally a gain (provided, of course, that there are not still better uses for the scarce complementary factors). The neglect of "subsistence" production can lead to serious misunderstanding of the process of development and therefore to inappropriate policies and plans to accelerate development.

The absence of a Malthusian population problem may account for the fact that at least in West Africa people quickly react to economic incentives. It is a reasonably well-established observation that the construction of a feeder road will lead immediately to an increase in production and even in productivity. It is said that the acreage tilled by a male cultivator in, say, Northern Nigeria increases when a feeder road is built, which means that his productivity—measured per man or manday, but not necessarily per man-hour—increases. The reasons are evident. With a road available, he needs less time to go to his plot or to evacuate the crop and has more time for cultivation. It also means, *ceteris paribus,* that he receives higher ex-farm prices. One can argue therefore that his product per man-hour goes up as well, if the time spent on activities ancillary to production is properly counted.

I suggest that this effectiveness of economic incentives, the absence of which is frequently deplored in other parts of the world, is connected not merely with social surroundings but with the absence of population pressure as well. Population pressure means that increased production is absorbed by increased population. Why should a cultivator exert himself if he cannot see the fruits of his labor? The "grinding poverty" and the reported apathy of Asia may well have their root here. In Africa south of the Sahara, at least one's own family benefits from increased exertion. More land can be taken into cultivation. Increased prices for one's product can be translated immediately into more capital formation and higher consumption; they do not get absorbed in general population increases but accrue to the cultivator.[18]

In Africa it is not *as yet* exceedingly difficult to stay ahead of population increases; thus far, relatively minor investments—in feeder roads or land clearance—will do the trick, without the necessity for massive investments of the kind typified by dams or large-scale irrigation projects. For the planner, this suggests strongly the use of indirect rather than direct methods of moving the economy in the desired direction. It suggests limits to the extent of taxation, austerity as a method of raising savings, and so forth. Perhaps because the fact is too obvious, it is often forgotten. How else explain the frequent neglect of the so-called subsistence sector, or of investment in agriculture, or the investments in that kind of infrastructure which very directly assists agricultural production and productivity, creates markets physically, not just metaphorically, and raises the amounts of factors of production available to the economy? Where land is not scarce, a feeder road will do just that.

Although there is *not yet* a population problem, one will almost certainly arise unless policy makers plan against such an

18. There is some evidence that in India and Pakistan economic incentives work if they are allowed to, that is, if in fact the benefits from changed behavior accrue to the person who has changed it. Of course, the incentive must be economic and not merely technological. It is no use to suggest a technologically advanced program to a farmer if at the same time all benefits he might derive are taxed away directly or through lower prices.

Attention is drawn once more to Polly Hill's 1963 book, *The Migrant Cocoa Farmers of Southern Ghana,* for evidence of the economic rationality of West African farmers. Her Appendix VII.6 (pp. 214-217) on "Linguistic Economics" is particularly fascinating, showing as it does that the Twi language has perfectly good words for such "modern" concepts as capital, invest, save, interest, mortgage, and perhaps even "quantity discount" ("what is given into the bargain when a large quantity of anything is bought")!

event. It is virtually inevitable that public-health measures will lead to a population explosion, and it is only too well known that birth rates do not respond as quickly to changing circumstances as death rates.

Nigeria may be one or two generations ahead of a Malthusian situation. This is a period of grace for which many an Arab or Asian country would be grateful. The policy implications are that the period of grace must be used as effectively as possible to change the nature of the economy from one in which a population increase is a drag to one in which it is a stimulus.

This involves a great deal more than raising the rate of capital accumulation, though it surely involves that also. Characteristically, traditional economies respond to a population increase by duplicating existing organizations, much as Roman or Greek colonies were duplicates of one another. As advanced economies grow, however, significant changes in organization occur that allow the economy to grow faster than the increase in population. Large factories are not simply bigger versions of small factories; large industrial cities are not as a rule simply bigger collections of buildings. Even in advanced economies there comes a point at which the gains of an increasing population are outweighed by its increased cost. Certain social expenditures that are not necessary or are even wasteful for smaller numbers become essential when large numbers congregate. The debate in the United States on the starving of the public sector can at least in part be understood in terms of increased urbanization, that is, in terms of the cost of a population whose rate of growth has outstripped even the most optimistic projections of less than a generation ago!

That the change from a traditional to a modern economy requiries radical changes in attitudes can probably be taken for granted. It is likely, however, that a proper organization of the economy will force the development of these attitudes where they do not already exist. In the traditional pattern of some African societies the desire for education is very strong and leads easily to increased efforts. Yoruba mothers have traditionally been responsible for the education of their children and have traditionally taken an active and effective part in trading to fulfill their social responsibilities. This sort of attitude can be "transferred," while others must be changed. An African friend pointed out to me that in the old days a man with increased income got himself another wife; now he acquires more textiles and housing, "a step in the right direction."

The urgency of using the period of grace explains much of the insistence in this book on economic profits and economic profitability in planning and the resistance to any attempts to substitute other and possibly "higher" criteria, such as social benefits not measurable in money. No one denies that such benefits (or costs) exist and that there is something less than perfectly attractive about an insistence on economic profits and economic payoff. Yet no amount of good intentions can get around the basic fact that, in the words of a Communist slogan, "as we work today so we shall eat tomorrow." Only increasing productivity can provide the economic base for a good life, and that base must be created while the economy is as yet free of the Malthusian millstone. Fortunately, however, economic and non-economic benefits are by no means inconsistent.

With rapidly increasing population, social costs increase disproportionately. Water supplies, roads, sewerage, police and fire protection—all such facilities become more urgent as numbers increase. At the same time political problems become more prominent and the methods of dealing with them more costly. As society becomes progressively depersonalized with increasing numbers, the need for, and powers of, government become increasingly pervasive. If, when this happens, the economy has not been put upon a firm productive base, individual liberties, non-economic benefits, and the further growth of the economy itself are jeopardized.

II

Planning in Nigeria

A DEVELOPMENT plan cannot be a rigid blueprint for the future, to be followed come hell or high water. Even in centrally directed economies, plans are not always fulfilled, and they are revised continuously. In the words of the Nigerian Plan:

It is not given to man to foretell the future. By its very nature, development planning cannot be an exact science, since plans must be drawn up in the light not only of past experience and present circumstances, which are known factors, but also in the light of assumptions concerning the future—assumptions concerning world market prices, the pace of technological advance, the availability of capital and of manpower, trends in agricultural output and so forth. The assumptions underlying the preparation of this First National Development Plan have been based on the firmest evidence available, but the future may show many of these to have been mistaken. The prices for Nigeria's exports may be more or less favourable than seems likely at present. New technologies may emerge, new markets may spring up and old markets be lost, and new sources of potential wealth be discovered.

The Plan therefore has not been conceived as a law akin to that of the Medes and Persians, but rather as a flexible instrument. Flexibility, however, cannot be equated with arbitrariness. The Programmes of the four Governments within the Plan and the projects within those Programmes themselves will be constantly evaluated and refined in the light of achievements, prospects, and the changing pattern of needs and resources. But the ultimate goal of all development—the raising of the level of living and the acceleration of growth throughout the economy—can be achieved only if the overall Plan priorities are strictly observed. Particular projects may be discarded or curtailed, whilst others may be added or expanded. This is not important. In fact, the Governments recognise it would be a disaster to adhere rigidly to all details of the Plan now presented, for in the light of changing circumstances some projects now properly included may well be seen not to contribute to the achievement of rapid growth. This then is the aim of the First National Development Plan—to give a sense of direction to the economy, a sense of priorities and urgency and to enlist the support and co-operation of all sections of the community to work for a better future—their own future.[1]

In formulating their program, the planners must realize the limitations which reality puts upon them if their labors are to have any impact on that reality. *Inevitably, whatever can be done will be the result of a double compromise between conflicting political views and ends and between what is ideally desirable and what is possible.*

Unlike theoretical analysis, planning is a policy-directed activity, and it is directed toward the future. Planning and economic development take place in a particular situation and at a particular time. A theorist developing an explanatory model may perhaps choose his assumptions so as to bring a particular point into focus. Even he will want to choose "realistic" assumptions. A development planner, however, is not free to choose *his* starting position. What can be done is limited by the dearth of facts, the time available, the historic situation in which planners (and politicians) must make their decision, and the institutions within which they must work. All of these have their own logic and inertia, and they can be changed only slowly.

These are universally valid statements which this chapter tries to make specific by describing briefly the situation in which the Nigerian planners of the early 1960's found themselves and within which all decisions had to be made. It will specify the limitations which the past put upon them and the manner in which they had to make the best of the given situation within the time and with the staff available. Once again, the Nigerian

1. Federation of Nigeria, *National Development Plan, 1962–68* (Lagos: Federal Ministry of Economic Development, 1962), chap. I, p. 5, paras. 16-18.

case is both interesting in itself and, *mutatis mutandis,* characteristic of the problem.

A. GEOGRAPHY, CONSTITUTIONAL POWERS, AND PLANNING

The Federation of Nigeria became an independent nation within the British Commonwealth on October 1, 1960. It became a Republic within the Commonwealth on October 1, 1963. With approximately 55 million people, all but about 27,000 of them Africans, it is the most populous independent state in Africa, and its 356,660 square miles make it one of the biggest. The size of the country and the diversity of its factor endowments give it a potential for development of which many other African countries might well be envious. Its ethnic diversity and political diversity, as well as the regional differences in resource endowments, create numerous political and economic problems that were successfully handled in the early 1960's by a Federal constitution which recognized strong Regional prerogatives but which vested in the Federal Government all those powers that were essential to the maintenance and further development of nationhood.[2]

The Northern Region dominates the Federation in area, population, and politics. The final adjustment of the Regional boundaries was made in 1961, when the Northern Cameroons Trust

2. After the military revolt of January 1966 it could be seen that the peaceful resolution of the political crisis in the Western Region in 1962, of the quarrels over the validity of the Census in 1963 and 1964, and of the electoral crisis of early 1965 were but preludes to the 1966 coup d'état. The military revolt swept away the constitutional mechanism of resolving difficulties, as well as the politicians charged with the mediation of conflicts. But it did not require the outsider to abandon his cautious optimism about Nigeria as a political unit. Major General Johnson Thomas Umunakwe Aguiyi-Ironsi did not initially change the number of Regions or the Federal prerogatives. Neither did he interfere in any way with the civil service or the judiciary. Later attempts to establish a unitary state were resisted. The precise constitutional form of the future is still under study.

Territory which had been administered as part of Nigeria voted to join Nigeria, while the Southern Cameroons preferred to join the Cameroons Republic. The North's 281,782 square miles, many of them very dry sub-Saharan country, contain—according to the census of 1962–63—about 30 million people. The Hausa, Fulani, and Kanuri people predominate in numbers and power. Organized in Emirates and Native Authorities, the North is the poorest and least developed Region. It is also, however, a Region ruled by persons of considerable political acumen who understand power and who know the urgency of change.[3]

The vastness of the territory and the sparse population over large areas impose substantial strains on the development of transportation and other social facilities, and these are reflected in budgetary pressures. Groundnuts, cotton, and benni-seed are the major export crops; millet and guinea corn are the major domestic food staples, supplemented by livestock raising. Northern agricultural production consists overwhelmingly of annual crops. Tree crops are of minor importance. On the Jos Plateau, tin and columbite are mined by both traditional and modern methods, and tin is smelted in two modern installations. There are a few industries based on domestic materials. The major ones are the production of cotton textiles at Kaduna and the processing of groundnuts into oil and cake.

The agricultural economies of the three (formerly two) Southern Regions, by contrast, are based on tree crops. The Eastern Region, stretching from the Niger to the Cameroons border and north to within about 100 miles of the Benue River, encompasses 29,484 square miles and in mid-1963 had approximately 12.4 million inhabitants, chief among them the Ibo people. For planning, it is relevant to note that the political traditions of the Ibo

---

3. One finds occasionally the view that because the North is "backward" it will be dominated by the more "advanced" South. But surely, the relation between economic development and political power is more complicated than that. Machiavelli was not a capitalist either!

once created numerous small kingdoms, that they deserve their reputation for energy and local cooperation, and that they tend to live in family compounds rather than towns.[4] The strong sense of community has led to local efforts that have relieved the Regional budget of some capital expenditures for schools and feeder roads. Palm oil and palm kernels are the major agricultural exports; yams, cassava, and increasingly rice supplement palm oil as domestic staples. Petroleum and natural gas have been found in substantial amounts in the Niger Delta. The Eastern Region produces coal of low quality, and iron-ore deposits are known to exist. Industries are springing up in the major centers around Enugu, the Regional capital located in the coal-mining area, and around Aba and Port Harcourt. A new oil port has been constructed and a channel dredged. By 1966 an oil refinery in the Port Harcourt area will produce enough refined products for the major domestic uses. Oil and natural gas are also used for thermal generation of electricity and conceivably could become the base of a petrochemical industry in the distant future.

The Western Region as established in 1954 had 45,376 square miles, reduced to 30,095 square miles in 1963 when the Midwestern Region was created. Its population in mid-1963 was officially estimated at 10.3 million. It is dominated by the Yoruba, a town-dwelling people with old political traditions that have transcended the level of the clan or family. Cocoa, rubber, oilpalm products, and timber are the major export products, supplemented, as in the Eastern Region, by cassava and yams as domestic staples, which also include citrus fruit, pineapples, bananas, avocados, and rice. Some fishing is carried on. The west has most of the industries. It is the wealthiest of the Regions, since cocoa prices did relatively well after the war compared to those of other commodities.

4. For the political traditions, see K. O. Dike, *Trade and Navigation in the Niger Delta* (London: Oxford University Press, 1960).

The newly created Midwestern Nigeria has 15,281 square miles and in mid-1963 an officially estimated population of 2.5 million. The Region centers around Benin and is dominated by the Edo people. Rubber, oil-palm products, and the recently found petroleum make up its economic base.

There are finally the 27 square miles of the Federal Territory of Lagos with, in 1963, an estimated population of about 675,000 people. It is not only the seat of the Federal Government but also has the best harbor and is the headquarters and terminus of the country's railway system. Most industries are located either within its boundaries or in the Western Region immediately adjacent to it. It is the center for the commercial community and the seat of the Central Bank, and most of the expatriates live there.[5]

This sketch of the diversity of the country brings out one relevant fact for planning: Although all boundaries are arbitrary to a degree, the Regions are in fact reasonably distinct entities with special ethnic characteristics and each with a fairly clearly defined economic base. This diversity is also reflected in the constitutional arrangements within which planning proceeds.

Politically and economically, federalization means that in effect all those matters that are relevant to maintaining a nation and to giving direction to an economy are either Federal prerogatives or are dominated by the Federal Government. On the other hand, all those matters which are regionally distinct—education at the sub-university level, for example, and agriculture—are largely or entirely left to the Regions. Hence the lack of coordination among the Regions is much less significant than one might at first think, because it exists basically only in matters where

---

5. Throughout this book the term "expatriate" is used in its legal and political sense and is not meant to carry any literary or emotional overtones associated with a self-exiled figure who is rootless or prefers to let his roots sink in foreign soil. Typically an "expatriate" is a non-Nigerian living and working in Nigeria for a specific period or purpose and with the intention of returning to his native country.

each Region is a distinct entity. Where coordination nevertheless becomes important, it can be achieved quite easily within the present constitutional arrangements. This, too, is not unimportant, since young nations can ill afford too many and too drastic revisions of their basic laws.

Under the constitution, the Federal Government has certain exclusive powers. National defense, foreign affairs, the issue of money and the control of the banking system and credit, and exclusive control over foreign loans are the major Federal prerogatives. But even though the Federal and the Regional Governments have concurrent powers in many other matters, the Federal Government predominates in all those decisions which determine national coherence. The Electricity Corporation of Nigeria, the Nigerian Railway Corporation, Nigeria Airways, the Nigerian Ports Authority, the Nigerian National (Shipping) Line, and the Nigerian Coal Corporation operate over the whole country and have actual or virtual monopolies in their fields.[6] The Federal Government is responsible for the major trunk-road network, and it has exclusive jurisdiction in all telecommunications. Given these nation-wide powers—to which the newly established Niger Dams Authority should be added—the forces making for increasing national coherence are extremely strong, despite regional autonomies in other fields.[7] Moreover, in a few instances, of which the raising of domestic loans is probably the

6. On the Plateau in the North, a private company, the Nigerian Electricity Supply Corporation, organized in 1929, generates electric power, mainly for use in the tin mines. There are also some other industrial producers of power for their own use. At the time this is written Nigeria Airways is not yet a statutory corporation, although it is run as if it were one.

7. The threats of secession made during the electoral crisis of 1965 led to a realization that the consequences of a break-up of the Federation were really unacceptable to all. The purpose of this note is not to discuss the political developments which began to be chaotic and led to the coup d'état of 1966, but simply to point out that, in fact, the coherence of the country had already become quite strong under the Federal Constitution, despite political troubles, corruption, the misuse of power, and regional and tribal rivalries. This, at least, is and always has been my view, which I note even though future events may prove me wrong.

most significant, the Regions have voluntarily surrendered a prerogative to the Federal Government.

The major Regional prerogatives relate to agriculture and to primary and secondary education. There is no Federal Ministry of Agriculture. The Federal Ministry of Economic Development was responsible for basic agricultural research, but applied research was a matter for all Regions. In early 1965, after the Federal elections of 1964, the Ministry of Economic Development handed over its concern with resource policy to a newly established Ministry of Natural Resources and Research, a change which did not, however, involve a major shift in the constitutional division of power. (The Federal Ministry of Trade and Industry was at the same time also split into two ministries to deal more effectively with the increased burden of business.) A national agricultural policy can nevertheless be developed. Although the Regional Marketing Boards exert a major influence by setting the prices paid to producers, the Federal Government is beginning to influence these prices as part of monetary policy. In addition, the Plan provides for substantial loans and grants to Regional projects. This requires the formulation of criteria for such grants and thus can be made to serve the development of a national policy.

The Federal Ministry of Education is not directly responsible for primary and secondary education except in the Federal District. But it is responsible for the Federal Universities at Ibadan and Lagos, and was responsible for the Nigerian Colleges of Arts, Science, and Technology until they were regionalized. A national educational policy has been developed through the Ashby Report, which was followed up by a joint effort of the four governments that in turn led to a Federal document on *Educational Development, 1961–70*.[8] This document not only accepted

8. Sir Eric Ashby et al., *Investment in Education: The Report of the Commission on Post-School Certificate and Higher Education in Nigeria* (Lagos: Federal Ministry of Education, 1960); Federation of Nigeria, *Educatonal Development, 1961-70*, Sessional Paper no. 3 of 1961 (Lagos).

the Ashby Report in principle, while revising some of its targets upwards, but stated explicitly that it should form the basis for a *national* policy to be pursued by the Federal Government. The concrete expression of the national policy consists of subsidies to the Regions amounting to £5.092 million.[9]

Thus the actual constitutional setup within which national planning proceeds leaves important sections of the economy to the Regions and limits the national influence. Yet the limitation is neither absolute nor harmful wherever regional differences are so pronounced that the problems to be solved are very heterogeneous.

The constitutional division of powers is reflected also in the fiscal structure. The major income of the Regional Governments derives from their agricultural products, either as export duties or produce sales tax or as so-called "profits" of the Regional Marketing Boards. The Regions also collect direct taxes and receive a substantial portion of the import duties which are collected by the Federal Government and divided according to a complicated formula that varies for specific imports. The Federal Government derives its major income from customs revenues. In the very recent past, revenues from petroleum exploration and petroleum exports have become substantial. The importance of petroleum revenues will increase rapidly, as will also the income from company taxation.

Once again, planning must work within an already existing framework. Allocation of revenue sources can be changed only slowly and only by mutual consent of the Regional and Federal Governments. In practice, there are frequent meetings of the Ministers of Finance, and there are attempts at unifying certain tax structures such as income-tax rates. The Federal Government has some influence through its exclusive power over foreign loans and because subsidies to Regions are contemplated. Nevertheless, for better or worse, revision of the tax structures and in particular

9. *National Development Plan,* chap. VI, p. 88, para. 146.

of the formulae that distribute import duties occurs infrequently and becomes for a number of years a fixed datum for planning.[10]

B. INSTITUTIONS FOR PLANNING

Very few decisions can ever be made with a clean slate, and it is questionable whether a completely clean slate would allow many decisions to be made at all. When the Nigerian National Plan was being formulated, certain institutions had evolved out of past attempts, successes, and failures. What can be done at any one moment depends on what has gone before and on the

10. The basic document is Colonial Office, Nigeria, *Report of the Fiscal Commission*, Cmnd. 481 (London: H.M.S.O., 1958). The proposals of this report, which is normally referred to as the Raisman Report after its chairman, have been accepted.

An earlier *Report of Commissions on Revenue Allocation, Nigeria*, was published in 1950. Its authors were Professor J. R. Hicks and Sir Sidney Phillipson. Professor Hicks has published a section of it under the title "A Chapter in Federal Finance—The Case of Nigeria," in J. R. Hicks, *Essays in World Economics* (Oxford: Clarendon Press, 1959), pp. 216-236.

For a discussion of the fiscal effects of federalization, see Arthur Hazlewood, "The Finances of Nigerian Federation," *West Africa*, Aug. 27, 1955 (reprinted in Oxford University Institute of Colonial Studies Reprint Series, no. 14). In 1964, a new commission was set up, "headed by Mr. Kenneth Binns, Under Treasurer in the State of Tasmania, Australia, to review the basis of revenue allocation to the various Governments of the Federation. The Commission is requested, among other things, to review and recommend a formula for the distribution of the proceeds of mining and royalties and the funds in the Distributable Pool Account. In making recommendations, the Commission is to take into account the creation of the new Mid-Western Region, the sources of revenue available to each government, and the legitimate requirements and responsibilities of the various Governments." This quotation is from Central Bank of Nigeria, *Weekly Financial and Economic Review*, June 25, 1964. The Binns report appeared at the end of 1965 as K. J. Binns, *Report of the Fiscal Review Commission* (Lagos: Federal Ministry of Information, 1965). The recommendations essentially followed existing practice except that the shares of the Regions in the so-called Distributable Pool were slightly altered to take account of the new Mid-Western Nigeria and of the fact that the Cameroons ceased to be administered from Nigeria. It also suggested outright transfers by the Federal Government of £3.7 million to the Regions, and a number of alternative arrangements in case this suggestion should not be acceptable to the Federal Government.

data which happen to be available. This of course does not mean that institutions and data are accepted as permanent. But all changes take time, and one has to start where one is. It is the purpose of the present section to describe how the institutional framework affects planning decisions in the specific situation of Nigeria.

Deliberate development policy in the British Empire started with the Colonial Development and Welfare Act of 1929, but the Great Depression cut short any substantial aid to the colonies. The Colonial Development and Welfare Act of 1940 substantially enlarged the scope of assistance to the colonies, both as to amounts involved and the variety of schemes eligible for loan or grant financing, but World War II made it little more than a declaration of intent. Deliberate development really got under way only with the third Colonial Development and Welfare Act, of April 1945, which made £120 million available to the colonies collectively for the ten fiscal years ending March 31, 1956.

As the result of this act, each colony was asked to produce a Ten-Year Development Plan. Nigeria's Plan envisaged expenditures of £55 million (out of an increased total of £180 million actually made available for all seventeen colonies), of which £23 million was to come from funds provided under the Colonial Development and Welfare Act.[11]

Already in 1948, a Select Committee of the British House of Commons pointed out with respect to Nigeria's Plan that:

65. The allocation of expenditure on the Ten-Year Plan . . . does not give anything like a complete picture of the future development of the territory. The Plan does not propound a complete strategy of

11. *A Ten-Year Plan of Development and Welfare for Nigeria, 1946,* Sessional Paper no. 24 of 1945 (Lagos: Legislative Council, 1945), as amended by the Select Committee of the Council and approved by the Legislative Council on 7th February, 1946. The act provided £120 million, but Britain subsequently approved the expenditure of £180 million, the aggregate amount called for in the seventeen plans submitted—see *Fifth Report from the Select Committee on Estimates* (Session 1947–48; Colonial Development, H.C. 181 [1948]), p. vii.

development; it is merely an aggregate of proposals for spending money.

66. This piece-meal approach to the problem of planning is evident in the text of the Plan. It begins by laying down the maxim that development should be conceived as a military operation, but proceeds without any attempt to appreciate the situation or define the objectives. Admittedly, there is a list of "certain fundamentals" which must be put right before any policy of wide economic development can be usefully considered. Beginning with water supply, the list goes on with education, agriculture, forestry and veterinary services—in fact through the whole gamut of possible development . . . This is not planning.

67. This is not to say that these various kinds of proposed expenditure are unnecessary; all of them are desirable, and most of them are urgent. The point of criticism is that if the Ten-Year Plan were carried out overnight the improvement in the condition of the mass of Nigerians would be barely perceptible . . .

The select committee drew attention to the very serious underspending and pointed out that it was "the symptom of a wrong approach to development," of envisaging planning essentially as a governmental operation, and moreover that the planning proceeded from the top down instead of from the grassroots up.[12]

The criticisms voiced were both appropriate and, in a sense, unfair. The fact was that no one had much experience with planning or planned economic development. The only existing examples of planning, that of the Soviet Union and that of Britain in wartime, were of questionable relevance to the situation in which Nigeria found herself.

The experience with the Ten-Year Plan of 1945 led to a revision for the years 1951–1956;[13] but, with impending regional-

12. *Fifth Report,* just cited, pp. xviii-xix, viii.
13. *A Revised Plan of Development and Welfare for Nigeria, 1951–56,* Sessional Paper no. 6, 1951 (Lagos: Government Printing Office); IBRD, *The Economic Development of Nigeria* (Lagos: Federal Government Printer, 1954).
Concerning *The Economic Programme of the Government of the Federa-*

ization, a new approach was needed. The International Bank for Reconstruction and Development (IBRD) was invited in 1953 to make a report, and this report in turn led to four Governmental Programs for the years 1955–1960. The nearing of independence in 1960 and the fact that the program targets had not been met made it desirable to extend the Federal program period to 1962, so that the next plan would be a truly Nigerian effort.

By the time the present National Development Plan, 1962–1968, came to be formulated, a number of institutional changes had been made to facilitate the planning process. A Federal Ministry of Economic Development had been created, and there were corresponding ministries in the East and West, while in the North planning was, until 1962, a function of the Ministry of Finance. A Joint Planning Committee (JPC) had been set up, which was an interregional body at the top civil-service level, under the chairmanship initially of the Governor of the Central Bank and later of the Economic Adviser to the Federal Government. It served to coordinate Federal and Regional efforts. The secretariat of the JPC was provided by the Federal Ministry of Economic Development, and within that ministry the Economic Planning Unit (EPU) was specifically charged with developing both the Federal Program and the National Plan. The JPC itself reported to the National Economic Council (NEC), an inter-

---

tion of Nigeria, 1955–60, Sessional Paper no. 2 of 1956 (Lagos: Federal Government Printer), there were up to 1962 five annual progress reports. See also Eastern Region of Nigeria, *Outline of Development Plan, 1955–60* (Enugu, 1955; Sessional Paper no. 4 of 1955); Northern Region of Nigeria, *A Statement of Policy on the Development Finance Programme, 1955–60* (Kaduna, 1955); and Western Region of Nigeria, *Development of the Western Region of Nigeria, 1955–60* (Ibadan, 1956; Sessional Paper no. 4 of 1955).

No new program was issued by the Federal Government or the Northern Region Government, beyond the annual capital budgets and, in the case of the Federal Government, progress reports that now referred to the "Economic Programme for 1955–62." The Eastern Region produced a *Development Programme, 1958–62* (Enugu, 1958). Only the Western Region produced a Second Five-Year Plan. *The Western Region Development Plan, 1960–65* was published as Sessional Paper no. 17 of 1959 (Ibadan, 1959).

regional body on the ministerial level whose chairman was the Prime Minister of the Federation and whose other members were the three (later four) Regional Premiers, four other ministers from each Region, and four others from the Federation itself.[14]

Thus a framework existed through which ideas could be channeled from the field to the political level and vice versa and through which plans could be coordinated even in those areas in which the Federal Government had little or no jurisdiction, such as education and agriculture. The Federal constitution and the interregional character of the planning institutions forced the planners from the very beginning into a position in which they had to get a consensus of independent agencies and in which it was not possible to enforce their will from above, though they had no wish to do the latter. In effect, the federalized organization of planning forced the plan formulation to start from the grassroots, although admittedly these roots did not always go as deep as would have been desirable.[15]

14. For a more detailed description of the institutional planning setup, see Peter B. Clark, "Economic Planning for a Country in Transition: Nigeria," in Everett E. Hagen (ed.), *Planning Economic Development* (Homewood, Ill.: Richard D. Irwin, 1963), pp. 252-293.

15. Dr. Ojetunji Aboyade has suggested that the analogy of an air root reaching from a tree branch to the ground might be more appropriate at times. Peter B. Clark (cited in my note 14), appears to consider as a shortcoming of the organization what I would consider a strength, namely, the inability to impose one's will, the necessity to persuade and to participate in political give and take, the necessity of reaching a free consensus. I mention this not to criticize Mr. Clark but to suggest that the same facts can be interpreted rather differently according to the temperament of the observer. Thus, after explaining how coordination was deficient, Mr. Clark states, "Cooperation among governments in following the policy guidelines agreed upon in the National Economic Council was excellent" (p. 263), as indeed it was. But does this not indicate that coordination worked, despite Regional autonomy? Direction was central, but the steps were worked out in a decentralized and delegated manner.

Similarly, after stating that ministers were "position oriented, not achievement oriented," and that they promoted their pet projects, Mr. Clark correctly states that "when the time for final decisions came the ministers collectively respected the economic arguments put before them and made difficult decisions regarding the final composition of the government plans"

From the beginning, development of the National Plan was seen as a fourfold exercise: (1) the formulation of capital plans for the Governments and Statutory Corporations in as integrated a manner as was possible under the circumstances; (2) the projection and shaping of the ordinary recurrent budgets; (3) the development of consistent economic policies; and (4) the building of an institutional framework within which policies could be executed and capital works would be fruitful.

The final shape of any plan depends, of course, on what happens at the political level to the proposals made on the technical level, and the Nigerian Plan is no exception. But success in getting a "technical" plan adopted is more likely if both the "grassroots" and high-level policy makers are drawn into the formulation of the plan in the first place. Acceptance will also depend on the extent to which work at all levels has already resulted in the development of ideas and plans. Planners are dependent on the ideas originating in the working ministries, and it is irrelevant to pretend that a meaningful plan can emerge from their brains alone like Pallas Athene springing from the head of Zeus.

In the specific situation of the Nigerian Plan, a number of important studies had been initiated and were bearing fruit when the Plan was being hammered out. These studies themselves had developed out of past experiences, and this gave rise to the feeling that specific knowledge in certain crucial areas would be needed in the future. At the same time, the very availability of these studies had an important influence on the specific content of the National Plan.

This point seems worth stressing because any real situation is

---

(p. 264). But what meaning is there in contrasting achievement and status, when status depends on achievement? And how else would a final decision be reached politically except by everyone's fighting for his pet project? Nonsense decisions proliferate only when political power is concentrated to such an extent that discussion becomes impossible or when advisers fail to give honest advice.

characterized by two inescapable limitations to action. The first, already mentioned, is that one never can start with a clean slate. The second is that the choices for future action are circumscribed by the alternatives that have been prepared or that can be prepared within a reasonable time span. In a particular situation it is impossible to consider *all* possible alternatives, because it is impossible to know them. This impossibility must be allowed for in the theoretical framework applied to planning, and it is central to the approach to be outlined in Chapter III. The real choices are among *known* alternatives. One choice included is of course to postpone action until further data are accumulated and thus to widen the areas of choice in the future.

To return to the specific Nigerian case, the available data included not merely information about exports and crops under the jurisdiction of Marketing Boards. An economic survey had collected essential data and represented, as it were, a dry run for future planning. The national accounts for 1950 through 1957 became available during the planning exercise itself. A transport development survey was essential for the formulation of transport policy as well as for the establishment of priorities of road construction.[16] Studies of the Niger and Benue rivers and a projection of electricity demand were available; studies of the proposed Niger Dam had been made; and many aspects of government policy as well as technical and economic aspects had been gradually clarified over the years.[17] The problem of educa-

16. *Economic Survey of Nigeria 1959* (Lagos, 1959); also P. N. C. Okigbo, *Nigerian National Accounts 1950–57*, published [December 1961] by the Federal Ministry of Economic Development, printed by the Government Printer, Enugu, Eastern Nigeria. Dr. Okigbo has also provided a short discussion under the same title in a volume for the International Association for Research in Income and Wealth—L. H. Samuels (ed.), *African Studies in Income and Wealth* (London: Bowes & Bowes, 1963), chap. 12, pp. 285-306). See also H. Robinson, S. Smith, and Kenneth Clare, *The Economic Coordination of Transport Development in Nigeria* (Stanford Research Institute Project no. 1-3280 (Lagos: Federal Ministry of Economic Development, 1961).

17. These river studies cover several large volumes. No references are

tion and high-level manpower had been discussed by Sir Eric Ashby, its budgetary implications had been worked out by J. N. Archer, and governments had made policy decisions on the subject.[18] The Electricity Corporation of Nigeria, the Nigerian Railway Corporation, and the Nigerian Ports Authority had prepared long-term development plans of their own which provided a more than adequate start in their respective fields.

Although all of the documents and reports mentioned referred directly to government investments and policies, they were immediately relevant to the development of the private sector. Thus the transport study established priorities for road construction. It also laid down policies for financing that had a direct bearing on the budget and on the relation between the publicly owned rail transport and the privately run truck and water transport.

In addition, there were of course numerous studies and policy statements relevant to the private sector. The whole field of tax policy belongs here. The establishment of a Central Bank, a stock market, banking legislation, and so forth (see Chapter VI) influenced the formulation of the Plan and are an integral part of it. This statement is necessary because obviously "planning" for the private sector is not done in the same manner as for the public sector, and because a "plan" is all too often mistaken for a detailed blueprint for the whole economy.

From the outset, the planners made every effort to learn what the "middle ranks" were thinking—by visiting all the Federal and Regional ministries and statutory corporations, research institutes, and as many businessmen and officials in the field as was possible.

given because they have not been made generally available. The following are public documents: Federation of Nigeria, *Proposals for Dams on the Niger and Kaduna Rivers* (Lagos: Federal Government Printer, 1959); Federation of Nigeria, *Statement of Policy for the Niger and Benue Rivers*, Sessional Paper no. 3 of 1959 (Lagos: Federal Government Printer, 1959).

18. Ashby (cited in my note 8); J. N. Archer, *Educational Development in Nigeria, 1961–70* (Lagos, 1961); Federation of Nigeria, *Educational Development, 1961–70*, Sessional Paper no. 3 of 1961 (Lagos, 1961).

This served not only as essential briefing but also to establish a close working relationship between the central coordinators and the dispersed executors, who were frequently originators of ideas as well. In trying to learn about activities at this level the central planners found it possible to discuss what individuals and agencies hoped to achieve, why their particular approaches to a specific problem were chosen, what the possible alternatives were, and how various plans related to each other.

In short, by bringing the executors of plans into the planning process from the beginning it is possible simultaneously to pick their brains and to set them working in the desired direction. There is no doubt that in many respects the accomplishments of the Nigerian Plan, such as they are, should not be looked for in the Plan itself or even in the process of collecting, weighing, altering, and sometimes eliminating various elements as the Plan was formulated. The real accomplishments often consisted of unspectacular changes that occurred in some ministries and statutory corporations in the manner in which they themselves approached their tasks. Chapter V, on investment criteria, indicates how initiative at all levels was used to coordinate and thereby change specific projects.

The advantages of this decentralized approach seem to be so great that it would probably have been chosen even if the constitutional arrangements of Nigeria had not made it inevitable. In this manner much more of the knowledge of an economy can be utilized than would be the case with a severely centralized approach. Decentralization almost automatically allows concrete local knowledge of social and cultural factors to enter into the formulation of a plan, and many aspects of political feasibility and social equity can be built into its very structure.[19] Moreover,

19. More will be said on the equity aspects in connection with the discussion of taxation. See also W. F. Stolper, *Social Factors in Economic Development Planning, with Special Reference to Nigeria* (Addis Ababa: Economic Commission for Africa, E/CN.14/SDP/3, 1963). This is reprinted in *East African Economics Review,* XI (June 1964), 1-17.

it becomes possible to calculate the aggregate aspects of the economy, which are essential for an over-all view, from the bottom up. This in turn allows for more realistic planning than could result from starting with aggregates themselves. All these points are taken up in more detail in subsequent chapters.

I do not mean to suggest that decentralization works miracles or that the Nigerian situation was ideal. Planners must have institutional aids in addition to good personal relationships, and their contribution should not depend on the sheer physical stamina required for frequent travel. In Nigeria, greater centralization of the coordinating and directing functions could probably be achieved by an economic secretariat in the Prime Minister's office. I believe that persuasion remains a better and more efficient method of achieving coherence than imposing one's will. But in some instances only the prestige of the Prime Minister's office is likely to achieve speedy cooperation and final decisions acceptable to all parties.

C. RESOURCE ALLOCATION AS THE CENTRAL PROBLEM

Planning in Nigeria, was from the beginning, viewed as a general problem of resource allocation and mobilization rather than merely the development of capital budgets. It is therefore necessary to describe how the task of coordination in the public sector was approached at the stage of plan formulation. The questions asked of the individual ministries and other executive agencies all aimed at developing a total picture of resource use and resource availability. For that purpose it was essential not to distinguish between capital and recurrent budgets, between developmental and nondevelopmental expenditures, and indeed even between new proposals and carry-overs from the past.

The reasons are really obvious and can be stated briefly. First, all uses of resources compete at any one moment of time for all available resources. Second, it is a mistake to see development and growth exclusively in terms of increased capital formation, however important this may be. Agricultural and industrial extension services and technological education are always included among current expenditures. Yet they are among the most powerful income-raising expenditures that can possibly be made. Third, capital expenditures build up future recurrent expenditures. It will be argued later in detail that the resource limitation to social expenditures in particular comes from rapidly increasing demands on resources for current running expenses. The problem of time sequences—of designing a program in such a manner that taxable capacity would at least grow in step with, if not faster than, the increase in current cost—will also be taken up in some detail. Fourth, a point often overlooked, the amount of resources that can be raised will depend significantly on the rationality of their use. This point, too, is central to my argument. It is logical that ministers and parliaments should be more willing to vote for higher taxes if the public or private goods and services which the taxes will buy are desired by the people. It is also often enough true that in order to get desired public or private goods, farmers will work harder. This means that a poorly designed expenditure program will reflect adversely on the amount of taxes that it is politically feasible to collect. It also means that a tax adviser is doing only half his job if he develops a tax program without considering simultaneously the manner in which the taxes are to be spent. Such advice is likely to be politically explosive and economically unsound.[20]

The preparations for the making of the Nigerian Plan suggest why in an important sense the recurrent budget becomes the central problem of development planning, as important as, or

20. All these statements are really implicit in the approach to public finance developed by Richard A. Musgrave, *Theory of the Public Economy* (New York: McGraw-Hill, 1959).

more important than, the capital budget. The budgetary implications for both taxable capacity and recurrent expenditures determine to a large degree the composition of the capital program. Considerations of future taxable capacity largely determine how big the developmental and nondevelopmental capital expenditures can be, and where, either in the recurrent or in the capital budget, it is advisable to make any cuts that might become necessary. The effects of programs on recurrent costs fix the size of the governmental program, and the costs together with the balance of payments set the safe limits to foreign borrowing and to capital imports in general, as well as to the form of the capital imports. Even gifts of schools and hospitals rapidly create a need for domestic resources to keep the schools and hospitals running. The recurrent budget is also a major link with the private sector, since policies involving subsidies, taxes, tax concessions, and the rest have direct budgetary implications. In order to illustrate this point and to show how the problem looked at an early stage of Nigerian planning, I reproduce with minor omissions the instructions which I wrote early in 1961 for the staff of the Economic Planning Unit. These instructions accompanied the worksheets that were the first attempt at collecting the detailed information which would eventually be used to make the Plan:

PROCEDURE FOR THE DEVELOPMENT PROGRAM

The present exercise is designed to give an over-all picture of the Plan and of the financing needs for the next five years. [By the time the Plan was adopted, it had been stretched to six years.] As our exercise is shaping up it involves, as it should, the rational allocation of resources. I think it would be a mistake to try at this stage to separate some of the expenditures, label them more or less arbitrarily as "development expenditure" and treat them as if they could be discussed independently of the total resources picture.

2. The Plan will consist of: a Capital Budget; a Recurrent Budget; and Policy Recommendations. This is necessary in order to ensure that the resources available to Nigeria are used in a reasonable manner.

For present purposes, I have asked that all Ministry programs for the next five years to be collected: we must know their total capital programs as well as the expenditures which will be generated by the new programs and the expected recurrent expenditure for continuing programs. It is no use to say that some of the old programs are not economic development; if they are continued they require resources which compete directly with development requirements. If at too early a stage, we limit ourselves to what we conceive to be "development expenditure" we run the danger that any cuts—which there will inevitably be—will be made in the new Development Program rather than elsewhere.

3. I have further asked that any revenue figures are collected. This has the double purpose of enabling us to make payoff calculations and the much needed evaluation of the resources which will have to be contributed from outside a Ministry or public corporation. In other words, if the figures are collected as I have requested, we ought to be able to translate them into:

(1) the total Program
(2) a Capital and a Recurrent Program
(3) a Financing Program
(4) a Resources Picture, and
(5) a Regional distribution of the spending.

If the figures are collected as I have asked them to be, it will be comparatively easy to translate any program we wish into the customary budgetary process.

4. I am adamant on getting recurrent expenditures for two important reasons. First, some of the major economic development programs, particularly in agriculture, must be recurrent programs. We must get away from visualizing the economic development programs essentially as a series of real estate projects, and we must equally get away from the notion that "development" is something separate from the management of every day affairs of the Ministry, et cetera.

. . . .

5. The requested information for revenues has the additional purpose of drawing attention to important policy questions. For example, if the Ministry of Information requests too much money for recurrent expenditure on radio, we should be in a position to go back with a request that they reconsider their own salary policy, their own programming, and, possibly, the collection of license revenues. Similar

problems will arise with respect to staff housing. Even a casual glance at the tables which we have prepared indicates that much too much use is made of subsidies for recurrent purposes, and it is an elementary proposition that somebody has to pay for these subsidies. Under Nigerian circumstances, the payer is most frequently the farmer while the beneficiaries are a small number of urban dwellers. We must be able to pinpoint where the beneficiaries of an economic service are and where they do not pay for the benefits which they receive. The payments may, of course, be either through the market mechanism, as may for example be the case with radio licenses, or through taxation. The latter involves shifting more of the tax burden to local authorities in Lagos and elsewhere to pay for local services rather than for them to be subsidized by farmers.

6. This problem will become very urgent because the development program, on the one hand is very ambitious while the resources are relatively scarce. In the past, a major part of the resources have been accumulated by marketing board profits. With world prices falling, the marketing boards may cease to be a source of substantial development funds unless the prices paid to farmers are reduced. It is obviously necessary that we will advocate the reduction of marketing board prices paid to farmers, at least to the level where the marketing boards cease to lose money. It is therefore likely that we will have to suggest a further reduction to enable marketing boards to accumulate development funds. This is a politically serious decision which no Minister can be expected to suggest to the country unless he is prepared to put an equal burden on the urban dwellers. This means basically that subsidies are abolished or reduced wherever possible and that local authorities assume a greater burden.

7. I have outlined some of the answers which we may expect to get from the tables as we have set them up. The first priority is, I repeat, to get the size of the total program regardless of whether it is strictly development or not and regardless of how it is financed because we must get an over-all picture of the claims on the resources.

8. The second priority is to get the actual financing needs: in the case of most Ministries this will be equivalent to the total program, in the case of public corporations there will be substantial differences. Even at this stage, we are not yet interested in whether the total contribution required by the Federal Government is to be in the form of a grant or loan or whether the contribution required may be through an international bank loan or a loan negotiated on the open market.

9. The third priority is to derive from the tables a revised picture of the recurrent expenditure projections so that we may get a better understanding of the available resources. We have projections furnished us by the Ministry of Finance, and, as you know, the Regions have given us their projections. All these projections have been made on the assumption that there will be only normal growth and that only those programs which could be seen at the time at which the projections were made were included. The new figures will give us the implications of the new development programs on recurrent expenditure and will allow us to make a better estimate of budget surpluses for capital expenditure.

10. The fourth urgent need is to derive a Regional distribution of the capital expenditure. This is part of our terms of reference; it is clearly politically important; it will become more so when the Regional development plans are known and when the Regional needs for Federal assistance if any are clearer.

11. Of fifth importance is to develop the implications of the capital program for imported material requirements and manpower needs and, similarly, the implications of the recurrent programs. This is needed for the evaluation of the individual programs for balance of payments implications, for training implications, but also for suggestions of domestic industrialization . . .

12. The sixth need is to develop the revenue implications of the program.

13. The seventh will then be to take another over-all look and match available resources with needs.

14. It is understood, of course, that all breakdowns have to be phased.

It is obviously easier to ask questions than to get answers. At the same time, it is clear that successful planning cannot even start unless answers to the questions are forthcoming. Without such answers, programs remain hanging in the air, and if too many programs have no firm basis, the whole plan becomes an idle exercise with a great potential for harm. The inability to get certain answers itself inevitably must determine the shape of a meaningful plan.

No plan is the work of one man or of a small group of men. The Nigerian Plan, as finally approved by the Federal and the three Regional cabinets and the National Economic Council, and as passed by the various Houses of Representatives in April 1962, is of course no exception. Coordination will remain imperfect, planners have staff functions, and ultimate decisions will remain political. The size of the Plan itself was and continues to be a matter of dispute. Rather than cut it, the Government extended its life from five to six years, without everyone's having been aware of the implications which such a "simple" political decision has on time sequences, executive and taxable capacities, inflationary pressures, wages, policy, and indeed on the realism and relevance of the Plan.[21] Just the same, many economic arguments *were* considered in the working out of compromises. Ministers were receptive to the economic implications of their political decisions, and they did limit educational, health, and transport plans (to name only a few) to amounts which available resources made at the time seem possible.

Nevertheless it is a mistake to expect any real plan to be wholly rational in economic terms or to be wholly consistent. The economist may regret that this is so, and the politician may come to regret some of his decisions when they have begun to backfire, when they fail to achieve his political ends, and when they raise new and yet more disagreeable problems. But it is futile to discuss a real plan as if it were an academic exercise, for a real plan is inevitably a compromise. The purpose of this chapter has been to explain how specific situations could be handled, and in what sense the Nigerian Plan represents the double compromise among conflicting ends and between what was desirable and what was feasible. Some of the Plan's serious weaknesses are discussed in later chapters. I believe, however, that the manner in which the planning operation tried to come

21. See, for example, Sayre P. Schatz, "Nigeria's First National Development Plan (1962–68)—An Appraisal," *Nigerian Journal of Economic and Social Studies,* V (1963), 221-235; W. F. Stolper, "How Bad is the Plan?" *Nigerian Journal of Economic and Social Studies,* VI (1964), 261-276.

to terms with the political and economic realities of Nigeria has
some relevance for development efforts anywhere.[22]

22. It is obvious that as the former Head of the Economic Planning Unit
in the Federal Ministry of Economic Development I am in no position to
publish more data than are officially available. Nor do I intend to break any
confidences to which I was admitted. Thus it would be quite improper for
me to give an account of the many confidential discussions in which the
final Plan was hammered out. Though I was present at all meetings of the
Joint Planning Committee, I attended only the single meeting of the
National Economic Council in which the final decision on the Plan was
taken, and I was not present at any cabinet meetings or at any meetings of
the Economic Committee of the cabinet. No one except the participants
knows how decisions were arrived at during the meetings of the finance
ministers or of the four premiers. I saw my own minister, the Honorable
Waziri Ibrahim, frequently and at length, but I had virtually no contact
with other ministers, though I had many consultations with the permanent
secretaries of the other ministries and with the Central Bank.

My views on the size of the Plan were published with the permission of
the Honorable Waziri Ibrahim in his capacity as Federal Minister of Economic Development. My paper written for the United Nations Economic
Commission for Africa in 1961 under the title "Comprehensive Development
Planning," reprinted in *East African Economics Review*, I, New Series
(December 1964), 1-21, was similarly cleared, and it too represents my own
views and not necessarily those of the ministry.

The best published critique of the Federal Program was made by Dr.
Ojetunji Aboyade of the University of Ibadan, who, at the time of his
criticism, had no access to the whole Plan or the underlying documents. See
his "A Critique of the Plan," *Nigerian Journal of Economics and Social
Studies*, IV (July 1962), 110-115. His critique drew upon the general outline of the Plan given in my "The Main Features of the 1962–68 National
Plan," *ibid.*, pp. 85-91; and L. M. Hansen, "Methods of Economic Programming and Analysis in the Plan," *ibid.*, pp. 92-109. Dr. Aboyade later
became my successor as head of the Economic Planning Unit and thus had
access to unpublished information. He has expanded his criticism in his
book, *Foundations of an African Economy: A Study of Investment and
Growth in Nigeria* (New York: Frederick A. Praeger, 1966).

III

A General View of Planning[1]

THE actual planning problem consists of mobilizing and allocating resources for growth in the best manner that time and circumstances permit. Planning (and development) always occurs in a specific historic situation, and, as repeatedly emphasized, no one can escape the limitations of his starting point. The problems to be faced can nevertheless be more or less abstractly formulated. It is the purpose of this chapter to discuss the major theoretical issues raised by the particular way of looking at the operational problem and to suggest theoretically valid operational solutions to the problems with which planners are actually faced.

A. ABSORPTIVE CAPACITY

An obvious characteristic of any economy is that it constitutes a very complicated network of interrelationships. This is true even when there is a large amount of nonmarket production. One rarely deals with a distinct subsistence sector; mostly one finds people who can produce either for the market or for themselves and finds goods that may either be sold or directly consumed. Planning must somehow learn to allow for these interrelationships. The approach must be a general rather than a partial one.

1. An earlier version of this chapter appeared under the title "External Economies from a Planning Standpoint" in the *Zeitschrift für die gesamte Staatswissenschaft*, CXIX (1963), 195-217.

A second characteristic of any economy is that the interrelationships refer to different moments of time and are changing, i.e. that there are changing time lags. It is indeed one avowed purpose of planning to change the interrelationships in order to accelerate growth. The approach to planning ought therefore to allow specifically for time relationship.

A third characteristic of any economy is that at any one moment of time it has a given productive apparatus, a given stock of machinery and factories, a given number of people of various skills. It is further characteristic of underdeveloped economies that in their productive structure they lack certain, perhaps most, lines of production, and that, in Leontief's terminology, many cells of their input-output table are empty.

A fourth characteristic of all economies is that, except in wartime and in very exceptional circumstances, they are open. The degree of their integration into the world economy may vary with size, resource endowment, location, and what not, but outside influences are unavoidable. The need to trade may be a boon to the economy or a stifling limitation on its development, but it cannot be disregarded.

A fifth consideration—it is not just a characteristic of economies —is that planners are human and no man can know the future. It is obviously the purpose of planning to anticipate the future and if possible to shape it. But the farther the future stretches, the less likely it is that what will happen will coincide with what has been planned to happen.

It is difficult to see how anyone can object to these five points. Yet they seem to me to amount to a controversial approach to planning and development and to deserve extended discussion in this chapter. Obviously the approach followed is very similar to what is called "dynamic programming," and again it is difficult to object; for who could object to decision making over time?[2]

2. I use the term "dynamic programming" with considerable diffidence, and I avoid it as much as possible. On the one hand, I believe strongly that

What I wish to emphasize, however, is that specific propositions often may turn out to be inappropriate to an actual situation. In the process of translating a theoretical construct into a specific action program, arbitrary decisions and judgments can be minimized, but they cannot be avoided.

The dynamic approach to development planning requires the planner to have a time horizon. The most satisfactory time horizon in terms of logic is also the one that is practically impossible: infinity. Theoretically, it is necessary to specify a goal in the future which then can be approached in an optimal manner. Therefore, although the setting of such a goal cannot be avoided, it cannot be set in a realistic manner. Hence adherence to it in every detail would be a catastrophe. There are too many unknowables, not merely unknowns. This means that a good plan must allow for adaptive processes to take place and must ideally build them into the plan itself. It also means that the long run is seen essentially as a sequence of short-run decisions, each made as best as can be, each allowing for as much of the future as is visible now, but no more. Practically speaking, planning involves optimizing as one goes along.

Such a statement inevitably raises questions of plan goals and of optimizing over time versus optimizing at any one moment of time. A plan can formulate ambitious goals in a consistent

---

this approach to development is theoretically preferable to any other. On the other hand, it would be a serious pretense on my part to suggest that I understand the mathematics involved, though the basic ideas are clear enough. I leave the theoretical development to my betters: Chakravarty, Chenery, Eckaus, Lefeber, Leontief, Samuelson, Solow, and others, whose direct and indirect help is gratefully and admiringly acknowledged. I am, however, concerned with two aspects of their theoretical constructs. First, assuming that they are right, what can I *do* about it in the circumstances that have been sketched in the preceding chapters and that, *mutatis mutandis*, are general? Second, how do other policy prescriptions, such as "increase savings and investments," or "investments should be capital intensive," or "the shadow price of capital should be $x\%$" measure up against the implication of their theory? The theoretical framework of this book might be, somewhat bombastically, described as "the numerical approximation to the solution of a nonlinear dynamic programming problem."

manner. As argued later, the formulation of a bargaining plan as against a realistic plan means that what is planned will not be won—with serious undesirable consequences for priorities and resource mobilization.

This is not the issue here, however. In the present context it is clear that what happens in the economy depends on implementation rather than on goals. Obvious though this is, it means that even realistic goals can be reached or surpassed only if each successive step to achieve them is optimal.

I believe that the only realistic aim of a plan ought to be to ensure that the economy will grow at a certain minimum rate *or more*, that the economy should be put into a position where in successive periods an increasing number of economic choices become available, so that it becomes increasingly master of its own fate.[3] This I believe is achieved quickest if at any moment of time the economy achieves the largest short-run growth rate possible. Obviously it is logically possible that short-run maximization may not lead to maximization of the long-run rate and vice versa. I believe, however, that under realistic assumptions and with proper safeguards such a result can easily be avoided. In any case, achieving a short-run optimum is a necessary though not a sufficient condition for achieving a long-run optimum.[4] Steps must be taken over time. Step two cannot precede step one, and a faulty first step may make it impossible to take a better step later.

The maximum growth rate that can be achieved will be limited

3. Chakravarty puts it as follows: "There is nothing in the logic of economic analysis which dictates what should be the terminal condition . . . The main idea behind the choice of terminal conditions is to sustain the level of economic activity and/or to ensure growth beyond the planning period." S. Chakravarty, "Alternative Preference Functions in Problems of Investment Planning on the National Level" (mimeographed paper presented to the International Economic Association Conference on "Activity Analysis," Cambridge, Eng., 1963), p. 10.

4. This has been pointed out to me in a letter by Mr. Chakravarty. See also his paper, just cited.

by the structure of the economy, including both its openness and its productive capacities. Both will have a direct bearing on the absorptive capacity of the economy, i.e., on the rate at which investments can be pushed with a hope of stimulating growth.

Investment means the use of resources over time for the purpose of enlarging the productive capacity of a country and of enlarging the stream of outputs. Investments have gestation periods, and they have to be replaced. For technical reasons, it is sometimes impossible to invest in Industry A unless there has been a previous investment in Industry B. Sometimes the investments can be made simultaneously. Sometimes imports or exports can make up for insufficient inputs or insufficient markets.

However, it is clear that existing capacities will present bottlenecks which a good plan will try to break. Breaking them takes time. A simple application of more savings and more investment may help but cannot solve the problem. On the saving side, the form in which savings become available will be limited by the structure of the economy. If the economy can export freely, increased savings can take the form of convertible foreign exchange which in turn can be used to obtain any goods desired. But if the country cannot export freely, the increased savings have as their counterpart domestic resources which for technical reasons cannot be always easily converted into investments. This problem of lacking complementary goods is not solved by simply increasing the savings, and indeed, increasing the savings alone may make the solution more difficult. The solution requires the breaking of specific bottlenecks.

Similarly, an investment that will raise productive capacity and increase income cannot be made unless there is a market for the output. If there is such a market, the investment will be profitable. There may still be many obstacles to overcome, but they are of a different order and are not considered here. The important point in the present context is that absorptive capacity can be defined by the amount of investment which can be profitably undertaken, and the absorptive capacity so defined is *limited at any moment of time.*[5]

We need not linger on the precise definition of "profitability," since much more will be said about it later. Suffice it here to say that "profit" allows for interactions in the economy and for appropriate prices. *At any one moment of time* the amounts of output that can be sold depend on what happens elsewhere in the economy (and abroad if it is possible to export); but what happens elsewhere in the economy will itself depend not only on cross-reactions in the economy but also on the speed with which factors can be shifted and investments undertaken.

Now planning can do two things. It can act as a coordinating device which, if accepted by a sufficient number of decision makers, can induce them to make investments that mutually support each other. And it can act as a device to reduce risks of investment in the process. Both are important aspects of planning. Both use the price mechanism and act to make so-called external economies real. Both thereby act to speed the process of development.

But it is not possible to speed the process *ad libitum.* If investments could be made once and for all and needed no replacement while producing income streams in all eternity, one could wait until the market for the output has grown sufficiently. The inputs might have been made earlier than necessary and hence might have been inefficient, but eventually growth would catch up with them, and no irremediable harm would be done. But if investments must be replaced, they must earn their way during their lifetime. It is not always, not even frequently, possible

5. J. R. Hicks put his finger on this crucial problem a long time ago by pointing out that "economic growth is not merely a matter of investment as such, but of investment in ways that are sufficiently productive. We must distinguish between causes that make for a high rate of saving, and causes that make for ability to turn savings into highly productive investments." Hicks, *Essays in World Economics* (Oxford: Clarendon Press, 1959), p. 177. The essay from which this quotation is taken was written in 1957.

to speed up other investments so that they provide a market for the first one in time. This is simply inherent in the fact that *all* investments involve inputs and outputs over time. Consequently, if an investment is undertaken too early, the other investment will not have a chance to provide the necessary market. How fast other investments can provide the market will depend on the structure of the economy.

I have stressed the production aspects to indicate that even when shortages of demand in the Keynesian sense are eliminated, bottlenecks in the structure of production remain and define *at any one moment* the optimum size of a program. Even if investments lasted forever, an investment undertaken too early would reduce the rate of growth, at least temporarily, below the possible rate. For, suppose that the investment had been postponed. This would have allowed more consumption, which would have increased the market for some good or goods earlier, which in turn would have increased the investment opportunities. Since in fact investments do not last, the reduced demand implied in too early an investment may prevent the market from growing to sufficient size to make the investment profitable ever.

Absorptive capacity is therefore ultimately limited by the structure of the economy and the fact that investment decisions must be made over time. There are, of course, other limiting factors. Executive personnel are scarce and lose their effectiveness when overworked. Lack of executive capacity is a further limitation on absorptive capacity.

It is in this context that the impact which the openness of the economy has on absorptive capacity can be most sensibly discussed. There can be little doubt that integration into the world economy may increase the absorptive capacity of a country. For, potentially at least, international specialization permits the sale abroad of production that cannot be sold at home, and it permits the imports of complementary factors for the production of which the domestic market would be too small. The point goes beyond the traditional gains from trade because the gains now discussed also include gains from larger-scale production.

The market can be increased in two ways: by integration into the world economy or by growth of the internal market. The two are of course not inconsistent. Even if the market initially grows mainly by exporting, rising income will make the domestic production of additional goods possible.

The issue is not whether international trade is or is not an engine of growth. The issue is simply that economies *are* in fact open, whether a country likes it or not, and that they cannot avoid allowing for the openness in their investment decisions. Similarly, the issue is not whether to have import substitution or not but what kind of import substitution to have. As the domestic market grows, import substitution becomes inevitable in any case. The question is: how can the growth be achieved fastest?

Countries may have a difficult time integrating into the world economy, because they may have nothing to sell, or because the elasticity of demand for their products is low and the gains from trade go to others.[6] This may indeed be so, although it is also possible that the true elasticities are underestimated and that the inability to sell abroad is homemade rather than foreign-imposed. Nigerian exports have in fact expanded satisfactorily. If a country really cannot export, it probably finds it also exceedingly difficult to develop domestically. Chile is sometimes mentioned as a case in point.

It should be observed that regardless of the elasticities involved, a country still has to decide precisely which domestic industries to develop. If the foreign elasticities are low, that by itself should make domestic industries more profitable—provided, of course, that the domestic market is sufficiently big to sustain a

6. See, for example, H. W. Singer, "The Distribution of Gains between Investing and Borrowing Countries," *American Economic Review* (May 1950). Reprinted in H. W. Singer, *International Development: Growth and Change* (New York: McGraw-Hill, 1964).

domestic industry. But, as Lloyd Metzler has shown, if foreign elasticities are low, protection may backfire and make domestic industries less, not more, profitable.[7] Protection may therefore hinder domestic development under exactly those conditions which normally call forth recommendations for import substitution. This suggests that, paradoxically, a more thorough integration into the world economy may be more favorable to a policy of import substitution than a policy of withdrawal from the world economy!

To repeat, the real issue is what kind of import substitutes to produce and when, not whether to produce any at all. Economic development *means* acquiring a more complicated productive structure; it *means* producing goods at home that were once imported. But development will occur only if the investments produce profits over their lifetime, or at least if they avoid losses.

No wonder, therefore, that W. A. Lewis and Albert Hirschman used imports as a kind of market study to select those industries that might be economic out of all the industries for which imports have shown a demand to exist. No wonder that Sukhamoy Chakravarty uses the much-despised comparative advantage as a means of determining which cells in the input-output table to fill and when. No wonder that Hollis Chenery comes to the conclusion that countries could do much worse than specialize according to comparative advantage.[8]

7. L. A. Metzler, "Tariffs, the Terms of Trade, and the Distribution of National Income," *Journal of Political Economy*, LVII (February 1949), 1-29.

8. W. A. Lewis, *Report on the Industrialization of the Gold Coast* (Accra: Government Printing Department, 1953), reprinted 1962. A. O. Hirschman, *The Strategy of Economic Development* (New Haven: Yale University Press, 1958). Hollis B. Chenery, "Comparative Advantage and Development Policy," *American Economic Review*, LI (March 1961), 18-51. S. Chakravarty, *The Logic of Investment Planning*, Contributions to Economic Analysis, no. 18 (Amsterdam: North Holland Co., 1959).

Arguments have of course been put forth to the effect that the theory of comparative advantage is static and therefore automatically useless in dynamic situations and that specialization according to comparative advan-

This does not mean that free trade is the best of all possible development policies. It may mean that small countries with limited resource endowments cannot hope to develop except in the context of at least a regional grouping. It certainly means that "import substitution" as such is not an operational concept for development policy. The operational concept is profitability, and how to measure it in an actual situation comes up for consideration later.

If free trade does not work economic miracles, neither (as some writers and planners seem to imply) is the existence of international trade a flaw in the real world which the planners should correct. Some of the discussions come very close to suggesting that *any* kind of import substitution is good from the standpoint of growth and development of an underdeveloped country. Yet the countries increasing their income as well as their standard of living at the most spectacular rate are also countries in which foreign integration has been substantial. Hong Kong has absorbed millions of refugees successfully at rising economic levels. No doubt there were special circumstances: the influx of Chinese labor was accompanied by an influx also of Chinese capital and entrepreneurs. And one should probably not underrate the fact that Hong Kong is a gateway from and to mainland China. But how many economists can honestly say that fifteen years ago they believed it possible that Hong Kong, at an eightfold increase in population (compared to 1945) and with rising wages, would manufacture machines for local use and would successfully overcome discrimination against her exports by ad-

---

tage tends to freeze economies along existing lines of production. The brief discussion in the text indicates that this is not my view.

It may be of interest to point out that location theory also envisages the gradual growth of a complicated industrial structure in different areas of the world. The one-sentence paraphrase of location theory that corresponds to the statement that countries tend to specialize in lines of production in which they have a comparative advantage, would read: "A good is produced in as many locations as possible." See A. Lösch, *The Economics of Location* (New Haven: Yale University Press, 1954).

vanced countries? The conclusion is inevitable that the skill of the colony's administrators in promoting integration into the world economy largely accounts for the success of Hong Kong. Similarly, the rapid growth of Japan has been associated with a dramatic change in the commodity composition of her trade, which serves to show what can be done with good policies and good luck. Low elasticities of demand refer normally to raw materials. With increasing industrialization the argument that exports cannot be expanded because of inelasticities of demand, even where true with the existing structure of trade, loses much of its force. There is no reason why Nigeria or any other country should not be able to produce, even *now*, assembled products both for the domestic market and for exports.

The point of this lengthy digression is not to make a case for "exports as an engine of growth." But it is not only import structure that should change from consumption to investment goods in the normal course of development. Export structure should also alter. To come back to the point made before, import substitution by itself is not an operational concept, but profitability is, even though profitability considerations are likely to lead to import substitution.

The approach advocated here (which may be described as dynamic general equilibrium or dynamic programming with built-in adaptive processes) must be further analyzed with regard to external economies and the aggregative planning framework.

External economies were conceived by Alfred Marshall as a method of introducing the interactions in the economy into a partial equilibrium framework. The dynamic approach, as outlined, specifically allows for interactions and is therefore an operational way of dealing with external economies. Theorists distinguish between technological and pecuniary external economies, the former operating directly and without the market mechanism, the latter with and through the market mechanism. Tibor Scitovsky and others have pointed out that purely technological external economies are rare. Scitovsky also concludes, "Pecuniary external economies clearly have no place in equilibrium theory," and he points out that profits are a disequilibrium phenomenon.[9] It follows in the present context that allowing for interactions in the economy will in fact allow for external economies of a pecuniary type. It would therefore be as inappropriate to allow for them in *addition* to what can be calculated through interactions as it would be to forget the calculations of these interactions. The manner of the calculation of the profitability is therefore crucial.

Moreover, it is by no means certain whether or not allowing for repercussions will in fact increase or decrease the profitability of individual investments. Scitovsky points out that planning can provide a signaling system to supplement the price mechanism and thus improve the allocation of investments. He also notes that although from the standpoint of the world as a whole *all* economies and diseconomies ought to be allowed for, from the standpoint of any one developing country only those economies or diseconomies accruing to it are relevant.[10] And Marcus Flem-

9. Tibor Scitovsky, "Two Concepts of External Economies," *Journal of Political Economy,* LXII (April 1954), 143-151. Reprinted in A. N. Agarwala and S. P. Singh (eds.), *The Economics of Underdevelopment* (Bombay: Oxford University Press, 1958), where the quotation appears on p. 300. Scitovsky refers to J. E. Meade. "External Economies and Diseconomies in a Competitive Situation," *Economic Journal,* 62 (March 1952), 54-67.

10. Scitovsky, in *The Economics of Underdevelopment,* p. 306. He continues: "Accordingly, investment in export industries is always less, and that in import competing industries is always more desirable from the national, than from the international, point of view" (p. 307). It should be stressed that Scitovsky compares the national and international points of view. He does *not* say that investment in import-competing industries is always preferable to investments in export industries. This fact is worth stressing because the sentence reproduced has been quoted to me as suggesting that he does.

Scitovsky is also the author of a brilliant article on "A Reconsideration of the Theory of Tariffs," *Review of Economic Studies,* IX (Summer 1942), 89-110. Reprinted in American Economic Association, *Readings in the Theory of International Trade,* ed. H. S. Ellis and L. A. Metzler (Homewood, Ill.: Richard D. Irwin, 1949). There he shows that mutual tariff

ing's analysis shows that when repercussions on cost as well as demand are allowed for, "the introduction of unprofitable though efficient large scale production in one industry is more likely to reduce than to increase the profitability of other industries."[11]

Enough has been said to indicate that the approach outlined provides the signaling system needed and allows for repercussions. The approach therefore translates into operational terms the concepts of external economies and balanced growth—insofar as it is possible to translate a sophisticated theoretical argument into a rough and ready action program. Nothing in the theoretical discussion of external economies permits one to neglect profitability as a guide to action; nor does theory suggest that the acceleration of growth achieved by a "balanced" effort can be increased at will.[12] The approach to development planning sketched here may therefore be properly interpreted as a legitimate offspring of development theory which received its modern impetus from Allyn Young and Paul Rosenstein-Rodan.[13]

There is thus no inevitable inconsistency between the approach outlined and the writings on external economies and balanced

---

retaliation will leave all trading partners worse off than they were or would be in a free-trade situation. Is it inappropriate to suggest that retaliation triggered by deliberate import substitution may also leave everyone worse off?

11. J. Marcus Fleming, "External Economies and the Doctrine of Balanced Growth," *Economic Journal*, 65 (June 1955), 241-256. Reprinted in Agarwala and Singh (cited in my note 9), quotation on p. 290.

12. For a brief discussion of balanced growth, with an excellent bibliography, see José Maria Dagnino-Pastore, "Balanced Growth: An Interpretation," *Oxford Economic Papers*, XV, New Series (July 1963), 164-176.

13. Allyn A. Young, "Increasing Returns and Economic Progress" (Presidential Address, Section F of the British Association for the Advancement of Science, 1928), reprinted in R. V. Clemence (ed.), *Readings in Economic Analysis*, vol. I (Cambridge, Mass.: Addison-Wesley Press, 1950). Paul N. Rosenstein-Rodan, "Problems of Industrialization of Eastern and South-Eastern Europe," *Economic Journal*, 53 (June–September 1943), 202-211. Reprinted in Agarwala and Singh, cited in my note 9. It is hardly an exaggeration to say that modern development theory starts with this path-breaking article.

growth.[14] This is not necessarily true for a development approach that relies primarily on aggregative concepts. A word must therefore be said about the relationship which inter-industry economies and a dynamic general equilibrium approach bear to the aggregative national-income framework which is an equally indispensable tool for development planning.

The national-income framework uses aggregates, i.e., not basic elements. "Investment" and "national income" are not homogeneous concepts but are aggregates whose meaning derives from the nature of their components. From the purely scholarly standpoint of the teacher, a good deal is to be said for the simplifications that deal with such entities as wage goods, an investment good, an export and import good, and the like. At a particular level of abstraction, it is quite legitimate to eliminate the aggregation problem by simplifying assumptions.

However, once the concepts mentioned are to be quantified— that is, still on a scholarly level of abstraction and long before we have reached the policy level of making an actual economic plan—it becomes necessary to deal with the operational magnitudes of investment, national income, etc., as aggregates. This in turn means that the composition of the aggregates takes on great importance, and in fact the aggregates cannot be interpreted usefully unless their composition is understood and their method of aggregation is specified. Aggregation involves among other things the choice of a particular system of prices to weigh the components and to allow their combination.

The theoretical aspects of aggregation need not concern us here. Even before descending to the operational level from theoretical abstraction, however, it is essential to realize the futility of talking about totals without talking about the components.

14. The manner in which the concepts are applied at times is, however, hair-raising. It would be invidious to quote examples. It would be uncomfortably easy to do so.

The practical planning aspect is even more important. By forgetting that investment as well as national income is an aggregate, many who discuss development proceed as if the problem of development consisted essentially of increasing investments. The limits to investment are looked for in the available resources. This in turn reduces the problem to methods of raising savings and capital imports. Once resources available for investment are increased, an assumed capital-output ratio is thought to raise income automatically and proportionately.

This spending-for-its-own-sake approach can be improved by substituting a series of sectoral capital-output ratios for a single aggregate capital-output ratio. In fact, a breakdown of the ratio into a number of components is required under the balanced-growth approach. This, however, is not the sort of disaggregation which is at issue here.

Capital-output ratios (c/o) were originally intended to show what increases in physical capacities would be needed to achieve certain increases in output. As such they were defensible statements of a technological nature. A categorical statement, however, that a certain investment will automatically raise output or national income is different in nature. There is a logical discontinuity between saying that a textile machine of a certain specification can produce so and so many yards of a certain kind of cloth and stating that textile machinery not further specified worth x million can produce, per year and over its life, textiles not further specified valued at y million. The former statement is purely technological, but the latter is a combination of technological and economic statements.

The jump from physical units to values necessarily carries one into the domain of prices and cost-benefit calculations. Whether national income will in fact be raised by increasing investments depends on whether the investments pay off. It may well be true that $100 invested in textile machinery will produce $20 worth of textiles for six years, provided prices of textiles are constant. But if the textiles cannot be sold except at a loss, the effect of the investment will be detrimental to growth. Policy recommendations based on over-all or even sectoral capital-output ratios without underlying payoff calculations as to whether a particular output mix can be profitably achieved with a particular input mix are likely to lead to unrealistic results, to put it politely.[15] Policy recommendations regarding taxation and other methods of raising savings are likely to have pernicious results if they are not related to the possible use of these savings. Aggregative concepts are dangerous to use and impossible to interpret unless they can be linked to the micro-aspects of an economy.

Moreover, in an open economy, price effects, for reasons of internal logic, cannot be neglected. It may, after all, be no occasion for parades in Nigeria or Ghana that cocoa production will as the result of certain inputs increase by 50 percent, if Nigerians or Ghanaians do not consume cocoa and if the real resources which this rise of domestic production will buy abroad increase only 20 percent because of a change in the price of

15. There is a whole literature on the nature of capital-output ratios which makes other valid objections. C/O ratios assume, for example, that capital is the only determinant of output, that the labor inputs are constant, that the sectoral composition of capital remains constant, and so forth. I have not gone into these criticisms, on the assumption that they are well known. I am here mainly concerned to stress the relation between micro and macro concepts. In particular, between capital inputs and the final outputs there must be the intervening variables of profits and prices.

Hicks (note 5, above) has made the same point by saying that "there is in fact no guarantee that capital expenditure—or what the accountants are prepared to certify as capital expenditure—will help the development of the country significantly, or even at all . . . The error has been abetted by the practice of national income statisticians of valuing capital investment *at cost*. This, from their point of view, is natural; it is a thing which they are almost obliged to do; but one must still insist that it is a very dangerous proceeding. The gain (to the nation) from putting up a mill is not measured by the cost of the mill, but by its value in terms of future output; if the thing proves to be a white elephant, the investment that was embodied in it will be simply thrown away" (p. 176). Italics are in the original.

cocoa. From the standpoint of Nigeria's or Ghana's development, resources *available* are relevant, not resources produced.[16]

It would be easy in Nigeria to increase cocoa production by leaps and bounds with little additional inputs. Unfortunately, Nigerians do not drink cocoa or eat chocolate. The real alternatives would be to sell the cocoa at falling prices or to store it (at considerable cost in a tropical country). Storage would lead to considerable though quite spurious growth in the Nigerian accounts, particularly if the increase in unsold and unsalable stocks of cocoa would be entered in the national accounts at the price at which the rest of the cocoa was sold, that is, at prices that are high only because some of the cocoa was withheld from sale.

The point is obvious. Yet in the American national accounts agricultural products withheld from the market by the various agricultural programs are counted as part of GNP at market prices, and something like this seems to be done with coffee in the Brazilian accounts. In the case of the United States, the values involved are negligible. In the Brazilian case, they are probably not. In the case of Nigeria or Ghana, they certainly would not be.

Matters are actually still worse. "The use of a constant capital output ratio on the margin implies that additional output from an act of investment is constant in perpetuity." "The needed generalization," however, "consists in defining investment as a dated sequence of inputs and outputs."[17] Neither the input streams nor the output streams are regular, and the outputs certainly come in time after the inputs. Thus the prices at which inputs and outputs are measured will not necessarily be constant over time. The cost of investment is incurred *now*, but the results come later. To proceed in such circumstances without explicit

16. See H. W. Singer, as cited in my note 6.
17. S. Chakravarty, "Alternative Preference Functions" (my note 3), pp. 3, 4. The implications for shadow prices will concern us later.

payoff calculations and on the assumption of constant capital-output ratios is to invite disaster.

In this regard, it is most unlikely that *at any one moment* an economic plan can be enlarged without increasing the aggregate capital-output ratio. At least two phenomena must be considered. A project may require a great deal of investment and a long lead time before it produces any income. Or, an investment may not produce any net income at all, regardless of the lead period involved. Now imagine a double ordering. First, order projects in declining order of expected profitability over their lifetimes, finding a cutoff point where the return is less than the cost of capital. Second, rank the projects so selected in order of their capital-output ratios. Since the cutoff point of investment was where there was no net return, it follows that any additional investment undertaken will at the very best not produce net income. Additional investment may bring losses and thus reduce the net income of the economy, or it may be of the kind for which economic calculations cannot be made. (It goes without saying that the calculation of net return allows for interactions in the economy. The problem of shadow pricing is touched upon later.)

The capital-output ratio that is economically relevant—and which is the only one that can be measured—must therefore increase as a program is enlarged to include both delayed payoff projects and less profitable projects. The observed capital-output ratios do not, therefore, simply reflect the composition of investments with respect to sectoral capital-output ratios and length of gestation periods. They also reflect the efficiency and profitability of investments.

This analysis implies that there is an optimum-size program and that programs therefore can be too big. It is obvious that inclusion of loss investments will reduce the rate of growth and will hurt the development of a country—obviously after due allowance for interactions, a qualification that will not be repeated any more. How big a viable program can be depends on a country's absorptive capacity. The analysis implies also that the timing of investments is crucial and that the timing itself will be affected by both technological requirements of inter- action and profitability considerations.

Thus any well-thought-out development program that is based on detailed analysis of its individual components and tested for internal consistency can be enlarged only by adding investments that will not raise income at least during the period under con- sideration—say the next five or six years. Increasing an invest- ment program means in these circumstances in effect raising capital-output ratios. Plans which raise investments while keep- ing the capital-output ratio constant—and frequently rather low, to boot—must be viewed with suspicion. They are likely to be unrealistic, and they are likely to be inconsistent in at least one respect: since they assume that income will rise beyond what is feasible, they are likely to assume greater savings and internal mobilization of resources than can in fact be mobilized, which in turn is likely to make nonsense of the resource picture on which the investments depend.

This discussion also indicates why it is idle to criticize a plan for not assuming or postulating a higher rate of growth. The rate of growth to be achieved will depend in the short run on the level of spending, including the level of investments, be- cause in the short run the multiplier effects are likely to dominate. But a sustained rate of growth can be achieved only by adding to productive capacity and making profitable investments. Con- centration on profitability, not postulating larger rates of growth through more investments, will achieve maximum growth.[18]

18. I cannot resist adding a quotation from R. M. Solow's *Capital Theory and the Rate of Return* (Amsterdam: North Holland Co.; and Chicago: Rand-McNally & Co., 1964), although it appeared long after the Nigerian Plan was formulated and the present manuscript was largely completed. "Without any dubious 'measurement of capital,' within whatever tech- nological assumptions instinct and observation lead one to make, it is possi-

B. TIME SEQUENCES

Long-run equilibrium is usually defined as the solution which a system would reach as time approached infinity. Much of dynamic analysis deals with the effects over time of a particular event. The problem of planning (and of dynamic programming), however, is different. It has more to do with causes. It is the Schumpeterian problem of innovation, that is, of deciding when to introduce an investment. In Sukhamoy Chakravarty's formulation, it is the problem of the "structural break." For this reason it is essential to see the planning problem (and indeed economic development) as a multi-stage process. The long run has been described as essentially a sequence of short-run decisions. It now becomes clearer that the cumulative objective of these should be to make new and better decisions possible.

The fundamental development problem is to overcome the limited absorptive capacity of the economy, which is defined in terms of limited opportunities for profitable investment. Savings may be difficult to generate because of the low level of income, but they are also difficult to invest in a growth-inducing manner because of the inflexibilities in the economy, the difficulties in shifting factors of production to different uses, and the shortages of complementary factors.

Even if capital is given to an economy, it must be rationed in this economy as long as it is not also supplied in unlimited

---

ble to pose and to answer what I have claimed to be the central question of capital theory. What is the payoff to society from an extra bit of saving transformed efficiently into capital formation? This is more than a safe question to ask; it is an important one. I don't see how a nation can have a rational investment policy until it has found approximate answers to such questions as these: what is the social rate of return to saving? . . . What are the long-run consequences of long-term thrift?" (p. 34) How I wish I had been able to quote Robert Solow or John Hicks' *Capital and Growth: A Comprehensive and Comparative Survey of the Main Methods of Dynamic Economics* (London: Oxford University Press, 1965), whose authority might have prevailed where my unintentional originality did not succeed in carrying the day.

quantities. If, in a fairy-tale world, capital from abroad should arrive in a never-ending stream without cost and without limit, hardly a problem would exist. The economy could be subsidized at any level desired and tolerated by the donors, limited only by the speed with which imports could physically be pumped into the economy. Even if a prudent fairy godmother insisted that imports be used for investment, the only limit would be set by the availability of complementary factors which could not be imported. In the real world, however, where at best foreign capital is free but limited, an internal allocation problem arises. A decision must be made as to how much of this capital can be spent in a slow-payoff or no-payoff manner. The more is spent in such a manner at the expense of quicker and bigger returns, the less quickly the economy will grow. If projects of a slow-payoff or no-payoff character are added in the manner of the ordering suggested in the preceding section, the capital-output ratio (calculated *ex post*) will increase, but the growth rate of the economy will not fall. If the returns of additional projects are negative, the growth rate itself will be less than it could be with a smaller investment program. That much is self-evident. The slower the economy grows, the less quickly will it be able to generate internal savings for development. In a vicious circle, the less quickly internal savings are generated, the slower the economy can grow.

Two possible misunderstandings must be prevented.

First, the argument being developed here refers to a program, not a project. During any planning period, the projects considered will have varying lead times. At any moment of time a certain amount of resources is available. In matching the available resources to the desired plans, care must be taken that more resources become available during the next planning period. How much it is wise to spend on projects with a long lead time depends on the resources available, how many projects that will increase available resources are under way, and at what rate inputs needed during later plan periods can be supplied.

Second, a distinction should be made between those investments for which profitability calculations can be made and those for which it is impossible or repugnant to do so, primarily in the fields of education and health. Profitable investment remains desirable in general. Yet investments in education (to stick to this example) must be made if only to provide the skilled manpower that will eventually be needed. It is, of course, theoretically possible to calculate the benefits to an economy of better health and education. Skilled manpower is a "product" of schools. Hard-headed businessmen quite out of sympathy with "milk for Hottentots" provide balanced meals in subsidized canteens in order to keep their employees efficient. There is something repugnant, however, in figuring the profit on something one feels is basic to the workings of a society. The reason for distinguishing nonprofit investments is not that the returns from health or education may lie so far in the future that, with given interest rates, too little would be invested in them. The argument is that *as far as possible* the decision on investments in health and education should not be made on economic grounds at all. This personal view, to which exception can easily be taken, does not of course mean that the economist abdicates in these fields.

In the present context, it is sufficient to indicate that investments in education should be related to the long-term needs of the economy for skilled manpower. Resources allocated to such investments will compete in a double manner with investments in directly productive projects. First, at any one moment of time, the various projects compete for resources. Second, and more important, projects in education or health build up recurrent costs very much more quickly than they build up taxable capacity. They will therefore reduce available resources for growth needed to employ the educated. Hence if too many resources are allocated to education, the educated manpower will go to waste. If too few resources are allocated, the manpower for growth will not be forthcoming. This means that the output of nonpriceable goods and services can be logically related to the allocation of resources for directly productive investments through the consideration of the budgetary effects and effects on future resource needs and resource availabilities. A fuller discussion is postponed to Chapter V.

A number of objections have been made to the proposition that as many resources as possible should initially be channeled into directly productive investments with as high an economic profitability and as quick a return as possible. In dealing with these objections, I should reiterate plainly that the word "initially" is meant to convey my conviction that in the West African context, in the oil countries and perhaps also elsewhere, the profitable outlets for capital are at present smaller than the resources that can be raised for investment. In line with the previous discussion, this does not mean that the education and health sectors should be starved. The disagreement centers around other factors.

It has been objected, first, that insistence on profitability, and if possible quick profitability, as an investment criterion is equivalent to insisting that the economy stay frozen in its present line of specialization. Furthermore, comes the question, what about a growth path which in the short run leads to slower rates of growth than its alternative but in the long run leads to higher levels of income?

These objections seem unreal when one remembers how concretely planning must proceed. It is hardly sufficient to be told that the losses of a particular investment project will somehow turn into profits at an unspecified date and in an unspecified manner. The planner must insist on knowing when (roughly when will do) and how (roughly how will do) losses are going to give way to profits. In other words, the planner must insist on being as specific as possible, and must reject as an irresponsible misuse of resources anything as vague as what has just been mentioned. Moreover, as stressed before, the planner is trying to formulate a program of many interrelated projects, related to the private sector by economic policies. His calculations are, of course, made with different time horizons. Thus the calculations for the proposed iron and steel complex for Nigeria, calculations for which L. M. Hansen was responsible, were made under a number of assumptions to 1980, i.e., with a time horizon of twenty years. Surely, it is unreasonable to ask for more. This means that rudimentary dynamics are introduced into the planning process numerically and in the form of time sequences. In any specific case, therefore, the approximate date at which it will become reasonable to introduce new structural changes into the economy—Chakravarty's structural break—can be roughly specified. (To give an example of how the planner could be truly helpful, profitability calculations on the replacement of all DC-3's used by Nigeria Airways indicated that by waiting an extra year, not more, economic losses could be turned into economic profits.)

The desire to specify a time path and to develop a program rather than a project implies a more or less clearly formulated target in the more or less distant future. But this long-term target need not be very precise. For the basic function of the long view is to serve as a check on short-run decisions so that they do not lead into a trap at a later stage, when further growth might be prevented. It never can make continuous new short-run decisions unnecessary.

The theoretical literature has on the whole assumed that the choice before the planner is to introduce an investment now or never, and the problem of time sequences is sidestepped. Despite such notable exceptions as Chakravarty's fine analysis of the structural break, much discussion proceeds as if one had to decide today on either of two paths, one of which rises more quickly in the immediate future, while the other lifts more gradually but eventually overtakes the first and leads to faster growth later. It is, of course, important to trace through the consequences of a new investment. Nevertheless, this view blurs the much more important problem of the choice of the time to introduce a new investment. Setting up the problem as if investment decisions had to be made once-and-for-all actually misses the essential point.

From the planning standpoint, you want to raise income as fast as possible, which, given proper policies, will generate as fast as possible further savings which then should be allocated to stimulate further growth.[19] The planning problem is visualized as a sequence of steps which allow new and better decisions to be made in each succeeding period. This aim of planning is relevant in the present context; presumably the long-run aim is to make people better off. The planner strives to increase the resources available for allocation, and he strives to increase the internal mobility of factors (in the economic sense) so as to widen the possible choices.

Once time sequences are recognized as essential, long-term planning appears in its true colors as a series of short-term decisions rather than as a choice of alternatives made once and for all. Conceivably in planning practice there is a danger that the short-run decisions which maximize short-term growth will preclude later and better decisions. It need not be so. The reverse is at least as likely. It may be—and this is my experience—that a long-term decision made too early will in fact reduce the chances of growth by siphoning off too many resources in the early stages in the form of subsidies, with the result that the

19. The problem of possible conflicts between maximizing savings and maximizing income is sidestepped here, but more is said later in connection with investment criteria, shadow prices, and monetary and fiscal policies.

economy never reaches the point at which the long-run decision becomes profitable.

The objection that sticking to a short-term growth criterion prevents an economy from becoming flexible overlooks three factors. One is that imports are available to achieve flexibility. The second is that the long-term alternative which may be inadvisable now may become advisable later. It is not rejected forever, but only for the present. Third, "short-term" offers no license for wandering along from day to day, since all decisions relate to a program that itself contains projects with different time horizons. Thus, the training of manpower needed a few years hence is a long-term proposition. But the issue to be faced by the planner is not whether he wants to include technical training, say, but only how much. The planner both recommends a long-term investment *and* breaks it down into steps that gradually increase the program as needed.[20]

The issue can perhaps be clarified by a graph along the lines of Figure 1. On the vertical axis is plotted Gross Domestic Product or output or any other acceptable quantification of growth; on the horizontal axis is time. The "either-or" argument is indicated by the solid lines I and II. Line I pictures the results of an investment program which pays off faster in the immediate

20. It is true that later developments could be hampered because, say, the necessary manpower has not been trained years before. But my discussion refers to an investment program, and in the program a sufficient number of trainees can be included. The program, it should be repeated, consists of a series of interrelated projects with different time horizons. The problem is essentially marginal; i.e., it relates to questions of the "more or less" type, rather than to questions of the "either-or" type.

To give a realistic example, there is no doubt that high-level manpower is urgently needed in Nigeria. There is no doubt that eventually the five universities planned are needed and may even turn out to be too few. There is equally no doubt in my mind that long-run development in Nigeria would be accelerated if for the time being only two or three universities were developed and the others waited for a higher-income level and the availability of more students.

future; Line II shows the results of an investment program that will overtake I at a later period.

This picture is deliberately unfavorable to my argument, since it assumes—what is questionable in practice—that Program II

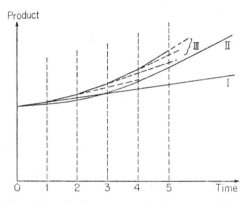

Figure 1.   Hypothetical alternative time patterns of investment.

will in fact eventually lead to higher growth rates and since it omits the repercussions throughout the economy of an initially slower rate of growth on taxable capacity, recurrent budgets, levels of consumption, incentives, and so forth. All these repercussions are already assumed to have worked themselves out positively to give the result pictured by Line II. Such strong assumptions hide major planning and development problems that are encountered the world over.

But assume for argument's sake that all is well in these respects. It is still true that the decision on the program represented by Line II could have been taken, say, a year later, in which case still higher levels of income could have been achieved in any given subsequent year. I cannot imagine a situation in which it would be impossible to start the program pictured by Line II in Years 1, 2, or 3. I cannot imagine a situation in which a program that makes an economy more flexible suddenly hits a dead end and in which future decisions are foreclosed forever if they are not made in period 0.

Moreover, new additional short-term and long-term decisions could have been framed in successive years to take account of the higher income. Higher incomes mean that markets have grown faster; hence more enterprises in a greater variety of production have become profitable faster. Higher incomes also mean potentially more savings, hence less restriction on growth from the resources side. New decisions (put into effect more rapidly the faster income is allowed to grow) could have brought real income to yet higher levels. They could have increased the viability of the economy, both financial and structural, even further. This is pictured by the group of dotted lines labeled III which start successively in new years.

In "Austrian" terms, this is equivalent to lengthening the period of production as income and, with it, savings rise. In Communist terms, it is equivalent to saying that one must establish first a firm productive base for the economy, before one can afford social luxuries and before one can "redistribute" ("umverteilen") the product. In terms of capital-output ratios it is equivalent to saying that by making at any one moment of time the best possible (i.e., practicable) decision on payoff, it is possible successfully to go in for larger and larger c/o ratios.

In other words, as more and more resources become available, it is economically possible to include in any program more and more investments with large capital-output ratios or with slow or no income generation. Development is, of course, not expected to make the aggregate capital-output ratio for the economy increase. On the contrary, if my analysis is right, the object of development is to make the economy more flexible and to open up increasing possibilities. As productivity increases and income rises, increasing numbers of investments will become profitable, absorptive capacity will increase, the speed with which resources can be shifted to different uses will increase, and, it is to be hoped, more and more investments with shorter payoff periods and lower capital-output ratios will become feasible.

In terms of modern theory, this means establishing the best practically possible approximation to a dynamic sequence which, instead of sacrificing short-run growth in hopes of a later and unspecified acceleration, gathers momentum through a sequence of paying projects. In budgetary terms, taxable capacity must be increased first, and a program must be reformulated annually in the form of reconsidered capital and recurrent budgets.[21]

This sort of planning is neither as improvised nor as short-sighted as it might seem, for, as has been stressed, payoff calculations for different projects will establish different time horizons. But it is an approach that allows the use of the best information available at successive moments of time and that allows a continuous rational adaptation to situations which the planning process itself has changed. It makes the theoretical discussion of the "structural break" operational. It is a practical way of making dynamic programming decisions.

The ability to improve a development program as circumstances warrant is of great importance. Suppose a program has been worked out. It has been phased over the years, its implication for the budget have been determined, and so forth. Suppose that the program now turns out to be too large, because of unrealistic targeting, scheduling, etc., or because of changing conditions. It is then illusory and harmful simply to stretch the plan for another year. Of course, there is no magic in a fixed planning period of five, six, or whatever number of years. But the only sensible way of "stretching" a plan inevitably involves a reworking of all time sequences, since it is most unlikely that a simple proportional cut throughout the program will work. Stretching without changing the structure is asking for trouble,

21. There is, of course, nothing sacred about an interval of one year. Supplementary appropriations are a common device.

for it attacks the symptom rather than the cause of the disease. With stretching, priorities get changed, the growth of taxable capacity and available resources changes, and sense can very quickly become nonsense.

The implications of this analysis are that it is dangerous to formulate a bargaining plan and then to proceed as if it were a realistic plan. It seems better to aim for minimum targets that can be fulfilled or surpassed rather than for maximum targets that cannot be met. In the former case priorities can still be improved and growth accelerated. In the latter case priorities are bound to be distorted, and the growth rate achieved will be less than was possible. These points are taken up again in the context of tax policy.

Approaching long-run development as a sequence of short-run decisions within a rational time sequence has the advantage of making it feasible to deal with possible nonlinearities in the system. (I have run several times into the criticism that the planning approach followed in Nigeria neglected nonlinearities.) The difficulty with the concepts of nonlinearities and the absence of long-run equilibrium is that the terms hide a bewildering and intractable bundle of situations. Linearity and equilibrium are something specific and unique; nonlinearity and disequilibrium are not. There are any number of nonlinearities. There are at most only a few equilibrium situations. It is hopeless to deal with either nonlinearities or nonequilibrium in general. This means that even on a highly abstract level, one has to *specify* the nonlinearities or the nonequilibrium one talks about, before it is possible to say anything very useful or interesting. This very fact, however, makes it possible to allow for such situations in actual development planning. For it is frequently possible to deal with *specific* situations where one cannot deal with things in general. Since economic development and development planning are concrete activities relating to a specific geographic area at a given moment of time, the presence of nonlinearities, the

absence of long-run equilibrium, and even the existence of in-
divisibilities become less of a handicap to development planning
than one might believe at first blush.

Thus a planner finds himself being thrust into a given initial
situation and working within a limited time horizon. He deals
with factors and modifications which can be more or less known
and shaped through one's actions. What appear to be sweeping,
ill-defined, unmanageable general situations can sometimes be
converted into specific and hence manageable problems and
tasks. One does not, after all, have to make irrevocable decisions
for the whole future. Limited decisions can create new and, one
hopes, more favorable contexts in which to make the next set
of decisions.

The burden of the argument is, then, that nonlinearities can
be made manageable by making them specific. By considering
sequences for a limited time horizon, say five or six or fifteen
years, it is possible to alter the relationship in the interactions
from year to year, thus approximating as closely as is practically
necessary a nonlinear relationship. For example, in making profitability calculations, it is possible to use a single set of long-run
expected prices for the whole period, but it is also possible to
use different sets of prices for different years if one has com-
pelling reasons to do so.

C. SHADOW PRICES AND THE BUDGET

Since so much stress has been laid on seeing the long run as
a sequence of interrelated short-run decisions on profitability,
it is necessary to deal briefly at this point with objections that
involve the use of shadow or accounting prices. A more detailed
discussion of the use and effects of shadow prices in the African
context is postponed to Chapter V. Here it is appropriate to deal,
first, with the stability of shadow prices and, second, with their
budgetary implications.

Shadow or accounting prices are logically called for whenever market prices can be presumed not to reflect properly an existing situation—whenever wages are above and interest rates and exchange rates are below the levels they would reach in a perfectly competitive situation. Since reality is imperfect, this seems to leave a wide field to the use of accounting prices for the purpose of making economic decisions. Both the logical and the administrative difficulties are formidable, however. Logically, accounting prices should result from the solution of a complex inter-industry system of equations. The data for making such calculations simply cannot be assembled and are not likely to be available for the foreseeable future. Moreover, in the kind of dynamic programming approach that has been outlined, the shadow rates themselves are not constant over time, so that different sets of shadow rates should be used.[22] This raises formidable practical problems, and neglecting the time sequences of different shadow rates and using a single set of shadow prices may be worse than using the imperfect market prices. Therefore, although it is impossible to deny the imperfections of reality, the methods of improving on it may be so dubious that they lose much of their practical appeal.

If rules of jurisprudence were applied to economics, the critics

---

22. "Defining the time structure of an activity by a single number leads to great difficulties when we are trying to appraise investment projects on the micro-level by using the shadow prices derived as dual to the inequality constrained maximization problem in the quantity space. An investment project on the micro-level is always defined as a dated sequence *with the time distribution of inputs and outputs far from being a uniform one.* Because of this non-uniformity of the streams of benefits and also because the scarcities of relevant factors of production will be altering over time, the *use of a single set of shadow prices derived from a static maximization procedure may affect seriously the nature and timing of investment projects.*" S. Chakravarty, "Alternative Preference Functions," p. 4 (italics added).

See also S. Chakravarty, "The Use of Shadow Prices in Program Evaluation" and "An Outline of a Method for Programme Evaluation"—both originally mimeographed, M.I.T. Center for International Studies, 1960, now published as chaps. 3 and 4 of P. N. Rosenstein-Rodan (ed.), *Capital Formation and Economic Development* (Cambridge: M.I.T. Press, 1964). I am indebted to Professor Chakravarty for drawing my attention to his three papers, which make the points I have in mind so much more elegantly than I ever could.

of market prices would have to prove their case in specific instances. This is not at all easy to do. It is far from clear how one gets from criticizing a particular situation as imperfect to stating precisely what should take its place. Moreover, in actual situations one settles for the second best, as James E. Meade has called it, and the unattainable "best" becomes too easily the enemy of the attainable "good." Even if prices do not correctly reflect social cost or preferences, what is the realistic alternative? An arbitrary decision by the planner or politician may or may not be better. If it is an isolated interference, it will not do much harm. But if the price system is ignored on a wide range of commodities and services, very real dangers of inconsistency creep into planning. These dangers are well known to analysts of Communist planning, and so is their pernicious effect. The existing price system evolved by even an imperfect market has inestimable advantages: it is interpretable; it is internally consistent; and it can be used as a planning device.

Contrary to many a prejudice of both planners and anti-planners, the price system has no ideological content. It belongs exclusively neither to capitalism nor to socialism; but it must be used by both to achieve reasonable results. And it can be abused by either. Shadow prices can all too easily become inconsistent. If they go awry, one loses track of whether one's calculations of economic profit do or do not reflect a real situation and whether as the result of one's planning one does or does not come out with more resources than one had to start with. Then one can no longer gauge even approximately what the effects of policies on the balance of payments, taxation, and so forth will be.

There are, however, specific biases in actual prices that can and probably should be corrected. The problems that arise in this connection are dealt with more fully in Chapter V. Here it is sufficient to point out that the actual facts in a particular situation are more difficult to ascertain than might be expected. Thus is may seem "obvious" that true interest rates cannot be as low as the ones actually prevailing on an imperfect capital market to which only few privileged borrowers have access. And it often seems equally "obvious" that wages fixed by government are too high.

Nevertheless, reckoning interest rates and wages higher or lower than their market value and substituting shadow prices for market prices suggests indifference to the requirements of a truly general planning framework. This may seem a surprising statement, especially in view of the fact that Jan Tinbergen has certainly developed his ideas in a general equilibrium context and that shadow prices are supposed to be derived from an inter-industry system. Thus it is assumed as self-evident that shadow rates of interest should be higher than the borrowing rate of the government on international markets. But what are the repercussions? Leaving aside for the moment the fact that in Nigeria (and not only there) even charging the existing borrowing rate is a great improvement over the actual accounting practice, a higher "book" rate will not merely change factor proportions but will limit directly growth-inducing investments and shift the composition of an investment program toward investments for which calculations are not usually made. These investments are normally of the kind that raise recurrent budgetary cost and therefore curtail in the future the availability of resources for further investment. This in turn keeps future interest rates higher than need be and so on. This outline of events is of course simply an illustration of the dynamic nature of shadow prices, and it indicates that certain repercussions are not ordinarily allowed for in the literature on the subject. I return to this discussion in Chapter V.

The argument suggests that the imperfections of the capital market found and deplored in underdeveloped countries which permit some favored borrowers to get their funds at, say, 6 percent, while others must pay 15 percent or more, may be a blessing in disguise, provided the low-interest funds can be channeled into uses which increase the productive and taxable capacity of the economy and help to make the structure of the economy more flexible. A suggestive case in point is the policy of the West German authorities in the early fifties. There the capital market was split, with 6 to 8 percent loans being pushed into the major bottleneck sectors of coal, iron and steel, electricity generation, and shipbuilding; 2 percent loans being made available in limited amounts for so-called "social" housing; and everyone else forced to shift for themselves. The success of the policy, which by 1965 had led to a unified and substantially improved capital market, suggests that its application to underdeveloped countries might at least be considered in all those cases in which limited absorptive capacity is a real problem.[23]

In general, the systems developed to derive shadow prices are fairly simple (which may nevertheless leave them useful exercises). They assume usually only one type of labor or at best a few.[24] They show at best that income would rise by more than the subsidies required by the substitution of accounting prices for market prices. They never, however, relate the use of shadow pricing to the fiscal problem of *actually* raising the taxes or other funds to pay the subsidies on which a system of shadow prices operates.[25] Surely there must be some budgetary effects of a

23. See Wolfgang F. Stolper and Karl W. Roskamp, "Planning a Free Economy: Germany since 1945," in a forthcoming book edited by Henry Kissinger at the Center for International Affairs, Harvard University.

24. Hollis B. Chenery, George E. Brandow, and Edwin J. Cohn, Jr., in their *Turkish Investment and Economic Development* (Ankara: United States of America Operations Mission to Turkey, Foreign Operations Administration, 1953), allow for a shadow wage for unskilled labor in agriculture. But, they observe, "In industry, we have been unable to get an accurate breakdown of labor requirements according to the level of skill, and we have not made this correction" (p. 251). The other major corrections applied by these authors refer to the exchange rate and to the elimination of tariffs from prices.

25. For a different view, see A. Qayum, *Theory and Policy of Accounting Prices*, Contributions to Economic Analysis, no. 20 (Amsterdam: North Holland Publishing Co., 1960), particularly chaps. vii and viii. Mr. Qayum's excellent study, however, moves on a higher level of abstraction than the

planning decision that substitutes shadow for actual prices. How else would the manager of a plant that has been decided upon by assuming, say, a shadow price for labor lower than the wage he has to pay, meet his actual payroll? Fiscal problems in fact quickly become very serious, and a budget that is shot through with subsidies soon becomes uncontrollable. This in turn cancels the most effective method of controlling the waste of resources, and one source of waste—incorrect prices—has simply been supplanted by another—an unmanageable budget. In addition, it becomes increasingly difficult to separate those items which are "naturals" for subsidies—some education (not all), some health measures (not all), some housing (not all)—from others where special arguments of a different kind apply.

This does not exhaust the difficulties. Someone has to pay the subsidies. Subsidies represent real resources, and there are always alternative uses for real resources. Suppose a particular policy of taxes and subsidies requires a net subsidy from the budget. The budget at the same time must also provide for the running of the government, and it is usually expected to produce surpluses for investments. The choices before the policy maker are now whether to reduce public investment by the amount

---

comments made in my text. And his model implies either that the whole of the budget consists of subsidies and taxes or that the raising of taxes and payment of subsidies have no further repercussions. Thus he is concerned with cases in which the subsidies will be bigger or smaller than the taxes collected. But in terms of his analysis, the surplus or deficit has no further effect on output or employment.

Moreover, the only purpose of the taxes or the subsidies is to produce the proper prices in the economy. If, however, the net effect of a shadow-price policy is to produce a net burden on the budget, and if this budgetary burden has to be met by taxation (which presumably must be neutral in its price effects), the consequences can be very serious. Thus Qayum calculates in the most unfavorable case that "the financial burden to the state due to the execution of the policy reaches the maximum of about 2.6 per cent of the national product" (p. 93). Assuming that tax collections equal 20 percent of national product, this is 13 percent of the budget, which may have to be raised by additional taxation. It is difficult to see how such an increase could be neutral.

of subsidies or to raise taxes in a manner that is neutral with respect to the shadow-price policy to allow for the same amount of investments and the necessary subsidies. It would seem likely that the set of accounting prices that allowed for increased taxes and reduced consumption so as not to reduce the volume of public investments would have to differ from the set geared toward a reduction in investments and differ from the set that permitted deficit financing. It has to be shown therefore that the alternative uses of subsidies are less desirable. If a country's resources are already strained, the subsidies might be scraped together only at the expense of schools, hospitals, roads, or even of more directly income-creating uses.

Nor is it sufficient merely to show that income will rise through a program of subsidies. Unless taxable capacity increases apace, in a form that can be tapped by government, the program is administratively not feasible. The taxation out of which the subsidies are to be paid must be specified. If the increased income accrues to a few rich people, it is easy to make out a case for higher income taxation. But this is not necessarily a realistic assumption. It is much more likely that the increase in income will accrue to a relatively small number of urban workers (possibly among the rural unemployed before, if the facts of the case are favorable to the theoretical proposition), whose increased tax payments will amount to less than the subsidy required. There may be indirect repercussions on the income of local trades people, but they are not easily taxed either. Hence circumstances lead to the subsidy's coming out of the pockets of farmers, who not only will be forced to reduce their consumption (thus offsetting the indirect effects on traders!) but who are likely to reduce their efforts. This is not the usual "incentive effect" argument. The plain truth is that farmers everywhere are hard-headed people who will not use improved methods of production unless they are better off as the result of doing it, and who will limit their efforts if the results of the efforts are taxed away.

The drawbacks of shadow pricing must be recognized. The reader will notice a family resemblance between the last arguments and the discussion of the gains of international trade when, as a result of trade, some people are better off and others are worse off than before. There, too, it is not sufficient merely to show that income is potentially greater with trade than without, so that no one need be worse off, and some people could be better off. It must be shown also that there is a feasible way to achieve the required redistribution of income without at the same time reducing income to the pre-trade level. When all repercussions that a planner must consider are allowed for, taxation required for redistribution may well undo the effect of subsidies which on the face of it seem justified. It is obvious that correct prices are preferable to wrong ones. But tracing through the budgetary consequences in an effort to formulate policies to deal with them brings out immediately all the questions raised and thus reduces the practical appeal of shadow pricing.

In the African context (perhaps everywhere), factor substitutability and factor complementarity interact in a complicated pattern, and tax and monetary policies labor under severe limitations. For these reasons, extreme caution is necessary in interfering with the price mechanism, which has the advantage not indeed of perfection but of workability. One ignores the warning which prices give on profitability or the lack thereof, and on how to allocate resources rationally, only at the grave risk that priorities get distorted in unexpected places and that the problems are simply shifted to the budget or the balance of payments.

Finally there is the problem, already touched upon, of prices changing over time. This is true for both market and shadow prices. The importance of time sequences suggests that it would be dangerous to put future prices into present calculations without showing how to get through a series of such time sequences from the present to the future situation. For one has to start where one is, and one cannot change the world by a stroke of the pen. The planner's picture of a rosy future is worthless unless he specifies how the present situation can be transformed.

I V

National Accounting from a Planning Standpoint

THE primary purpose of this chapter is to describe the planning uses to which the National Accounts of Nigeria were put.

National accounts, like almost all aggregations used in economics, embody compound concepts: they are by definition statistical in nature, and their meaning depends essentially on how they are compiled. The underlying detail must therefore somehow be learned.

The Accounts of Nigeria were used in two basic ways. First, they were the most convenient framework within which past developments could be assessed. Second, they were the most convenient framework in which the consistency of the detailed policy decisions for the future could be tested.[1]

---

1. The pioneer work dealing with the problems of national accounting in the African context is Phyllis Deane, *The Measurement of Colonial National Incomes* (Cambridge: Cambridge University Press, 1948). All investigators producing actual accounts face the same problems. See, for example, A. R. Prest and Ian G. Stewart, *National Income of Nigeria 1950/51*, Colonial Research Studies, no. 11 (London: H.M.S.O., 1953); and Alan Peacock and Douglas Dosser, *National Income of Tanganyika, 1952–1954*, Colonial Research Studies, no. 26 (London: H.M.S.O., 1958). For the differences in the approaches followed in English-speaking and French-speaking territories, see Peter Ady and Michel Courcier, *Systems of National Accounts in Africa* (Paris: O.E.E.C., for the Commission for Technical Cooperation in Africa South of the Sahara, 1960).

See also "National Accounts in Africa and Relevant ECA Activities," *Economic Bulletin for Africa*, vol. I, no. 2 (June 1961). This publication gives an account of the estimates of social accounts available for all African

In Chapter III, the difficulties of using aggregate concepts for operational purposes were briefly discussed. These difficulties will be further elaborated in the context of national accounting. Although projections more or less mechanically arrived at were an essential step in the study of problems confronting Nigeria's policy makers, this step did not take much time. Beyond this, the study of past trends and in particular of past investments suggested that the interpretation of the aggregative concept was crucially affected by the underlying micro-economic relationship. The example of Nigeria may serve to show the kind of logical problems that is universally encountered by planners and that development theorists, too, must take into consideration.

A. PAST DEVELOPMENTS AS A GUIDE FOR THE FUTURE

There are two important and related reasons why the study of past development is essential for an assessment of the future. One is that a bench mark has to be determined in as great detail as possible to be useful. The other is that past decisions will determine future developments, and new decisions have to come to terms with the inheritance from the past. It is therefore natural that the planners should first have familiarized themselves with the details of the national-accounts calculations for 1950–1957 by Dr. Pius Okigbo and should have brought the

---

countries as of 1961. It therefore supplements the Ady and Courcier study, from which it quotes *in extenso* and which is indispensable for methodological detail.

See also Economic Commission for Africa, *Report of the Working Group on the Uses of National Accounts in Africa*, E/CN/14/84 (Addis Ababa, 1961). The International Association for Research in Income and Wealth has sponsored *African Studies in Income and Wealth*, ed. L. H. Samuels (London: Bowes & Bowes, 1963), with studies by Richard M. Barkay, "The Statistical Macro-Economic Framework Needed in Development Planning in Africa"; G. C. Billington, "A Minimum System of National Accounts for use by African Countries and Some Related Problems"; Pius Okigbo, "Nigerian National Accounts, 1950–57"; Jan G. Stewart, "Consumer Demand in Nigeria"; and others.

estimates up to date.[2] The estimates of Gross Domestic Product by industrial origin have since been revised by the Federal Office of Statistics (Table 1). The estimates of GDP by category of expenditures in 1957 market prices are reproduced from the Plan (as revised by the Federal Office of Statistics) as Table 2. The major differences in GDP as between the estimates made by the Economic Planning Unit for 1958–1960 and the revised estimates made by the Federal Office of Statistics are that the latter has revised downward the capital formation estimates. The overall differences are not startling.

It would be tedious to describe in detail the methods used by the Economic Planning Unit to expand the Okigbo estimates of GDP for the years 1958–1960. Suffice it to point out, first, that a great deal can be done by using the statistical and human resources at the disposal of a planner and, second, that the essence of the exercise is not merely to arrive at the final tables but to gather detail underlying the calculations. The exercise is invaluable for getting a feel for what went on and is going on in the economy, what is and what is not known, and how parts of the economy fit together. At every turn arbitrary decisions must be made; yet if such decisions are unavoidable, it seems better to make the degree of one's ignorance explicit.[3]

There are practical reasons for this. Decisions on the size of the plan, on priorities, and on feasibilities are inescapable. They all depend on one's knowledge of the economy. Any shred of in-

2. P. N. C. Okigbo, *Nigerian National Accounts 1950–57*, published [December 1961] by the Federal Ministry of Economic Development, printed by the Government Printer, Enugu, Eastern Nigeria. The study was originally set up by Okigbo and E. F. Jackson, Director of the Oxford Institute of Statistics, who was responsible for much of the organization. The final formulations rested with Dr. Okigbo, later Nigerian Ambassador to the Common Market and Economic Adviser to the Prime Minister. See Okigbo's short discussion in *African Studies in Income and Wealth* (just cited), pp. 285-306.

3. Mr. Barkay has put the point succinctly: "In development planning to be wrong is permissible; what is not permissible is to be unaware." Richard M. Barkay, in *African Studies in Income and Wealth*, p. 69.

Table 1. *Nigeria's Gross Domestic Product by branch of activity at 1957–58 prices*
(£ million)

	1950–1951	1951–1952	1952–1953	1953–1954	1954–1955	1955–1956	1956–1957	1957–1958a	1958–1959a	1959–1960	1960–1961	1961–1962	1962–1963
Agriculture[b]	377.6	415.0	430.5	446.0	471.3	483.9	459.8	471.4	542.2	526.2	549.4	573.5	604.3
Livestock	60.1	57.7	52.5	53.5	55.7	56.5	57.6	57.7	52.3	58.7	61.0	63.8	61.1
Fishing	9.7	9.8	9.9	10.0	10.2	10.3	12.6	13.3	15.0	15.0	15.0	15.0	15.0
Forest products	9.4	12.0	10.1	11.9	12.3	13.4	13.6	14.6	10.4	13.1	14.6	13.3	13.7
Mining and oil exploration	7.6	7.6	8.2	7.9	8.1	9.0	9.6	9.4	7.0	6.6	8.4	13.8	18.2
Manufacturing[c]	3.9	4.0	5.8	6.3	7.9	8.7	12.0	10.9	23.0	27.7	32.5	35.9	37.0
Public utilities (electricity & water)	c	c	c	c	c	c	c	2.2	2.4	2.9	3.6	4.5	5.2
Communications	2.7	2.7	3.0	2.9	2.6	2.4	2.6	3.1	2.9	3.1	3.2	3.5	3.7
Building and civil engineering	20.3	25.4	19.4	25.9	37.8	38.3	36.5	43.0	22.9	32.1	33.3	27.5	29.2
Ownership of buildings	8.9	9.1	9.2	9.4	9.6	9.7	9.8	10.3	7.9	8.6	9.3	10.0	10.7
Transport	28.6	34.0	35.3	45.4	50.9	60.2	65.1	74.6	29.1	32.3	37.3	43.0	42.8
Crafts	15.8	15.9	16.0	16.1	16.2	16.4	16.5	16.7	20.4	20.4	20.4	20.4	20.4
Missions	6.9	7.0	7.6	7.8	8.7	11.4	12.7	15.9	18.1	21.6	23.3	24.6	26.7
Government	15.0	16.4	19.9	16.5	17.6	23.4	28.7	30.5	29.1	36.3	35.0	38.0	40.0
Marketing boards	41.0	10.5	28.0	28.8	42.7	25.0	44.9	11.7	0.7	11.6	5.8	—5.1	3.2

Table 1. (Continued)

	1950–1951	1951–1952	1952–1953	1953–1954	1954–1955	1955–1956	1956–1957	1957–1958a	1958–1959a	1959–1960	1960–1961	1961–1962	1962–1963
Banking, insurance, professions	1.5	1.2	1.3	1.7	1.7	2.1	2.2	2.5	3.1	3.7	3.7	4.0	4.2
Domestic service	4.4	4.4	4.4	4.7	4.8	5.0	5.7	5.5	3.7	3.7	4.0	4.0	4.2
Miscellaneous services	0.9	1.0	1.1	1.1	1.2	1.5	1.9	2.0	1.8	2.1	3.7	3.6	4.0
Land development	8.2	8.2	8.2	8.2	8.2	8.2	8.2	8.2	b	b	b	b	b
Distribution, residual error, etc.	64.6	98.3	122.6	105.7	104.7	112.7	74.1	106.5	108.0	112.6	117.8	121.7	128.7
GDP at factor cost	687.1	740.2	793.0	809.8	872.2	898.1	874.1	910.0	900.0d	938.5d	981.3d	1,014.0	1,072.3

General note: Nigeria's fiscal year runs from April 1 to March 31. Thus the 1950–51 fiscal year falls mainly in the calendar year 1950 and is often written simply "1950," as in the principal source document for this table. Some of the data that had to be used in building up the annual totals—particularly in manufacturing and agriculture—are for 12-month periods differing from the Government's fiscal year; but the errors involved are not cumulative.

a. There is a break in comparability between the years ending 1957–58 and those beginning 1958–59, because of different methods of estimating and improved coverage. Also, Southern Cameroons is included in the tabulations up through 1957–58 (the total for the territory amounting to about £20 million for that year) and excluded thereafter.

b. For 1958–59 and after, land development is included in agriculture.

c. For 1956–57 and earlier, public utilities are included in manufacturing.

d. The GDP estimates I made for planning purposes in 1961 excluded the distribution category and totaled £835 million in 1958–59; £865 million in 1959–60; and £935 million in 1960–61. If the official estimate for distribution is added, these figures come close to those in the table, for they become £943 million in 1958–59; £978 million in 1959–60; and £1,053 million in 1960–61.

SOURCES: P. N. C. Okigbo, *Nigerian National Accounts 1950–57*, published [December 1961] by the Federal Ministry of Economic Development, printed by the Government Printer, Enugu, Eastern Nigeria, p. 21 (table IV.2, table VI.35); Federal Republic of Nigeria, *National Development Plan Progress Report, 1964* (Lagos: Federal Ministry of Economic Development, 1965), p. 2; *Annual Abstract of Statistics, 1964* (Lagos: Federal Government Printer), p. 144.

Table 2. *Nigeria's Gross Domestic Product by category of expenditure at 1957–58 prices*

	1950–1951	1951–1952	1952–1953	1953–1954	1954–1955	1955–1956	1956–1957	1957–1958	1958–1959	1959–1960	1960–1961
					(£ million)						
Consumers' expenditure[a]	609.4	650.2	695.9	717.3	774.6	805.5	798.9	815.5	830.0	830.0	870.0
Government expenditure on goods and services	24.0	26.8	33.5	29.9	31.2	45.5	43.8	47.6	56.7	70.0	77.0
Gross fixed investment in Nigeria[a]	48.4	59.9	75.0	79.9	92.9	102.6	108.0	113.0	122.3	136.7	158.0
Increase in Marketing Board stocks	—7.3	6.3	1.5	—0.1	—6.2	4.6	—4.8	9.1	—0.3	n.a.	n.a.
Plus exports (f.o.b.)	99.9	93.6	111.7	114.8	131.9	126.9	138.5	129.1	144.0	163.0	171.0
Final expenditure	774.4	836.6	917.6	941.8	1,024.4	1,085.1	1,084.4	1,114.3	1,163.2	1,208.9	1,276.0
Less imports (c.i.f.)	75.1	82.6	108.3	114.1	131.6	163.3	180.9	175.6	182.0	212.0	253.0
GDP at market price[a]	699.3	754.0	809.3	827.7	892.8	921.8	903.5	938.7	970.7	987.7	1,023.0
					(Percentage distribution)						
Consumers' expenditure as % of GDP	87.1	86.2	86.0	86.7	86.8	87.4	88.4	86.9	85.5	84.0	85.0
Government expenditure on goods and services as % of GDP	3.4	3.6	4.1	3.6	3.5	4.9	4.8	5.1	5.8	7.1	7.5
Gross fixed investment in Nigeria as % of GDP	6.9	7.9	9.3	9.7	10.4	11.1	12.0	12.0	12.6	13.8	15.4

Table 2. (Continued)

	1950–1951	1951–1952	1952–1953	1953–1954	1954–1955	1955–1956	1956–1957	1957–1958	1958–1959	1959–1960	1960–1961
	(£ million)										
Total available resources[b]	749.6	825.8	914.2	941.1	1,024.1	1,121.5	1,126.8	1,160.8	1,190.7	1,248.7	1,358.0
	(Indices)										
Index of GDP	100	108	115	118	127	131	127	132	139	141	146
Index of available resources	100	110	122	126	137	150	150	155	158	167	181

	1958–59	1959–60	1960–61	1961–62	1962–63
Consumers' expenditure	825	825	910	947	984
Gross fixed investment	109	127	127	140	137
GDP	900	939	981	1,014	1,072

n.a. = not available.

Note: On fiscal years, see Table 1, "General note."

a. Revised estimates of consumers' expenditures, gross fixed investment, and GDP are given in Federal Republic of Nigeria, *National Development Plan Progress Report, 1964* (Lagos: Federal Ministry of Economic Development, 1965), p. 10. These estimates, over a five-year period, in £ million at 1957–58 prices, are as follows:

b. "Total available resources" equals consumers' expenditure, plus government expenditure on goods and services, plus gross fixed investment in Nigeria, plus increase in Marketing Board stocks, plus imports.

SOURCES: Federation of Nigeria, *National Development Plan, 1962–68* (Lagos: Federal Ministry of Economic Development, 1962), p. 13 (table 2.5); P. N. C. Okigbo, *Nigerian National Accounts 1950–57*, published [December 1961] by the Federal Ministry of Economic Development, printed by the Government Printer, Enugu, Eastern Nigeria.

formation is useful if only enough such shreds can be gathered within the matrix of national accounting. Then a picture of the economy emerges. Without a framework, individual pieces of information remain largely meaningless. The picture may be blurred and uncertain, but it is essential to have one if the programs to be developed are not to hang in the air.

The study of past developments revealed a number of disturbing features. GDP in constant prices had increased from 1950 to 1960 at an average rate of a little more than 4 percent. But the rate of increase had been substantially bigger until 1954— about 6 to 7 percent. The growth thereafter had been very slow, averaging only about 3 percent since 1954, although it had picked up at the end of the decade.

Ironically, the growth rate fell after 1954 when the International Bank for Reconstruction and Development made a report, *The Economic Development of Nigeria*. The fall was accompanied by a change from an export to an import surplus. Gross domestic investments at the same time grew rapidly as a percentage of GDP—from 6.8 percent in 1950 to 9.7 percent in 1953 and to 12 percent in 1957, the last year of the Okigbo estimates. The rate of increase in the investment ratio was somewhat slower between 1953 and 1957 or 1958 but seemed to rise again thereafter.

During the whole period, the availability of resources had increased substantially more than GDP, as declining export surpluses changed to import surpluses accompanied by a decumulation of sterling assets (Table 3). Except for 1957, real imports increased, moreover, steadily and substantially, as Table 2 shows. This indicated not only that the cushion of sterling reserves made it possible to ignore the fluctuations in export earnings but also that the level of investment was at no time limited by a shortage of foreign exchange.

Thus past developments indicated that an increasing domestic-investment ratio had been accompanied by a declining rate of

Table 3. Nigeria's sterling balances, 1950–1964
(£ million)

	Mar. 1950	Mar. 1953	Mar. 1954	Mar. 1955	Mar. 1956	Mar. 1957	Dec. 1958	Dec. 1959	Dec. 1960	Dec. 1961	Dec. 1962	Dec. 1963	Dec. 1964
Marketing Boards	39.3	51.6	60.6	74.0	67.1	37.9	31.7	35.2	19.2	−0.4	1.1	4.9	2.4
Currency Board	32.8	55.5	66.1	54.0	58.2	61.0	70.0	27.4	10.0	6.8	—	—	—
Federal Government		47.7	62.7	47.3	49.3	52.0	47.2	29.6	27.0	27.1	28.0	10.5	4.3
Regional government		5.4	7.7	23.2	26.7	41.5	31.5	31.6	23.3	19.5	8.5	7.0	5.1
Local government		3.1	2.9[a]	3.1	3.0	3.3	3.5	3.5	3.9	3.9	3.9	2.2	—
Regional Production Development Boards (corporations)	38.5	15.1	12.7	13.0	10.3	9.2	6.3	5.3	1.9	1.3	0.6	0.2	6.7
Other official		11.9	14.6	19.5	16.3	11.4	9.4	11.2	8.7	9.4	6.6	4.4	
Total official	110.6	190.3	227.3	234.1	230.9	216.4	199.6	143.8	94.0	60.8	48.7	29.2	18.5
Post Office Savings Bank and net balances due from banks abroad	13.2	16.4	16.4[b]	29.0	25.5	22.6	14.0	72.7[c]	78.5[c]	90.2[c]	69.4[c]	64.7[c]	58.4[c]
Total official and banking	123.8	206.7	243.7	263.1	256.4	239.0	213.6	216.5	172.5	151.0	118.1	93.9	76.9

a. Lagos Town Council not available.
b. Net balances of banks only. Post Office Savings Bank included with Federal Government.
c. Including Central Bank overseas assets.

SOURCES: *Nigeria*, "Commonwealth Development and Its Financing," no. 5 (London: HMSO, 1963), p. 48 (table 15); *Digest of Statistics* (Lagos: Federal Office of Statistics), January 1963, p. 16, and October 1964, p. 16; *Economic Indicators* (Lagos: Federal Office of Statistics), July 1965, p. 24.

99

growth; that the increased domestic investments were at least in part purchased with a decline in foreign assets; and, worst of all, that the domestic-savings ratio had not increased at all.[4]

These facts indicated, therefore, that, in the face of an anticipated further deterioration in the terms of trade, it would be difficult to maintain, let alone exceed, the growth rate of 4 percent which had been achieved in the past and which the Government had proposed to the planners as a tentative target rate. The gap between domestic savings and domestic investment made it unrealistic to plan on any substantial increase in the latter. Furthermore, as it had taken an increasing rate and amount of investment to produce a falling rate of increase in GDP, it seemed most unlikely that stepping up investments by itself

---

4. One can obviously question particular numbers. However, the manner in which the calculations were used did not depend on the actual numbers. Suppose subsistence production, which forms a substantial part of the total, had been bigger than estimated. Investment in the subsistence sector would certainly not have added much to the investment estimates, which had been directly arrived at by calculating the activities of government, including the Statutory Corporations, the major companies, and—much more roughly —other enterprises and personal investments. Investments in the subsistence sector consist mainly of land clearance and a few purchases from the money economy. They might have increased total product substantially. Therefore investment ratios would have been smaller than calculated. Consumption expenditures would have been raised by the same amounts as total output, since subsistence production is, by definition, entered identically on the production and consumption side. Thus average and marginal savings rates would also have been lower.

Yet, from the operational planning standpoint, all of this would not matter greatly. What matters for planning purposes is that (a) domestic investments were by 1960 a substantial proportion of total product and (b) that this proportion had increased steadily over the 1950's. These two facts could be estimated beyond doubt. It does not matter from the planning standpoint whether domestic-investment ratios increased from 7 percent to 15 percent or from 6 percent to 12 percent. What matters is that they doubled. Nor does it matter greatly whether domestic-savings ratios were 10 percent or 8 percent. What matters is that they were initially larger and at the end of the period substantially smaller than domestic-investment ratios and that they had not changed significantly. In other words, what matters from the planning standpoint is not whether the particular numbers arrived at are errorless but whether the error in calculations remains roughly constant throughout the period.

would produce the desired target rate of growth. A first analysis of past investments and their distribution did not permit any easy optimism about these investments' bearing fruit during the forthcoming plan period. The figures unequivocally indicated that a rate of growth for the economy of 4 percent or more could not be achieved even with increasing investments unless the *composition* of investments was substantially changed.[5]

The measurement of investments and an analysis of the relation of investment to growth forced upon the planners a rethinking of the concept of "investment" itself. In principle, the Nigerian accounts were compiled in accordance with the definitions proposed by the United Nations—"in principle" signifying that the intentions of the estimators, for obvious and sufficient reasons, could not always be carried through in the African context. The recently revised official estimates of "Gross Capital Expenditure" in Nigeria are given in Table 4.

Economists have been interested in investments for two reasons: as an addition to productive capacity and as a determinant of the level and fluctuations of income. The two are not identical, and what is relevant for the one is not necessarily relevant for the other. From the standpoint of either business-cycle or income-determination theory, what matters is durability and the motives that lead to the particular expenditures or investments. From that standpoint, expenditure on durable consumer goods shares all the essential characteristics of investment: purchases can fall to zero, replacements can be postponed or accelerated, and the motives that lead consumers to spend on consumer durables are more akin to the motives that lead entrepreneurs to invest than to those that lead consumers to buy food.

---

5. It might be added that, even with the resources available to government, a valid estimate of the sectoral distribution of government investments is extraordinarily difficult to make. For a thorough analysis of investments, see Ojetunji Aboyade, *Foundations of an African Economy: A Study of Investment and Growth in Nigeria* (New York: Frederick A. Praeger, 1966).

Table 4. Nigeria's gross capital formation at 1957–58 prices
(£ million)

	1957–58	1958–59	1959–60	1960–61	1961–62	1962–63
A. Visible sector	75.7	87.4	100.3	104.5	118.5	116.1
B. Invisible sector	23.6	21.1	27.0	22.4	21.6	21.0
Total	99.3	108.5	127.3	126.9	140.1	137.1
of which: (a) Public sector	38.2	49.5	63.8	60.8	55.5	55.0
(b) Private sector	61.1	59.0	63.5	66.1	84.6	82.0
of which: (1) Land, agriculture and mining development	10.8	14.1	12.0	10.9	27.4	22.4
(2) Buildings	30.7	35.6	44.8	44.7	42.8	46.9
(3) Civil engineering works	23.1	23.6	29.0	27.6	27.1	29.6
(4) Plant, machinery and equipment	26.5	23.8	32.7	32.7	32.6	32.7
(5) Vehicles	8.2	11.5	8.7	11.0	10.3	5.6

SOURCES: These preliminary new estimates of capital formation have kindly been made available by the Federal Office of Statistics. Previously published estimates refer to "Main Sector" and "Other Enterprises and Personal Investments." Previous estimates of total capital formation for the four middle years shown above were, in £ million: 1958–59, 120.1; 1959–60, 133.5; 1960–61, 154.5; 1961–62, 172.1. *Digest of Statistics* (Lagos: Federal Office of Statistics), October 1964, p. 85. See also *Annual Abstract of Statistics, 1964*, p. 146, and *Economic Indicators*, July 1965, p. 32.

The effect of investment on income and income fluctuations is linked to multiplier effects. This means, basically, that it is linked to aggregate spending. Any increase in spending will raise national income according to the relevant marginal propensities involved. But this is hardly growth. The fact that the rate of increase of Nigeria's national income had started to decline suggested strongly that past increases had been at least to some extent the result of a multiplier effect which was being exhausted. Unless, therefore, something was done about the *composition* of investments, there was a real danger that a constant stream of investments would simply lead to a constant level of income. The growth effects of investments cannot be taken for granted.

When the acceleration principle is introduced into the picture in the manner of Samuelson, the picture is not essentially modified.[6] Productive capacity now indeed figures in the analysis, but in an essentially harmless manner: only the demand for investments is introduced.

Difficulties arise when a stream of investment necessary to maintain full employment itself leads to an increase in full-employment income, and these difficulties have given birth to the Harrod-Domar type of growth theory. Productive capacity is introduced by means of the capital-output ratio, which has been critically discussed before. Analysis of the actual Nigerian figures suggested, for the reasons given, that productive capacity had not increased satisfactorily. Neither the weather nor the deterioration of the terms of trade that had occurred could be entirely blamed for the falling rate of growth. The conclusion followed inevitably that the growth-inducing aspects of investment required utmost attention.

6. Paul A. Samuelson, "Interactions between the Multiplier Analysis and the Principle of Acceleration," *Review of Economic Statistics*, 21 (May 1939), 75-78. Reprinted in Gottfried Haberler (ed.), *Readings in Business Cycle Theory* (Philadelphia: Blakiston, 1944).

When planners focus their attention on productive capacity rather than aggregate spending, they are reminded what "underdeveloped" means. Where in an advanced economy they might prime the pump by stimulating construction, they may find that the country in which they are working lacks even a local building-materials industry. Providing better houses will serve as an incentive to production. Like any durable good, it will, of course, produce a stream of services which is part of GDP. But when major components of modern construction must be imported, an increase in domestic investment may be to a substantial degree offset by a decrease in overseas assets. So, although domestic income will rise as spending on residential construction increases, this spending itself will depend on the ability to maintain the necessary imports. In the absence of a domestic building-materials industry, residential construction can be used only to a very limited extent to raise income. The issue is not merely that because of the high import content the multiplier effect of construction will be reduced. The point is that construction, or any other kind of investment, must as far as possible be judged by its profitability, and that when this cannot be done, it is better treated as consumption rather than investment. In any case the absence of a domestic building-materials industry makes it impossible to use construction as a *stabilizing* device.

This is not a sterile question of definition. Practically speaking, the major problem in Africa is the enlargement of productive capacity in an international context and the creation of an expanding market, not merely the maintenance of aggregate spending. If a competitive construction-materials industry does not exist, planners should aim at creating one. More important, the economic payoff of *all* investments has to be increased if development is to keep going. Only the creation of competitive productive capacity can justify the imports needed for investments.

The need to shift the composition of any investment program toward directly productive investments became all the more urgent in Nigeria when the figures indicated that, at least as far as the public sector was concerned, a number of factors would combine to make it difficult to raise the rate of saving sufficiently. Sterling reserves were slowly being depleted (Table 3) and could be counted upon only to a limited extent for financing the planned expenditures. Past investments, particularly in education and health services, would continue to build up recurrent expenditures rapidly even if no further investments in these sectors were undertaken, thus making it increasingly difficult to generate budgetary surpluses for developmental investments proper unless the investments could be made to raise taxable capacity.[7] Domestic-saving ratios would have to be increased, whether in the form of private savings or of government surpluses (including funds accumulated by self-financing statutory corporations). But this would compete with the increasing needs for ordinary budgetary expenditures unless the necessary shift in the composition of investments was achieved. On top of this, it was necessary not only to mobilize as many resources as possible domestically but to plan for private as well as public capital imports if the target rate of growth was to be achieved.

Development planners everywhere will recognize the dilemma. The usual answer is: raise taxes and restrict consumption. Yet I believe it politically as well as economically dangerous to im-

7. Even if the building of schools and hospitals had ceased altogether, the increase in the number of students and patients, upgrading of teachers, normal salary increases with seniority, and increased staffing ahead—as the institutions already in operation approached full utilization—indicated a substantial future growth in the recurrent budgets of the regions. In the Eastern Region, in which the community spirit is particularly fine, the construction of local schools was done entirely by community effort and did not appear in the Regional capital budget to any significant extent. Recurrent expenditures, however, were carried entirely by the Regional budgets to such an extent that education requires more than 40 percent of ordinary expenditures in the Eastern and Western Regions. Other capital expenditures may have less dramatic effects on the budget, but the principle is the same. It has been stressed and will be stressed over and over again that the ordinary budget is of central importance to development planning.

pose a high degree of austerity, particularly when the investments to be financed have a very uncertain growth effect.[8]
Unless consumption is allowed to rise somewhat, political unrest
(often bursting out in strikes) is inevitable. Economically, increasing production (particularly of agricultural export products
but also of domestic goods) depends, I am convinced, not only on
weather and technical know-how but also on incentives in the
form of real goods and services. Hence too many restrictions on
the consumption of the mass of producers are likely to lower
production, canceling out the gain in resources which was the
purpose of the restrictions to begin with. Farmers can hardly be
induced to shift increasingly from subsistence to market production unless this shift is made worth their while. I do not see how
the productive capacity of an underdeveloped nation can be increased and how agriculture, the most important sector, can be
modernized unless real goods and services are increasingly provided to the farmers.

Against this view, it is sometimes argued that stopping the
conspicuous waste of the richer people might allow a reduction
in aggregate consumption while at the same time permitting
increased consumption of those sections of the population responsible for most of the production. Now, obviously, no moral
justification exists for conspicuous waste anywhere. But, in the
first place, if we knew little about GDP in Nigeria, we knew
even less about income distribution. When we found that an
estimated £472.8 million out of the £810.4 million spent on
consumption in Nigeria by Nigerian residents went for subsistence food valued at retail prices, we judged it highly unrealistic to rely on income redistribution.[9] Whether drastic in-

8. The personal tone is necessary because this view is not generally
shared. The point is more fully developed in Chapter VIII.

9. See Okigbo, *Nigerian National Accounts, 1950–57*, pp. 100 ff., for a
breakdown of consumer expenditures.

come-redistribution measures are administratively feasible in Africa is open to doubt also.

The analysis of the situation suggested that it was not merely desirable but crucial to hold down the growth of government consumption. This in turn pointed back to the importance of shifting the composition of investments away from administrative and social expenditures toward self-financing investments.

It is obvious that administration must be made as efficient as is humanly possible. Budgets can be relieved by shifting some expenditures to individual consumption and local authorities. The collection of school fees is an outstanding example of a transferable task. The issue is not whether expenditures on education are investment or consumption or whether they should be undertaken by government or privately. The issue is simply how the desire for education *and* development can be made to help maximize the mobilization of resources.[10]

An inspection of the budgets usually shows that they contain hidden subsidies. In many countries it can be observed that rising incomes do not lead to increasing rates of savings. Frequently taxes are high while public savings are low. When sub-

---

10. Dr. F. Snapper, at present with the Statistical Office of the Ministry of Economic Affairs and Planning in Victoria, Cameroons, has written to me about an interesting historic example, which, with some modifications, makes the same point: "Suppose it is profitable to start an umbrella factory . . . However, the Government will miss its revenue on imported umbrellas and therefore is not able to provide the recurrent expenditure for a university . . . Assume that the University and the umbrella factory would be established in the same town. What do you think that the citizens of that town would choose? I can give you a well-known historical example of Holland in 1574, which at that time was a poor country engaged in a deadly struggle against mighty Spain.

"In that year the city had resisted the Spanish armies after a siege in which that city had suffered tremendously. The Prince of Orange, in order to recompense the city, offered the citizens the choice between 10 years of freedom of all taxes or a University. As Dutchmen, the citizens of Leyden are supposed to be very materialistic, but notwithstanding that they chose the University, and so the now well-known University of Leyden started."

sidies transfer tax monies to inefficient enterprises, such a result must be expected. In Nigeria, and certainly not only there, it could be further observed that subsidies in effect go from the poor to the rich. Thus in Nigeria road users did not pay for the maintenance of roads, and telephone users did not return the full cost of the services they received. Neither car owners nor telephone subscribers could very well be considered too indigent to pay. There seemed to be a good case for charging the true cost of economic services to users and letting the shifting of costs in the economic system take care of itself.[11]

The tax question also leads naturally into the problem of how producer prices paid by Marketing Boards affect Board "profits," and in connection with this a consideration of export tax revenues is in order.[12] The expected deterioration of Nigeria's terms of trade was likely to affect adversely both Marketing Board "profits" and export taxes. Marketing Boards had already spent most of their sterling assets (Table 3). Import requirements for development would be increasing at a time when exports could not be increased substantially. With due allowance for individual differences, this problem, too, arises in many places besides Nigeria and unavoidably forces the planners' attention back to the composition of investments. Once more it becomes important to ensure that investments will increase available resources, stim-

---

11. On this point, see Chapter VI, section C. Cf. also W. F. Stolper, "Social Factors in Economic Planning, with Special Reference to Nigeria," *East African Economics Review*, XI (June 1964), 1-17, a reprint of a document prepared for the Economic Commission for Africa, Addis Ababa.

12. Export taxes depend in some cases not only on the value of exports but also on the price of the exports, which introduces an element of tax progression. On cocoa beans, for example, export duties are "10% ad valorem while the value . . . does not exceed £150 per ton with an additional one tenth of 1 per cent for every £ or part of a £ by which the value . . . exceeds £150 per ton, provided that the amount of duty chargeable shall not exceed 20 per cent of the value." *Nigeria Handbook of Commerce and Industry*, 5th ed. (Lagos: Federal Ministry of Information, 1962), p. 279. Similar progressions apply also to groundnuts, palm kernels and palm oil, and so forth. Progressivity with respect to price and to income are, however, not necessarily the same thing.

ulate export production, and help to hold imports down. But these aims are consistent only if export production remains competitive and import substitution is profitable.

It may seem a long way from the percentage of gross fixed investment in GDP to the determination of a tax policy which advocates the abolition of hidden subsidies to telephone users and automobile owners. But is it? The major purpose of making a study of past performance of the economy in terms of such national accounts as can be gathered is to learn what can be learned for the future. If increasing investment ratios are needed to get decreasing rates of growth of income, some searching questions must be answered about likely trends of the terms of trade, the composition of investments, and the nature of policies. If there is a choice between crude estimates for a series of years and an accurate estimate for a single year, the former seems clearly preferable. There is much to be learned from a study of development over time. The "minimum system of national accounts" is both feasible and a powerful tool for planning analysis, and its usefulness depends not on great accuracy concerning absolute levels but only on a reasonable reliability of trends and of the relations of the components to one another.

B. PROJECTIONS: FIRST APPROXIMATIONS

The analysis of Nigeria's developments yielded the basic assumptions for the future. The projections were made in two steps. The first step can be described as a semi-mechanical projection to see what were the implications of assumptions derived from the analysis of past investments. The second step was a consistency test in which the implications of possible plans and programs were matched against the implications of the assumptions derived from the analysis of the past.

The purpose of the first approximation was simply to determine the required import surplus, given certain assumptions about the Plan. The assumptions were specifically, first, that there would be no price changes; second, that gross fixed investment would be 15 percent of GDP; third, that GDP would rise at 4 percent per annum; fourth, that private consumption would be allowed to rise at 3 percent per annum; fifth, that government consumption of goods and services would gradually increase by one half of one percent per annum from the 1960–61 level; sixth, that inventory accumulation would be one half the change in gross fixed investment. Given these assumptions, the total of resources required could be calculated; and the import surplus required to sustain the level of consumption and investment postulated could be found as a residual.

The assumptions flowed from the results of the analysis of the past. The comparatively high investment ratio already achieved would be difficult to raise further in the face of depleted sterling assets and lagging savings. (Revisions indicate that the investment ratio was probably 13–14 percent rather than the 15 percent originally estimated.) Similarly, there would be difficulties in achieving, let alone surpassing, a 4 percent per annum rate of growth of GDP, the target initially set.

Letting total private consumption rise at 3 percent per annum was intended to allow for the population increase and a modest increase in consumption per capita. However, the actual population of Nigeria was unknown, and there was no agreement on the probable rate of population increase. In view of these uncertainties the postulated increase of 3 percent seemed minimal.

The model obviously had to allow for an increase in government consumption of goods and services. The planned rise of one half of one percent per annum, chosen in this semi-mechanical manner, was, of course, arbitrary. However, new investments generate additional recurrent cost.

Virtually no information exists about inventory accumulation. A perusal of detailed import statistics over the years suggested that there must have been imports for inventories in some years, followed by a decline of inventories in others. This seemed the only possible explanation for some of the violent fluctuation in imports of individual commodities shown by the statistics. However, although these statistics were inadequate for estimating inventory accumulation accurately, it seemed essential to allow for inventory accumulation so that any future official calculations might be fitted into the model. The assumption that inventory accumulation is equal to half the increase in gross fixed investment was, of course, arbitrary; it was, however, not unreasonable to think that further attempts would be made to gauge inventory accumulation. In any underdeveloped country with relatively poor communications, inventories of substantial size have to be kept. Textile factories that in England would keep two days' supply of spare parts on hand must in Nigeria keep enough to last nine months. Similar figures apply to tobacco factories and steel mills. It takes that long to order and get the parts from overseas.

The calculations made on all these assumptions are reproduced in Table 5. Thus the table represents the semi-mechanical projection mentioned earlier. The calculations indicated not only a substantial balance-of-payments gap but also an unchanging domestic-savings ratio. Moreover, relatively minor variations in the assumptions had major effects on the model. Thus, if total private consumption were allowed to rise by 3.2 percent per year (see Alternative B in the table), the balance-of-payments deficits would increase substantially, year after year, whereas with a rise in consumption held to 3 percent per year, the deficits would slowly decline. Relatively minor variations in all other assumptions promised to lead to similarly important consequences in the model.

This sensitivity to relatively minor changes in assumptions suggested, first, that it was essential to project the budgetary and balance-of-payments implications as carefully as possible (see Section C, below). Second, it was essential for safety's sake

Table 5. Prospects for the Nigerian economy (projections made in 1961, at 1960-61 prices)

	1960-61	1961-62	1962-63	1963-64	1964-65	1965-66	1966-67	1967-68	1962-63 through 1967-68
ALTERNATIVE A: CONSUMPTION TO INCREASE AT 3% PER YEAR (£ MILLION)									
Private consumption increasing 3%	922.0	949.7	978.1	1,007.7	1,037.7	1,068.9	1,100.9	1,133.9	6,327.0
Government consumption increasing 0.5% starting with 8% in 1960-61	85.0	92.6	102.3	112.6	123.6	135.4	147.8	161.0	782.7
Gross fixed investment (GFI) at 15% of GDP	158.0	173.6	180.5	187.7	195.2	203.0	211.2	219.6	1,197.2
Inventory accumulation, 1/2 of change in GFI	10.0	7.8	3.5	3.6	3.8	3.9	4.1	4.2	23.1
Resources required	1,175.0	1,223.7	1,264.4	1,311.4	1,360.3	1,411.2	1,464.0	1,518.7	8,330.0
GDP increasing 4%	1,112.5	1,157.0	1,203.3	1,251.4	1,301.5	1,353.6	1,407.7	1,464.0	7,981.5
Import surplus required	—62.5	—66.7	—61.1	—60.0	—58.8	—57.6	—56.3	—54.7	—348.5
ALTERNATIVE B: CONSUMPTION TO INCREASE AT 3.2% PER YEAR (£ MILLION)									
Private consumption increasing 3.2%	922.0	951.5	981.9	1,013.4	1,045.8	1,079.3	1,113.8	1,149.4	6,383.6
Resources required	1,175.0	1,225.5	1,268.7	1,317.3	1,368.4	1,421.6	1,476.9	1,534.2	8,387.1
Import surplus required	—62.5	—68.5	—64.9	—65.9	—66.9	—68.0	—69.2	—70.2	—405.1

Table 5. (Continued)

	1960–61	1961–62	1962–63	1963–64	1964–65	1965–66	1966–67	1967–68	1962–63 through 1967–68
PERCENTAGE DISTRIBUTION, ALTERNATIVE A									
Private consumption	82.9	82.1	81.3	80.5	79.7	79.0	78.2	77.5	
Government consumption	7.6	8.0	8.5	9.0	9.5	10.0	10.5	11.0	
GFI	14.2	15.0	15.0	15.0	15.0	15.0	15.0	15.0	
Inventory accumulation	0.9	0.7	0.3	0.3	0.3	0.3	0.3	0.3	
Import surplus required	−5.6	−5.8	−5.1	−4.8	−4.5	−4.3	−4.0	−3.8	
Total	100.0	100.0	100.0	100.0	100.0	100.0	100.0	100.0	
Private and government consumption	90.5	90.1	89.8	89.5	89.2	89.0	88.7	88.5	
PERCENTAGE DISTRIBUTION, ALTERNATIVE B									
Private consumption	82.9	82.2	81.6	81.0	80.4	79.7	79.1	78.5	
Import surplus required	−5.6	−5.9	−5.4	−5.3	−5.1	−5.0	−4.9	−4.8	
Private and government consumption	90.5	90.2	90.1	90.0	89.9	89.7	89.6	89.5	

SOURCE: W. F. Stolper, *Prospects for the Nigerian Economy: Principles and Procedures Adopted in Projecting National Accounts* (Apapa: Nigerian National Press, Ltd., 1962), pp. 12–13, table A. In this separately printed appendix to the National Plan, the figures for 1960–61 differ from those for 1960–61 given in my Table 1 because, instead of being in 1957–58 prices (as in Table 1), they are in 1960–61 prices.

113

to make all projections conservatively. Third, even the "mechanically" arrived-at figures showed how important it was to assure
that GDP would *in fact* rise by 4 percent or more, which in turn
led to even greater concern with the composition and the size
of the investment program.

The composition of investments became important in yet another respect not so far touched upon. Earlier, no assumption
was made as to what proportion of investments should be public
and what proportion private. But one way to stretch available
resources would be to increase the private share of investments
and thereby limit the increase in government absorption. This
could be done by shifting public investments in a direction that
would generate lower budgetary charges. It could also be done
by restricting the amount of government investment, stimulating
private investment, or doing both at the same time. If private
investment were stimulated, the budget would not be charged,
and, moreover, what would have been final charges on output
would become intermediate goods that did not enter the final
calculations, or at least that would be self-financing.

Such shifting may seem to be a trick, sleight of hand. Yet this
is only partly true. From an accounting standpoint, where one
deals with the fact of the case *ex post*, it obviously makes no
difference how an economic activity is organized—at least it
should not make any difference. From a policy standpoint, however, there is a difference. The manner in which production is
organized and in which payment is arranged will affect the
resources that can be mobilized and will affect savings ratios.
Thus school fees belong to private consumption, but taxes to
pay teachers belong to public consumption. Road and bridge
maintenance paid for out of taxes is government investment, but
tolls are collected out of private consumption. An electricity department or a telephone system that is run as a ministerial department becomes a charge on the budget. When a facility is
reorganized as a private company or a public statutory authority,

the same payments become in part intermediate goods. In some respects the reorganization is merely a bookkeeping maneuver, but when it leads to a reorganization of resources and a reconsideration of price policies, it has a direct effect on what will happen in the economy.

Thus even the "mechanical" projections can be shown to have several important planning purposes. It is now necessary to turn to the next procedure which, so to speak, plays the record backward.

C. PROJECTIONS: CONSISTENCY OF THE PLAN

The major purpose of national accounts is to provide a framework within which the consistency of plans can be tested and the size of the plans determined. The basic projection of resource availability meets from the very beginning almost insurmountable difficulties. The resources that will be available for the various plan purposes and for consumption consist of total production less exports but including imports. Though this statement merely relates well-known national accounting identities, the translation of the statement into a testable numerical pattern meets certain logical difficulties.

First, the investment of a certain portion of GDP, 15 percent in the case of Nigeria, is a target variable which becomes, for the present purpose, an assumption. Suppose, it is argued, that the target will somehow be met. The division of the investment between public and private is not yet specified. This division results initially from the amount of the government plans; the percentage of private investment becomes a residual to make total gross fixed investment 15 percent of GDP.

Second, the assumption that a 15 percent investment ratio will, on the average, produce a 4 percent rate of growth in GDP over the years, continues to hang largely in the air. The implied gross incremental capital-output ratio of almost 4 is high by international standards and yet reasonable considering the large proportion of investments that do not pay.

In Chapter III, serious doubts were expressed about the logic of c/o ratios. They were not used as a planning device. It seems therefore necessary to justify further the initial assumption that GDP would grow by 4 percent per year as the result of investing year after year 15 percent of that growing GDP. Suppose the exact composition of past and planned public and private investment was known: that is, how much investment of what kinds took or would take place, and when and where. Suppose, further, that all investment proposals were sufficiently thought through so that the timing and size of the output stream were known. In such a case, future income streams could be calculated, and the rate of growth of GDP could itself be derived instead of having to be assumed, *provided there were no price changes.* The c/o ratios would become simply *ex post* calculations, summarizing the effects of investments on income.

In the situation that actually confronts a planner, it is not always possible to make such calculations, although in some cases a pretty good approximation can be achieved.[13] Private investment plans cannot be known in sufficient detail and, in any case, are subject to indirect controls only.

When starting to check the consistency of the total program, it must be assumed that governmental plans and policies toward the private sector have already been sifted and adjusted so as to make the desired rate of growth in the economy at least a strong probability. As far as public investment is concerned, unprofitable investments in that part of the governmental program that is subject to economic calculations will have been eliminated and some limitations will have been put on the other parts of public investment that require resources but do not lead

---

13. In Tunisia, for example, it was possible to make a reasonable guess as to the amount and timing of the outputs which past investments would produce in the future. In Nigeria, lack of data and staff made such a detailed study impracticable.

to increases in either taxable capacity or to any direct or quick rise in income. As far as the private sector is concerned, certain private plans will be known, and for the rest, some limitations on taxation will have been accepted to induce the needed private investment.

In other words, the desire to achieve a certain growth rate will have led to a number of decisions on the plan's composition and timing and on economic policies that seem to be required to achieve the over-all target. This will of course be a long way from the desired degree of detailed knowledge. But one of the virtues of national accounting is that it continually forces a reconsideration of plans.

Price developments are another matter that cannot simply be assumed away. In the present context, the problems connected with implementing monetary policy are of secondary importance. What matters is estimating the resources that will be available for the various purposes envisaged. Since the economies of underdeveloped countries depend to such a large degree on exports and imports, and since they are normally not in a position to influence either their export or their import prices, the projections of their terms of trade become particularly important. From the standpoint of determining the availability of resources, it makes no difference how exports in constant prices move. The important thing to know is the amount of real resources that are likely to be available to the economy. The projection of real resources available requires, therefore, for reasons of internal consistency, that price changes of exports and imports be introduced into the projections.[14]

14. The Economic Commission for Africa has recently pointed out that "Another basic assumption is the financing of the Plan by export earnings; it is glaring to note that although the earnings of many primary commodities were fluctuating and at times falling during the last decade, the planners still count on increasing earnings at constant prices with an increase in output." Economic Commission for Africa, *Outlines and Selected Indicators of African Development Plans*, E/CN.14/336 (mimeo., 1965), p. vi.

One also needs detailed projections of the import surplus likely to arise as the result of the plan. The import surplus, found as a residual in the first projection, must now be estimated independently and fed back into the calculations. This calculation, which will be presently described, serves also to coordinate private and public plans.

In certain approaches to development problems, particularly those associated with Dr. Raúl Prebisch and the Economic Commission for Latin America, the development of substantial import surpluses is considered essential for the success of development plans. For Nigeria's planners the calculations of the import gap had a threefold function. One was to determine the effect which the Plan would have on imports and exports, with the ultimate objective of modifying specifications either to minimize the likely import gap or to maximize the growth of the economy for any given import surplus. The second function was to help determine the size of the Plan itself, since capital imports had to have some relation to the mobilization of internal resources. Because it was (and is) unlikely that more than half the capital expenditures in Nigeria can be financed from abroad, this itself limited what one might call the permissible balance-of-payments gap. The third function was to ensure that the import gap would in fact lead to the kind of growth which would eventually make the continuation of capital imports other than on commercial terms unnecessary.

An import surplus of goods and services represents real resources that are available to the economy. There are, however, certain unrequited exports that lead to entries in the balance-of-payments on the debit side. In particular, interest payments and repayments of capital represent resources that must be produced but will not be domestically available either directly or indirectly through imports. From a planning standpoint, it is essential to adjust the GDP concept to allow for these unrequited exports. The information needed to make this adjustment is immediately relevant for the determination of the proper size and composition of a development program. For, in order to make such an estimate, it becomes necessary to decide how much of the program should be public and how much private; what proportion of the public program should be financed domestically; what proportion of the foreign financing should (or could) be financed by ordinary loans and what part by low-interest long-maturity loans. If, as has been suggested by the IBRD, debt service should not exceed 10 percent of export earnings, a limit to foreign borrowing will quickly appear to set still another limit on the size and composition of the plan. To be sure, the 10 percent limit is arbitrary, and all figures dealing with the future are uncertain. The point is simply that whatever figure is chosen, there will be a limit; and whatever projections are made, they must be internally consistent.

It is next possible to calculate in considerable detail the ramifications of a plan with respect to government consumption as defined in national accounts. By deducting the projected investments and government consumption from the adjusted GDP as described before, the possible private consumption can be found as a residual. If, as in the case of the Nigerian Plan, this residual shows an average increase of only 2.8 percent per annum, the specifications are too big and lead to inconsistencies in the sense that there are not enough resources to achieve simultaneously the desired growth of 4 percent in unadjusted GDP and 3 percent in consumption, and a GFI ratio of 15 percent.[15]

It will, of course, not do to say that all projections are suspect —as if this were not perfectly plain. Nor will it do to suggest that Nigeria's import surplus has somehow got to be bigger. The import surplus, after all, has been independently calculated—

15. Therefore, advocating a *smaller* plan is not the same thing as advocating a small one. The planners believed that the smaller plan was very big indeed, as big as resources and executive capacity could possibly stand. This view was not entirely accepted. Only the future can show who was more realistic.

the details of this and other calculations and their rationale will be discussed presently—so as to be consistent with a 4 percent rate of growth and with the rest of the assumptions. To state that the calculations underestimated the needs and treat this as if it were simply an arithmetical error misses the purpose of the exercise. The point is simply that a disaggregated calculation reveals internal inconsistencies. Moreover, if real imports are increased in any manner except by gifts or because the projected terms of trade were unduly pessimistic, the unrequited exports will soon increase, which, in turn, will affect the adjusted GDP. On the other hand, if the size of the program is reduced, the growth rate need not be affected, provided the cuts are made in the purely administrative and social sectors and provided the program originally contained projects with no foreseeable growth effect. There are several possible adjustments, and it is precisely the function of the calculations to bring these possible adjustments and their implication into the open.

Table 6 shows the projections made for Nigeria. The conclusions derived from that table were stated in the Annexure to the Plan as follows:

In other words, the consistency test shows that not sufficient resources will be available under the assumptions made to achieve all Plan targets at the same time, and that therefore adjustments in the targets must be made. It is evident that the investment targets can be cut only at the risk of failing to achieve the overall targets set for the economy. Various possible means of achieving the desired objectives would be either:

(a) to ensure that the composition of investments will shift sufficiently in the direction of directly productive investments of high return, and that expenditure on projects of low return is minimized so as to induce an increase of the growth rate of the economy beyond the 4 percent projected, thus increasing the resources available to the economy for all purposes; or

(b) to increase the balance of payments gap which must be financed by various means in order to make the additional resources available; or

(c) to restrict the growth of Government Consumption to set resources free for other purposes. To restrict Government Consumption means specifically that the growth of the projected recurrent expenditures will be held below the presently projected levels; or

(d) to accept a rate of growth of Private Consumption below the aggregate rate of increase of 3 percent per annum initially assumed; or

(e) of course, a combination of these courses.[16]

I turn now to a more detailed description of the manner in which the import and export projections were made and in which government consumption was estimated.

Nigeria exports a great variety of products. Cocoa, palm kernels, palm oil, groundnuts, groundnut oil, rubber, cotton, and tin accounted in 1960 for about three quarters of Nigeria's exports, and by 1967 petroleum exports are likely to displace cocoa as the largest single foreign-exchange earner.[17] In addition, there are by no means negligible exports of groundnut cake, logs, wood products, cotton seed, and cattle hides and goat skins.

The projections were made for about twenty products that in 1960 accounted for over 90 percent of total exports, and they were made separately for quantities and values where possible. This sort of detail is necessary for a number of reasons.

16. W. F. Stolper, *Prospects for the Nigerian Economy: Principles and Procedures Adopted in Projecting National Accounts* (Apapa: Nigerian National Press, Ltd., 1962), p. 8, para. 23. The inconsistency revealed by the calculations was one of the factors that led to the stretching of the Plan from five to six years. Unfortunately, time did not permit the staff to work out the proper adjustments and time sequences, and this, for the reasons discussed in Chapter III, produced certain further inconsistencies in the Plan as published. A reader of Chapter V of the *National Development Plan, 1962–68* might bear this in mind. The wording of the Annexure as quoted above has been altered in a very minor way for smoothness, without changing the sense in any respect.

17. Already in 1961, petroleum exports amounted to £ 11,545,000 and had become the fourth biggest export after (1) groundnuts and groundnut oil and cake, (2) cocoa, and (3) palm oil and palm kernels. Here are the figures for these four exports in 1961, 1963, and 1964, respectively: Groundnuts and groundnut oil and cake, £ 39,166,000, £ 45,880,000, and £ 47,020,000. Cocoa, £ 33,746,000, £ 32,360,000, and £ 40,100,000. Palm oil and palm kernels, £ 33,118,000, £ 30,790,000, and £ 31,710,000. Petroleum, £ 11,545,000, £ 20,140,000, and £ 32,060,000.

Table 6. Consistency test prepared in 1962 for projections of the Nigerian economy
(in 1960–61 prices)

	1960–61[a]	1962–63	1963–64	1964–65	1965–66	1966–67	1967–68	1962–63 through 1967–68
SOURCES OF AVAILABLE RESOURCES (£ MILLION)								
Real GDP increasing 4% per year	1,112.5	1,203.3	1,251.4	1,301.5	1,353.5	1,407.7	1,464.0	7,981.5
Less resources required for debt service	—	−5.1	−5.9	−10.9	−16.4	−26.6	−27.9	−92.8
Equals "adjusted" GDP	1,112.5	1,198.2	1,245.5	1,290.6	1,337.1	1,381.1	1,436.1	7,888.7
Add import gap (balance-of-payments deficit as independently estimated)	62.5	83.9	77.6	76.1	74.7	86.4	81.8	480.5
Equals available resources	1,175.0	1,282.1	1,323.1	1,366.7	1,411.8	1,467.5	1,517.9	8,369.2
USES OF AVAILABLE RESOURCES (£ MILLION)								
Gross fixed investment (GFI) at 15% of adjusted GDP	158.0	179.7	186.8	193.6	200.6	207.2	215.4	1,183.3
Inventory accumulation, ½ of change in GFI	10.0	5.7	3.6	3.4	3.5	3.3	4.1	23.6
Government consumption[b]	85.0	110.2	118.9	132.9	145.4	162.4	173.3	843.1
Private consumption (residual)	922.0	986.5	1,013.8	1,036.8	1,062.3	1,094.6	1,125.1	6,319.1
INDICES								
Adjusted GDP	100	107.7	112.0	116.0	120.2	124.1	129.1	—
Resources available	100	109.1	112.6	116.3	120.2	124.9	129.2	—

122

Table 6. (Continued)

	1960-61[a]	1962-63	1963-64	1964-65	1965-66	1966-67	1967-68	1962-63 through 1967-68
GFI	100	113.7	118.2	122.5	127.0	131.1	136.3	—
Government consumption	100	129.6	139.9	156.4	171.1	191.1	203.9	—
Private consumption	100	107.0	110.0	112.5	115.2	118.7	122.0	—
YEAR-TO-YEAR CHANGES								AVERAGE
Adjusted GDP	—	100	104.0	103.6	103.6	103.2	104.1	—
Resources available	—	100	103.2	103.3	103.4	103.9	103.4	—
GFI	—	100	104.0	103.6	103.6	103.2	104.1	—
Government consumption	—	100	107.9	111.8	109.4	111.7	106.7	—
Private consumption	—	100	102.8	102.3	102.4	103.0	102.8	2.8
PERCENTAGE DISTRIBUTION (ADJUSTED GDP = 100%)								
GFI	14.2	15.0	15.0	15.0	15.0	15.0	15.0	15.0
Inventory	.9	.5	.3	.3	.3	.2	.3	.3
Government consumption	7.6	9.2	9.5	10.3	10.9	11.8	12.1	10.7
Private consumption	82.9	82.3	81.4	80.3	79.4	79.3	78.3	80.1
Import gap (balance-of-payments deficit as independently estimated)	—5.6	—7.0	—6.2	—5.9	—5.6	—6.3	—5.7	—6.1
Private and government consumption	90.5	91.5	90.9	90.6	90.3	91.1	90.4	90.8

a. The figures for 1960-61 are included for comparison. Figures for 1961-62 were not published. The purpose of this table was to show the implications of the Plan from 1962-63 to 1967-68.

b. Assuming a slippage of 5 percent.

SOURCE: W. F. Stolper, *Prospects for the Nigerian Economy: Principles and Procedures Adopted in Projecting National Accounts* (Apapa: Nigerian National Press, Ltd., 1962), pp. 14-15, table B.1.

First, prices depend on what happens not only to a country's supplies and demands but also to world supplies and demands.

Second, what happens to any index of export prices will depend on the composition of that index, that is, the changing importance of individual exports. It will therefore not do to assume a blanket decline in export prices and to apply this to exports as a whole. Such a procedure would suggest the wrong policy implication. The procedure used in Nigeria allows for a changing composition of exports. With such a procedure, an export-price index can be calculated *ex post* with any weight desired, but such calculation becomes merely an interesting academic exercise of only limited practical significance.

Third, what happens to export earnings—which is what is relevant from the planning standpoint—will depend on both export prices of individual products and on quantities. Prices are largely outside the control of a country like Nigeria. Export quantities there depend partly on the weather, partly on the plans for agriculture, partly on the plans for industrialization (cotton processing, expression of groundnut oil, tin smelting, rubber manufacturing, petroleum refining are the outstanding examples), and partly on policies relating to the rate of growth of consumption, including Marketing Board price policies. As has been stressed, many of Nigeria's export products are also domestically consumed.

One major reason for projecting export quantities, therefore, is that Nigerian plans will affect them directly. Hence the effect of the Plan itself must be built in the export projections. World prices, on the other hand, are at best only indirectly affected by Nigerian action. There are at least two further reasons for making a detailed projection of export quantities. A rational development of the transport programs—ports, roads, railroads, and to a lesser extent, air traffic—depends on forecasting the movement of quantities (see Chapter V). Then, too, tax revenues of the Regions are determined partly by export values, partly by export quantities, and partly by prices received.

The bulk of Nigeria's exports are agricultural. Under the Nigerian constitution, agriculture is a regional matter. The reliability of the export projections will depend, therefore, on the information received from the Regional planners, who in turn must depend on their research institutions and the plans of their ministries of agriculture. Where there are domestic uses of exportable products, it is equally necessary to get information on plans for these domestic uses. This raises questions of profitability, which the Regional planners must have considered. Detailed projection of export quantities thus becomes an important means of coordinating private and governmental plans throughout the Nigerian economy.

Petroleum exports were much the simplest to project. After many years of fruitless search, Shell-BP discovered large reserves of oil and natural gas, and substantial quantities of petroleum were being produced and exported by 1961.[18] A fair estimate for the expected production in the 1960's was supplied by the oil companies. Since a refinery was planned to come into operation by the end of 1964 or thereabouts—it actually started operating late in 1965—it was necessary to deduct the amount of crude petroleum to be used domestically rather than exported. The feedback into the transport program came mainly through planned dredging operations to keep open a channel at Bonny, the specialized oil port.

For the Eastern Region, oil-palm products are the most im-

18. The initial explorations were made by Shell-BP and Mobiloil. Under the agreement with the Nigerian government, Shell-BP had to give up half its original drilling concessions in 1962. In 1962, "Altogether 10 continental shelf oil prospecting licenses, three land and territorial waters oil prospecting licenses and 14 oil mining leases have been granted to five oil companies." *Nigeria Handbook of Commerce and Industry,* 5th ed. (Lagos: Federal Ministry of Information, 1962), p. 141.

portant single crop. Plans envisaged new plantations, the rehabilitation of palm groves through a subsidized program of
thinning out of wild palms, and the introduction of hydraulic
handpresses which could raise both the yield and the quality
of palm oil from any given amount of fruit. Weather apparently
has little effect on output—or else it is too even in the belt in
which palms are grown. In any case, yields in tons of palm
kernels and oil were calculated to 1977 and combined with other
information to make export projections of this important crop.[19]

In the Northern Region, cotton and groundnuts are of major
importance. The Northern Region planners collected information
on what was known about yields and acreages of all major
export and domestic crops; what the research institutes knew
about raising yields; how fast this information could be transmitted to the farmers; what were the plans of extending acreages; and what the likelihood was of achieving the intended
aims. They also collected information on the weather and made
an average allowance for probable crop failures. In addition,
plans for domestic uses of what were primarily export products
were taken into account. For tin, some information on the
International Tin Agreement and the technical possibilities of
expanding production had to be considered.

The projections of export quantities not only correlated Regional plans but to a considerable extent also allowed for the
effect of public policies on the private sector; for almost all
agricultural production is private, as well as the production of
mineral oil, tin, logs, and plywood, and together they account
for the overwhelming part of total product.

19. Obviously projections allowed also for the expected production in the
other Regions. The Eastern Region calculations have been published in the
Eastern Region Plan, chap. vi, tables 2-4. Tables 5 and 6 give the projection
for rubber, tables 7 and 8 for cocoa. Appendix VII of the Western Region
Plan gives data for cocoa, rubber, and oil-palm programs. Calculations for
the Northern Region were available only for internal use.

The calculations of the value of exports involved the use of projected long-run prices. There is no sensible way to project year-to-year fluctuations in prices or output; average prices will have to be sufficient. But neither is it necessary to project a single long-run price for the whole period. In at least one instance a different price was used for the valuation of exports for the later part of the planned period than for the earlier part, because there was reason to believe that the world supply situation would change significantly.

To find approximate long-run prices is normally beyond the resources of an individual country. The prices themselves are determined by world demand and supply. To forecast them accurately requires constant expert attention to complicated systems of demand and supply equations. Some commodities, such as cocoa, have no close substitutes. Nigeria is the second largest supplier after Ghana and undoubtedly has some influence on the price. Production conditions are about the same in Nigeria and Ghana, so that their supplies tend to vary in the same manner from year to year. Other commodities, such as oil seeds, have very complicated markets, and for technical reasons animal and vegetable fats from the tropics, the temperate zone, and the cold regions all compete closely.[20] Clearly, to project what will happen even under simplified assumptions is beyond the capability of any underdeveloped country. Fortunately, the Food and

20. J. C. A. Faure, of Unilever (Raw Materials) Limited, on page 9 of a paper delivered at the 1960 Congress of the International Association of Seed Crushers in London, listed the world's oils and fats as follows: *"Edible" Type oils:* Cottonseed, Groundnut, Soya Bean, Sunflower, Olive, Sesame, Rapeseed, Maize, Teaseed; *"Palm" oils:* Coconut, Palm Kernel, Palm Oil, Babassu Kernel; *Industrial Type oils:* Linseed, Castor Bean, Tung, Oiticica, others including Niger, Hempseed, Penda seed; *Animal fats:* Butter, Lard, Tallow; *Marine oils:* Whale, Fish.

All of West Africa supplies about one fourteenth of the total supply of oils and fats (excluding the Soviet Union), the United States about a fourth, and Western Europe about a seventh. Detailed country figures appear on page 8 of Mr. Faure's paper.

Agriculture Organization, the IBRD, and the U.S. Department of Agriculture offer long-run price studies.[21]

Through the long-run price forecasts of such agencies, the exports of an individual country are effectively placed into a world-wide context, and until such time as there is joint action among the sellers, it becomes permissible to treat the individual country as a "quantity adapter," which can sell at the predicted prices all it actually offers to the world for sale. In any case, as far as it is humanly possible, the effects of the actions of the country on the price it is likely to receive have already been allowed for by the method of forecasting the price.[22] If there are no changes in import prices, the value of exports at long-run prices represents the amount of real resources available to the economy out of its sales abroad.

In the Nigerian case, long-run prices were conservatively estimated. This caution seemed consistent with viewing the Plan as an interrelated system, not of equations, but of inequalities (see Chapter III). It also served to identify the likely trouble spots and to anticipate the trouble by planning for the worst case. If developments turned out to be better than assumed, this would be all to the good.

The projection of imports raises many more difficulties than the projection of exports. The problem of long-run import prices is, for practical purposes, insoluble: imports consist of too great

21. FAO produces bulletins on cocoa and oil seeds giving all the existing information available on prices, production, demand, and stocks. The IBRD makes commodity studies. The U.S. Department of Agriculture publishes surveys of agriculture in various parts of the world. The International Association of Seed Crushers has annual conferences at which long-term projections are released. These are among the major resources available to the planners.

22. It is necessary to make a further qualification. The Marketing Boards in the former British African territories did, of course, try to sell at the best price obtainable and they sometimes withheld sales for short periods. They did not, however, sell in a sheltered market characteristic of the sales of French-speaking countries to France, nor did they try to fix world prices. If there are sales to a sheltered market, the problem of price forecasting is simplified.

a variety of goods, with too many quality differences and with too much technical change that must be expected even over five or six years. The only feasible procedure is to assume that the prices of individual import categories will remain constant. As Table 7 indicates, the index of Nigerian import prices did not in

Table 7. Indices of Nigerian export prices, import prices, and terms of trade, 1948–1963

Calendar year	Export prices		Import prices		Terms of trade	
1948	100	—	100	—	100	—
1949	104	—	102	—	102	—
1950	115	—	105	—	110	—
1951	157	—	130	—	121	—
1952	163	—	137	—	119	—
1953	142	—	122	—	116	—
1954	158	100	114	100	139	100
1955	(139)a	88	(112)a	98	(125)a	90
1956	(131)	83	(114)	100	(115)	83
1957	(133)	84	(116)	102	(114)	82
1958	(134)	85	(113)	99	(120)	86
1959	(141)	89	(111)	97	(128)	92
1960	(142)	90	(116)	102	(122)	88
1961	(133)	84	(116)	102	(114)	82
1962	(126)	80	(115)	101	(110)	79
1963	(133)	84	(122)	107	(110)	79
1964	(136)	86	(125)	110	(109)	78

a. Figures in parentheses were calculated to provide a continuous series, after basis of index was changed.

SOURCE: *Digest of Statistics* (Federal Office of Statistics, Lagos), vol. 13, no. 3 (July 1964), p. 53 (tables 26 and 26A); vol. 14, nos. 1 and 2 (January and April 1965), p. 61 (table 6.17A).

fact change much between 1954 and 1962. But it cannot be ascertained whether this was because the prices of individual imports had not changed, or because price changes offset each other, or because the composition of imports changed by the substitution of cheaper for more expensive goods so that import prices remained constant in the face of generally rising prices.[23]

23. Between 1954 and 1961, import prices of SITC Classification 0 (food) remained roughly constant; prices of SITC 1 (drink and tobacco)

Imports depend on relative prices. Imports for consumption depend also on income. Imports for investment, however, do not depend directly on either but hinge upon private and public investment plans. Obviously, private investments in Nigeria will very much depend upon possible investors' assessment of the future development of the country. This dependence can only be imperfectly formalized by making investment a function of income over a plan period of five or six years. This is all the more true if there is direct or indirect public assistance to private investments which will affect the marginal efficiency of the investments directly—and independently of national-income changes.

In the planning process, therefore, the behavior of imports over the past decade was studied, almost commodity by commodity, to see what could be learned. The first major lesson was that yearly fluctuations were highly erratic and seemed to result partly from the introduction of new tariffs, partly from inventory accumulation and decumulation. The second lesson was that, with rising income, imports of higher-quality foods were obviously substituted at a rapid rate for lower-grade traditional foods.

---

rose almost 20 percent; SITC 2 (crude materials) rose almost 25 percent; SITC 3 (minerals) remained constant. Import prices of SITC 4 (animal and vegetable oils and fats) fell by 25 percent, and SITC 5 (chemicals) did not change. SITC 6 (manufactured articles classified by material) fell by about 10 percent, but SITC 7 (machinery and transport equipment) rose about 20 percent, while SITC 8 (miscellaneous manufactured articles) rose about 10 percent. Between 1961 and 1963, there were further substantial price changes in individual categories.

For the period 1948–1954, imports of food, drink, and tobacco rose almost 35 percent; textiles and clothing fell about 4 percent; metal and engineering products rose over 30 percent; and the total of all these classifications including miscellaneous items rose less than 20 percent. Federation of Nigeria, *Digest of Statistics,* July 1964, p. 53.

When the import projections described in the text were finished, two sets of terms of trade projections were made, one based on the actual composition of imports and exports in 1960, the other one based on the projected composition of 1967. Although both calculations showed a deterioration in the terms of trade, the degree of deterioration varied substantially according to the composition of trade chosen as a weight.

Import projections were made for almost forty subgroups. The test for the degree of disaggregation was whether there existed any scrap of information which would be relevant to that particular subgroup of imports. To give an obvious example: the plans for expansion of the railroads were known in detail and hence also their import need for locomotives, cars, rails, and so on.

The projections were made in three steps. Initially, it was assumed that there would be no substitution of domestic production for imports and no change in tax and tariff policy. Next, the anticipated import substitution was calculated. This in turn involved correlating both private and public plans. The Federal and Regional ministries of commerce and industry kept rosters of production plans for much of the modern private sector. It was known, for example, that Dunlop and Michelin would start to produce rubber tires both for domestic use and for export. The expected composition of the output of the oil refinery was known. There was a considerable number of other more or less definite private projects. Less certain projects were not included because, as explained before, it was thought best to be conservative and to overestimate imports. Finally, the import needs of the import substitutes were added. The machinery required to produce the import substitutes had already been taken care of when the effect of the planned investments on imports were calculated. The new production of import substitutes, however, would require additional imports: wheat instead of flour, carbon black for rubber tires, etc. Sometimes estimates could be made in detail; at other times rough adjustments had to suffice.

The description of the procedures followed indicates that the balance-of-payments projections in fact involve the correlation of all public plans *and* of the private sector. Both export and import projections fed directly back into the transport plans, particularly of the Ports Authority. The detailed projections of both exports and imports were essential in order to project government revenues. None of these essential uses could have been achieved by simple aggregate projections. It is obvious that many of the estimates were necessarily crude. But this does not change the fact that only detailed projections are useful and can be made internally consistent. It is these detailed projections that were entered into the initial consistency test summed up in Table 6.

D. INFLATION AND THE CONSISTENCY OF THE PLAN

An attempt was made to estimate the effect that domestic price rises caused by inflationary finance might have on the balance of payments. The issues implicit in the attempt are many. Obviously there are different kinds of price rises. If prices to consumers increase because duties and taxes are increased, the effect on the balance of payments can be presumed to be favorable. Consumers cannot shift to imports, because the price relevant to them is the landed price including all duties and tariffs. There may be an increase in imports if the taxes hit only domestic products. But this is not a realistic contingency in a situation in which tariffs are both a major source of government revenue and a protective device.

A general price rise must come from an expansion of the domestic money supply, including an increase in the velocity of money. The major sources of such an expansion are: an increase in export quantities with no change in the prices received by the exporters; a rise in producer prices granted by Marketing Boards in the purchase of the major Marketing Board crops; and purchases by the banking system of government paper.

The problems arising out of monetary and fiscal policies will be dealt with in Chapter VI. The present objectives are more modest. Suppose prices of consumption, investment, and so forth rise as the result of inflationary policies by government, which need not be further specified. More money is paid out, wages rise, and the increased income spills over into imports. Suppose that both consumers and investors, including the government, insist on carrying out their planned purchases in real terms. Assume that there are no changes in import tariffs or taxes. What will be the effect on the balance of payments?

In the Nigerian economy, the prices of exports are determined outside the domestic economy, and so are the prices of imports. In the absence of higher duties and excise taxes and of changes in the exchange rates, the landed prices of imported consumer and investment goods will therefore be unaffected by domestic inflation. Any price rises that will occur must be due to a domestic wage-and-profit component or must concern domestically produced goods. In these circumstances there must be a substantial spilling over into the balance of payments, mainly for consumption purposes.

The calculations made in the Nigerian Plan Annexure indicated that a very substantial increase in the balance-of-payments deficit would result even from modest price increases. The estimates have been subjected to an intensive critique by Clive Gray, whose criticisms are acknowledged as on the whole valid. For this reason the original calculations are not reproduced. Mr. Gray, using J. J. Polak's model of the connection between money supply, income, and imports, pointed out that some of the inflation must show itself in the "adjusted" GDP—that is, some of the inflation must be domestically absorbed.[24]

24. Clive S. Gray, "Credit Creation for Nigeria's Economic Development," *Nigerian Journal of Economic and Social Studies,* V (November 1963), 247-353. Mr. Gray wrote: "In the construction of his model, Stolper's first error lies in calculating current-price total available resources under inflation in a way which begs the question . . . A second and even more glaring error of procedure . . . is to subtract constant—rather than current—price GDP from current price total available resources" (pp. 323, 324). I admit to the second, but not necessarily to the first, error. As the text indicates, even the second error was not entirely stupid. When a price index is built up from sectoral price changes, the price inflator applicable to "adjusted GDP" may be close to zero!

For the original inflation model, see J. J. Polak, "Monetary Analysis of Income Formation and Payments Problems," *International Monetary Fund*

An attempt was made to calculate such a price inflator for adjusted GDP on assumptions consistent with the projection of the Plan, in particular with the assumptions that prices of export products would fall and prices of imports would remain constant.

Index numbers are tricky to use and trickier to interpret. Suppose we take the expenditures on GDP in 1957 in current prices, as given by P. N. C. Okigbo, and apply price increases—at the same percentage of consumption of domestic goods as in 1957— to an index calculated for the period 1962 to 1968. In 1957, total consumer expenditures were £815.5 million, of which £657.0 million was on domestic goods and £158.5 million equaled the Nigerian retail value of imported goods—the c.i.f value of which was £88.1 million.[25] Domestically produced goods were thus 80.5 percent of total consumption. Suppose that for investments the domestic component is 50 percent, for inventories 100 percent, and for government consumption also 100 percent. Suppose further that export prices fall 20 percent over six years—an arbitrary assumption for purposes of illustration, though a realistic one—and that import prices remain constant while domestic prices rise 1 percent.[26] The hypothetical GDP price index is calculated in Table 8. Applying this price index to the projections of GDP made in constant prices still leaves a very substantial increase in balance-of-payments effects, as indicated in Table 9.

Only a superficial difference separates the foregoing analysis from Gray's analysis, a difference resulting entirely from the purpose of the calculation. Gray, following Polak, points out that an

Staff Papers, vol. VI, no. 1 (November 1957), pp. 1-50. See also J. J. Polak and Lorette Boissoneault, "Monetary Analysis of Income and Imports and Its Statistical Analysis," *IMF Staff Papers,* vol. VII, no. 3 (April 1960), pp. 349-416; J. Marcus Fleming and Lorette Boissoneault, "Money Supply and Imports," *IMF Staff Papers,* vol. VIII, no. 2 (May 1961), pp. 227-240.

25. The retail value of imported goods is calculated from Okigbo, *Nigerian National Accounts 1950–57,* pp. 100-103 (table VII.1).

26. Since the actual price assumptions made for the Nigerian Plan are confidential, it is necessary to state that they differed from the assumptions made in the text and in Table 7.

Table 8. Construction of a hypothetical price index of Nigeria's Gross Domestic Product for 1962–63 to 1967–68, assuming as weights the actual percentage distribution of GDP in 1960–61

(Also assuming that domestic prices will rise by 1 percent per year cumulatively, import prices will remain constant, and export prices will decline by 20 percent over six years, i.e., by 3.3 percentage points per year)

	1960–61	1962–63	1963–64	1964–65	1965–66	1966–67	1967–68
Private consumption							
Domestic goods	68.4 ⎫ 85	69.1	69.8	70.5	71.2	71.9	72.6
Imported goods	16.6 ⎭	16.6	16.6	16.6	16.6	16.6	16.6
Investment							
Domestic	7.5 ⎫ 15	7.6	7.7	7.7	7.8	7.9	8.0
Imported	7.5 ⎭	7.5	7.5	7.5	7.5	7.5	7.5
Government consumption (all domestic)	7.5	7.6	7.7	7.7	7.8	7.9	8.0
Inventory accumulation (all domestic)	0.4	0.4	0.4	0.4	0.4	0.4	0.4
Exports	16.7	16.1	15.6	15.0	14.5	13.9	13.4
Index of export prices assumed	(100.0)	(96.7)	(93.4)	(90.1)	(86.8)	(83.5)	(80.2)
	124.6	124.9	125.3	125.4	125.8	126.1	126.5
Less imports	−24.6	−24.6	−24.6	−24.6	−24.6	−24.6	−24.6
Price index of GDP	100.0	100.3	100.7	100.8	101.2	101.5	101.9
Price index of consumption	100.0	100.8	101.6	102.5	103.2	104.1	104.9
Price index of investments	100.0	100.7	101.3	101.3	102.0	102.7	103.3
Price index of government consumption, inventories	100.0	101.0	102.0	103.0	104.1	105.1	106.2

Table 9. *Effects of price inflation on balance of payments*[a]

(£ million)

	1960–61	1962–63	1963–64	1964–65	1965–66	1966–67	1967–68	1962–63 through 1967–68
1. Private consumption[b]	922.0	994.3	1,030.0	1,062.7	1,096.3	1,139.5	1,180.2	—
2. Investments	158.0	180.9	189.2	196.1	204.6	212.8	222.5	—
3. Inventory accumulation	10.0	5.8	3.7	3.5	3.6	3.5	4.3	—
4. Government consumption	85.0	111.3	121.3	136.9	151.4	170.7	184.0	—
5. Resources required	1,175.0	1,292.3	1,344.2	1,399.2	1,455.9	1,525.5	1,591.0	—
6. Less adjusted GDP	1,112.5	1,201.8	1,254.2	1,300.9	1,353.1	1,401.8	1,463.4	—
7. Equals gap to be financed	62.5	90.5	90.0	98.3	102.8	124.7	127.6	633.9
8. Less gap previously calculated (Table 6)	62.5	83.9	77.6	76.1	74.7	86.4	81.8	480.5
9. Equals effect of price rises	0.0	6.6	12.4	22.2	28.1	38.3	45.8	153.4

a. Price assumption as in Table 8.
b. For lines 1–4 and 6, the price indices calculated in Table 8 were applied to the figures in Table 6.

136

increase in the money supply must quickly find its way into imports. Certainly, instances could be cited in which inflationary finance has produced increases in GDP with only small price rises, but this occurred at the expense of the loss of all foreign assets and with the help of very substantial amounts of foreign aid. The calculations made in the Plan were not meant to suggest that the additional imports would necessarily be forthcoming. They did intend to show, however, that the control of the balance of payments would rapidly become a very difficult problem. In inflationary situations, the choice rapidly becomes one of (1) controlling prices, by allowing imports to satisfy the additional demand, or (2) controlling imports, thus allowing prices to rise. If balance-of-payments restrictions have to be imposed, the inflation itself becomes self-defeating, except to the extent to which it leads to greater domestic output. As will be argued in Chapter VI, such an increase is most unlikely.

The calculations made for the Plan assumed specific price rises, but made no specific assumptions about the increase in the money supply needed to bring about the price rises. Gray has made such calculations. It is interesting to note that his approach and the corrected approach just outlined give very similar results, his calculation of additional imports being £132.2 million instead of the £153.4 million shown in Table 8.[27]

27. Gray, "Credit Creation," p. 325.

V

Investment Criteria from a Planning Standpoint

A. THE PLANNING FRAMEWORK

IN the preceding chapters, the information at hand and the institutional framework of planning were described and their effects on the working procedure discussed. The use of the national accounts was analyzed and the general approach of the planners presented. In the present chapter the problems which arise in the application of investment criteria will be taken up. As before, theoretical arguments and factual information are intimately interwoven. This is deliberate: the relevance of a theoretical argument lies in its applicability in an actual situation.

The argument of the present chapter is that "economic" or "social" profitability, calculated so as to allow for interactions in the economy and for proper pricing, is the only operational criterion for determining the size and composition of an investment program.

Since this chapter is not concerned with the technical and accounting aspects of determining cost and returns, it is not necessary to dwell on particular methods of calculating the payoff of a project. The terms "economic" and "social" are used interchangeably and are meant to convey that prices used to gauge payoff should reflect actual scarcities and not be arbitrarily assumed *ad hoc*. Section E will have more to say about certain problems of "proper" pricing which have already been touched upon in Chapter III from a different angle. The interactions of various projects must be taken into account in order to compute indirect benefits and cost. Calculations must proceed realistically. If, say, a discounted flow method is chosen, depreciation ratios, allotted periods of economic life, time lags, and so forth should reflect actual conditions. The techniques of making such calculations are, however, outside the scope of this book.[1]

The argument goes further: I would assert that calculating the economic profit of individual projects puts these projects into a consistent general framework, so that such calculation provides in effect the solution of a general system of equations. And I would argue that in the application of profitability the calculation permits one simultaneously to determine the size and composition of a program and the factor proportions to be employed. It is unfortunately necessary to state at the very outset that "profitability" so understood has no ideological content. "Profitability" simply measures the fact that a particular deployment of resources does or does not lead to an increase in available resources. If it does, the use of resources is defensible; if not, the expenditure cannot be defended except as consumption. The Soviet discussion on pricing and efficiency should make it clear that insistence on profits is not a capitalist prejudice.

Neither do the arguments presented here mean that subsidies are not justified. However, the question of whether a particular

1. The term "social" is used interchangeably with "economic." Of the very extensive literature on investment criteria I mention only: A. E. Kahn, "Investment Criteria in Economic Development Programs," *Quarterly Journal of Economics*, LXV (February 1951), 38-61; H. B. Chenery, "The Application of Investment Criteria," *ibid.*, LXVII (February 1953), 76-96; S. Chakravarty, *The Logic of Investment Planning*, Contributions to Economic Analysis, no. 18 (Amsterdam: North Holland Co., 1959); Otto Eckstein, *Water Resource Development: The Economics of Project Evaluation* (Cambridge, Mass.: Harvard University Press, 1961).

Though the term "social" has no moral or political implication in the present context, the tone of the argument indicates that the moral aspects are nevertheless not neglected.

employment of resources should or should not be undertaken is logically and factually separate from the question of who should pay for it. Nor does the argument imply that only profitable projects should be undertaken. However, the decision about non-economic projects is a decision about ends, not means. And if a decision to implement an unprofitable project is made because it will open up profitable investment elsewhere in the economy, this fact ought to be observable and ought to be measured in the payoff of these other projects.

The discussion in Chapter III has indicated that it is essential to consider the allocation of resources for growth as a whole, regardless of whether this allocation refers to capital or consumption, to government consumption or to governmental budgets. In particular, therefore, the potential repercussions of any project should be studied not only with regard to other investments but also with reference to effects on taxable capacity, budgets, and the size of the government program. This becomes all the more important when very substantial investments must be made in sectors which have at best only indirect effects on growth and in which it is either impossible or repugnant to make economic calculations. These investments have serious budgetary repercussions which link them with economic investments more narrowly defined.

The analysis of past developments in Nigeria strongly suggested that the projected growth rate of 4 percent could be achieved or surpassed only if the composition of expenditures in general and of investments in particular could be shifted drastically in the direction of projects with the highest and quickest economic returns possible. Unless this were done, taxable capacity could not rise sufficiently, and the rise in recurrent budgetary expenditures resulting from the investment program would quickly limit the amount of resources available for the enlargement of the nation's productive capacity. To some extent, the problem of obtaining resources could be met by capital imports, but this would meet definite balance-of-payments limitations aggravated by an expected deterioration in terms of trade and a reduction in the sterling reserves controlled by Nigeria.

Investment criteria in the more narrow sense (to return to definitions), refer to a government capital program. They become relevant to the private sector through taxes or through direct or indirect subsidies. A policy of shadow prices can be imposed upon the private sector only through a system of taxes and subsidies. The size and composition of the private investment program can be influenced by similar means, even when introducing shadow prices is not the objective. (It should be mentioned in passing, however, that a policy of stimulating private investments through making capital available at subsidized rates will be inconsistent with a policy of inducing labor-intensive methods of production by high shadow rates of interest.) In either case, taxation is required, which means less private consumption and/or less private saving. Thus the size of the program, the budget, consumption levels, and so forth become part of the picture within which investment criteria even in the narrow sense must be viewed. When the problem is seen in this manner, the composition of investments—with its effect on taxable capacity and recurrent budget, hence its savings potential—becomes itself a target variable for the planner. I refer once more to Chakravarty's discussion, on a very abstract level, of how, through various consistency tests, the size of a program becomes a function not only of foreign and domestic savings but of its own composition.

There is a limit to the "austerity" that can be sensibly imposed in circumstances in which, because of the particular stage of development of the economy, there are only a limited number of investments that have a positive return at any moment of time. The same is true when there is a severe shortage of executive capacity at all levels, both private and public, and when one of the major problems is to draw traditional producers increasingly into a more and more complicated market nexus and in general to induce increased production.

There are thus a certain number of objective limitations on the size and composition of a program and on the policies that it is rational to pursue.

First, it makes no sense to outline a program which cannot be realized. Yet such programs are frequently found. Executive capacity must in this context be interpreted economically rather than technologically. It is wrong to think primarily of a shortage of top administrators or managers. The real shortages—and they are shortages that foreign assistance can make good only with the greatest difficulty—are at the secretary or foreman level. Executive capacity refers not only to status and training but also to ordinary efficiency. It is comparatively easy to erect factories but hard to staff them with competent people. If the number is increased at any one moment of time, the added work force is necessarily less competent. If subsidies are required, the net effect is a reduction in output.

Second, if "traditional" producers are going to be drawn more and more into the market nexus, their real income has to increase. Real income means real goods and services. Farmers are quite aware of the choice of goods that exists. But they have no money illusion, and they need to be assured that an increase in their income as the result of their efforts can be translated into particular goods which frequently involve imports: cement houses with tin roofs; transistor radios; bicycles and motor scooters; electricity; education; and better communications.

If such goods are supplied at reasonable cost, effort and production will increase. An outstanding example is the desire for education. There is strong evidence that parents will work harder to finance schools and that they are willing to pay for them directly through school fees or indirectly through higher taxes.

All of this implies certain limitations on policy and the size and composition of programs. Reducing consumption below the level where it is felt that the saver will get a desired return will not lead to increased saving. It will very likely lead to reduced effort. An investment program which requires increased resources through additional taxation, say, becomes self-defeating if the increase in output due to the investment is less than the increase in production that could have been achieved by permitting a higher level of consumption.

Failure to achieve modernization of agriculture leads to complaints that the inborn or cultural conservatism of the farmers makes them reject good technical advice, but the real trouble is just as likely to be that the taking of the advice would not make the farmer better off. Naturally farmers are conservative. Being subject to vagaries of weather, insects, diseases, and other erratic phenomena, they must be cautious. Yet there is every evidence, in Nigeria at least, that once they are convinced that something will work and that they will actually be better off by following the suggested practice, they will employ the new methods. Cocoa farmers in Western Nigeria do use spray pumps; there are thousands of farmers in Bornu Province in the Northern Region using mixed farming methods. In other countries, too, it has been found that when annual increments in income can be expected, even quite small ones, farmers will improve and increase production.

Finally it must be stressed once more that both the general ignorance of many basic facts and the knowledge of others necessarily will determine the size and composition of a program, simply because they will have a decisive influence on the calculations that can be made at any one moment of time. The incomplete state of knowledge at any given time forces the decision maker into risky judgments. Ignorance will drastically limit possible investment, and facts that happen to be at the center of attention will inescapably bias investments in certain directions. This itself gives the highest priority to research.

B. PROFITS, FACTOR PROPORTIONS, AND IMPORT SUBSTITUTION

The preceding analysis has stressed the importance of the composition of the investment program and hence the importance of proper investment criteria. The size and composition of a program are interrelated, not only directly in that the total program obviously consists of the sum of individual projects, but also indirectly in that the size will depend on the composition through the effect of the composition on growth, on taxable capacity, on export earnings, and on incentives in the private sector.

This puts the burden of programming upon the analysis of individual projects. Through a stressing of interactions in the economy and adequate pricing both of the final output and of the multitudes of inputs, the project is put into a general context. Profitability, being the resultant of complicated interactions, becomes in fact the criterion which allows an individual project to be analyzed without forgetting the rest of the economy. The profitability criterion is indeed these interactions made operational.

It will not do, therefore, to distinguish between sectoral and project investment criteria. A sector is an aggregate which is defined by its components. The point, however, is not merely definitional; rather, it is connected with the earlier emphasis on limited absorptive capacity. There is no reason to push resources into any one sector if profitable uses of the resources cannot be specified. Though it is legitimate to ask what the sectoral contribution to GDP will be at the end of the development period, it makes no sense to establish a particular sectoral contribution as a plan target independently of an investigation of profitabilities.

To be sure, the Nigerian Plan establishes official priorities for agriculture, industry, and technical education. But this was not meant to define sectoral criteria in the theoretical sense. Rather, it expresses, on the one hand, a determination to put modernization of the economy ahead of possible conflicting aims (such as a rapid increase in social welfare) and, on the other hand, a desire to push as many resources as possible into directly productive investments rather than into so-called social infrastructure with its much delayed and uncertain effects. It is, however, also true that the Nigerian Plan allocates large sums to agriculture and industry, the specific uses of which are not further specified.[2]

The basic aims that have to be constantly kept in mind are the achievement of a certain growth rate (or more) and the rapid enlargement of the choices available to the economy. There are also secondary objectives. Some are consistent with the primary objectives, such as to increase employment. Others may or may not be inconsistent with them, such as the simultaneous achievement of a more equitable income distribution.

In order to achieve a certain growth rate (or more) in a particular period, as many resources as feasible must be pushed into uses in which they will yield growth. From this point of view it is irrelevant what sector the employment is in and what kind of commodity or service is produced. The only relevant question is: will there be, as the result of a given deployment of resources, a subsequent increase in available resources and in the productive capacity of the economy? This will be the case only if the *actual* investments yield an economic profit. There is obviously no sense in simply pushing resources into the agricultural or any other sector unless their actual use creates more resources for future allocation. Therefore, in the design or evaluation of a particular development plan, just to consider the sectoral distribution of investments is not enough; the composition must be evaluated in detail.

If this point is granted, it becomes redundant to look for sectoral investment criteria. The proper sectoral balance is derived from the summation of the individual projects.

---

2. For example, £25 million allocated to agriculture in the Federal program and £10 million allocated to large-scale industries in the Western Region Plan have no specific content.

This approach means that there is only one legitimate investment criterion: economic (or social) profitability—that is, the
return on an investment, allowing for repercussions in the economy and adequate pricing. The points to be discussed are: first,
the relation of profitability to such other investment criteria as
factor proportions and the so-called reinvestment effects; second,
how this apparent project approach can be defended in the
name of program planning; third, how profit considerations are
relevant to non-economic sectors; and fourth, the problem of
shadow prices.

The problem of shadow pricing apart, there is no *logical* inconsistency between insisting on economic profitability and using
various factor-proportions criteria. But the criterion of economic
profitability has the inestimable advantage of being more general
and of being operational and quantifiable. The various factor
proportions are in fact not definable or quantifiable under the
conditions that interest a planner or a development economist.

One set of factor-proportion arguments suggests the execution of projects using much of the relatively abundant factor or
factors—say labor. The trouble is in assuming a knowledge of
what factor is abundant. The objections to all criteria of factor
intensity are familiar to any student of international-trade theory.
If one deals with two factors only, producing one good, and if
the technical possibilities allow for substitution so that the iso-
quants are concave upward, the entrepreneur, wishing to maximize profit or to produce a given output with minimum cost, will
combine factors in such a proportion that their relative prices are
equal to their marginal rates of substitution. As one factor becomes relatively cheaper, it will be increasingly substituted for
the other within the limits of technical possibilities. Even on this
level of abstraction the substitution of labor for capital or land,
as the relative price of labor falls, follows from profit maximization and is not an independent phenomenon.

When there are, however, three or more factors, it becomes

impossible even to define what is the abundant factor except *ex post*; that is, the abundant factor simply is the factor which, as the result of profit-maximization behavior, is the cheapest. Even on the simple level of abstraction of assuming one good and three factors, no clearcut answer as to the factor proportions can be given. Because complicated relations of competitiveness and complementarity become possible as the number of factors increases, one is forced to fall back on profit maximization as an operational tool.

When more than one good is produced, factor proportions in a particular line of production cannot be equated with factor proportions in the economy even when there are only two factors. For technical reasons, different goods require different factor proportions with the same set of relative factor prices, and the factor proportions in the economy become a weighted average of the factor proportions in the individual lines of production, the weights being the amounts of factors actually used, i.e., the size of a particular line of production. Thus, even on this very high level of abstraction, factor proportions used in the production of individual goods (i.e., the project criterion) and size of sector (i.e., the amounts of factors actually used) become inextricably and necessarily indistinguishable.

Thus the argument that labor-intensive industries should be pushed, though quite plausible in itself, lacks operational content. The matter is even more confused because the factor proportions that ought to be employed may be quite "perverse," as Romney Robinson has pointed out as the result of the startling finds of Leontief for the American economy, matched by equally "perverse" findings for the Japanese economy by M. Tatemoto and S. Ichimura.[3]

3. W. W. Leontief, "Domestic Production and Foreign Trade: The American Capital Position Re-examined," *Proceedings of the American Philosophical Society*, XCVII (September 1953); Leontief, "Factor Proportions and the Structure of American Trade: Further Theoretical and Empirical Analysis," *Review of Economics and Statistics*, XXXVIII (1959);

The point can be illustrated by an adaptation of a graph developed by Samuelson in another context. Assume, in Figure 2, that we are confronted with only two factors, called labor and capital (but do not forget that the complications arising out of the existence of more than two factors are great and may reverse any findings based on a two-factor model). Let the relation of wage rates (W) to interest rates (R) be measured on the vertical axis, and set the factor proportions of labor (L) to capital (K) along the horizontal axis. For technical reasons, some lines of

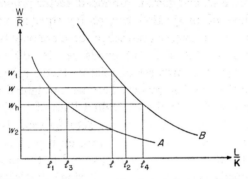

Figure 2. Factor proportions and relative factor prices, when goods can be uniquely ordered according to their factor intensities.

production will use more labor per unit of capital than others at any given level of relative factor prices. The correspondence of relative factor prices to relative factor proportions is shown by the series of declining lines. At relative wages w, good A will employ proportions of labor to capital l_1, and good B will use l_2.

The recommendation of saving capital and using labor intensively would seem to lead to the policy conclusion that only good B should be produced in the particular country. No one has,

M. Tatemoto and S. Ichimura, "Factor Proportions and Foreign Trade: The Case of Japan," *Review of Economics and Statistics*, XLI (1959); Romney Robinson, "Factor Proportions and Comparative Advantage," *Quarterly Journal of Economics*, LXX (May 1956), 169-192, and LXX (August 1956), 346-363.

in fact, made such an absurd suggestion. It may be objected that the factor-intensity argument is not meant to apply to sectors but only to a specific line of production. This is fair enough, but it will not do. For it is not possible to choose one line of production independently of others. The distribution of factors among different lines of production will depend on demand for the finished goods and the factor endowments in the economy.

Suppose that in Figure 2 relative factor proportions in the economy are l. Then, at any relative factor prices lying between the limits w_1 and w_2, both goods will be produced but with different factor proportions. If, for example, relative factor prices happen to be w_h, good A will be using proportion l_3, and good B proportion l_4.

If as assumed, all lines of production are ordered in ascending order of labor intensity and if therefore goods A and B represent the outside limits, factor proportions in a particular line of production and in the economy as a whole can coincide only if all the available factors are employed in the particular line of production, so that nothing is left for the production of other goods.

Even the theoretical applicability of the factor-proportions criteria is actually much more limited than indicated. In Figure 2 the lines never intersect; that is, it is possible to order goods uniquely in order of their factor intensity. But as Romney Robinson has pointed out, this is not necessarily so. When Samuelson's graphic representation is adapted to illustrate Robinson's point, the lines picturing the relationship between relative factor prices and factor proportions may cross even in the case of linear and homogeneous production functions—that is, even in the absence of economies of scale. Figure 3 offers an example of this.

If the economy in question has factor endowment l_1, relative factor prices will lie between w_1 and w_2, and good A is labor-intensive. With factor endowment l_2, good B is labor-intensive, and relative factor remunerations will lie within the limits of w_a and w_b. This, too, serves to underline that "labor intensity"

cannot be a primary consideration and in fact can be defined only
after all the other facts of demand, technology, factor endowment, etc., are defined. Thus one is once more thrown back to
the profitability criterion as the only operational method to determine what is to be produced and how much.

When one deals not with two but with several factors, even
the definition of relative scarcity is impossible. And if there are
economies of scale rather than linear homogeneous production
functions, the reasoning from factor intensities becomes com-

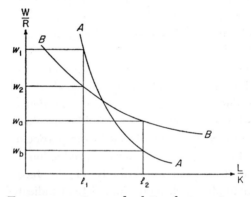

Figure 3. Factor proportions and relative factor prices, when unique
ordering of goods according to their factor intensities is impossible.

pletely inapplicable, and economic profits become the only possible criterion of what to produce and how to produce it.

This has a direct bearing on the issue of sector (or industry)
versus project (or line of production) priority. Even when only
two goods and only two factors are assumed—surely as simple
an assumption as one could wish to make—it becomes quite impossible to decide first on the good to be produced, and then,
having made this decision somehow, on the best method of producing it. Relative factor prices depend on the demand for the
factors. The demand for factors is derived from the demand for
final goods, which may come from abroad or from home or both.

The allocation of factors to one line of production will affect allocations to others. With economic phenomena thus interdependent, it can be seen that factor-intensity criteria are simply not operational. One is again driven back to the profitability criterion, which is both operational and general.[4]

Another type of approach stresses the effect of factor proportions not so much on the allocation of resources as on resource mobilization. Thus it has been argued that capital-intensive methods will lead to faster capital accumulation and hence faster growth through more reinvestment, because of the need, internal to the projects, of providing savings through charging for depreciation. The argument also stresses that capital-intensive methods will redistribute income in favor of groups with relatively higher savings ratios than would be the case with more labor-intensive methods.

A number of comments seem in order. Suppose the profitability of the enterprise is just enough to allow for replacement. Then the growth effect is nil, and the employment effect is limited at best to the constant employment for the project. Suppose the profitability is such that the enterprise can provide for its own expansion. This is, of course, highly desirable. But the profitability is what leads to the capital formation needed to achieve growth and higher employment. If the choice is between two projects which have equal profitability and which are in other respects identical except for the factor proportions, surely the project using less capital is preferable. Whatever the future savings may be, a larger *present* investment becomes possible and therefore more present employment and output. If profitability can be heightened through the use of a capital-intensive rather than a labor-intensive method, it should be employed for that reason. As already indicated, there is nothing in the factor-in-

4. It should perhaps be repeated that the shadow-price problem, and perhaps more generally the problem of evaluating profits properly, is a separate problem discussed in Section E.

tensity argument that suggests limiting production exclusively to those goods that can be produced with labor-intensive methods, and the definition of such methods has, in any case, been shown to be possible only simultaneously with a gauging of profitability.

The income-distribution effect of capital-intensive methods must also be questioned: a thousand "labor-intensive" projects using the same amount of capital as a single "capital-intensive" one will generate exactly the same amount of replacement funds and, depending on profitability, exactly the same amount of growth.[5] Whether the funds are used for growth or replacement or consumption will depend on price and tax and other government policies. Neither capital intensity nor size of the individual project nor a project's public or private nature has any logical or practical or political correlation with generating resources for growth.

To give an example, the Nigerian telephone system is run by the Ministry of Communications. Its receipts are treated as ordinary government revenues, and its costs come out of the governmental budgets. The day-to-day running of the system is charged to the recurrent budget; the capital (development) budget is charged with replacement or expansion. The system is not charging depreciation, and the financial surplus shown by the budget is misleading because of this fact and because, on the revenue side, the system is not reimbursed for the services it renders to the various government departments.

5. Obviously, variations on the theme can be played by allowing different lengths of life. Suppose you have an enterprise requiring 1,000 units of capital lasting twenty years, or ten plants requiring 100 units each, each lasting ten years. If the larger plant did not have to be replaced until the twentieth year but then fell apart like the one-hoss shay, whereas this was not true for the ten smaller plants, the replacement quota would become available for starting new enterprises. But these enterprises would have to earn enough above their own replacement cost to replace also the big one out of whose depreciation quotas they were replaced. Though we could get fluctuations in rates of growth, etc., the final and basic problem is to generate enough additional resources above replacement to lead to growth. The final criterion remains economic profit.

Now this is a most unsatisfactory state of affairs from many points of view that are discussed in another context (see Chapter VI). The important thing in the present context, however, is that a telephone system is highly capital-intensive. There is completely automatic service within the Federal Territory of Lagos, which has the greatest number of subscribers, within many of the other major population concentrations such as Ibadan or Enugu, to name only two, and even for long distance between Lagos and Ibadan. Yet the resources generated by the system under present accounting practice flow into the general governmental pool, from which they are reallocated in a manner which may or may not lead to increased savings but which certainly has nothing to do with the fact that the telephone system is capital-intensive.

Obviously, the situation should and can and in fact probably will be remedied. It is mentioned because, independently of any theoretical merits the capital-intensity thesis may have, logically as well as practically the generation of resources and the allocation between consumption and savings are different things which require different treatment. The income-distribution "effect" and the reinvestment "effect" are gratuitous assumptions; they are neither logical conclusions nor proven phenomena.

The Nigerian example is by no means particularly horrendous. Matters in Africa are much better than they apparently are in Latin America or India. In Nigeria, electric-power facilities, for example, not only pay their way but do contribute substantially to their own expansion. Nigeria accepts the principle that this should be so and that people benefitting from an expenditure should on the whole pay for it. Nigeria therefore accepts the idea that electricity rates and telephone rates, to name two, should be sufficiently high to generate adequate profits. This is not so elsewhere. In Latin America most public enterprises do not pay their own way, and to suggest that they should is considered almost immoral. Generating electricity or providing telecommunications are everywhere capital-intensive affairs (in com-

parison with other lines of production), and they are usually
government-owned. In Latin America and elsewhere, people who
can afford telephones or electricity are, on the whole, not among
the poorest—the farmers. Subsidies mean inflation and/or taxes.
The redistribution of income means in fact consumption, not
capital formation. The subsidies to public utilities are in fact a
transfer of income from the poor to the rich and from capital
formation to consumption, public or private.[6]

Since electricity and telephone service are normally sold on a
rate schedule, discrimination among users would be feasible, thus
allowing subsidies to particular industries while showing over-
all profits. Electricity and telecommunications are important incentives for businesses as well as private persons. At the same
time, the monthly charges for either are nothing to a business as
compared to the cost and handicap of operating without them.
A very few industries such as aluminum smelting or magnesium
production or heavy chemicals, use electricity as a raw material.
But, for most users, the cost of electricity is negligible, while the
cost of not having it is high. This means, in effect, that subsidizing
power rates to industries need not involve big sums.

To insist on economic profit in such cases brings an improvement in the relative position of the poor *and* an increase in
capital formation. It follows that neither capital intensity nor
public versus private investment makes the real difference.
Rather, economic profitability—charging users as a group for the
services they use—leads to expansion through self-financing. To
return to the real example of the Nigerian telephone system, obviously it should be reorganized with an accounting system which
would enable policy makers to come to rational decisions. How
to employ the funds generated by the system should (or could)
be seen in the context of general resource allocation in the economy. Again, the issue is not merely the problem of public control

6. On this point see Charles P. Kindleberger's conclusion on Germany
quoted in my footnote 4 to Chapter I.

to prevent the exploitation of the consumer by a natural monopoly, but has to do with the mobilization and allocation of resources and the putting of the burden of resources mobilization on the shoulders that can most easily bear them.

Even where electric-power generation or the telephone system are run as statutory corporations along business principles, they are responsible to a ministry. From the standpoint of developing a plan with reasonable priorities and from the viewpoint of raising and allocating resources, it is not necessarily logical to make the rate of expansion of a statutory corporation dependent on the resources it can raise itself. An electricity enterprise may require additional capital for further expansion, or (what is less likely) it may generate more resources than are required for expansion. In either case rate policy must be reviewed, and in either case government, through the ministries of finance and economic development, will have a say on how resources are to be raised and used. This is true even when the ministry of finance or of economic development is not the constitutional organ to which statutory corporations are responsible.

In connection with investments in the private sector, different policy issues arise. Cost accounting can be as faulty in the private as in the public sector, or as good. Decisions on expansion can depend as much on policies inducing or forcing private entrepreneurs to behave in a certain manner as on their inclination to do so without prodding. Small producers and consumers can be forced or induced to save proportionately as much as big ones. Thus the conclusion becomes inevitable that what matters for the proper allocation of resources is economic profitability; that the correct factor proportion should follow from this primary criterion; that factor-proportion criteria have no independent existence; and that if they are employed as independent investment criteria, they are almost certain to lead to internally contradictory and self-defeating results.

There is one further reason for rejecting arguments couched in terms of capital or labor intensity. One cannot really know whether a particular line of production is or is not relatively capital-intensive until one has worked through an input-output matrix which gives information not only on inter-industry flows but also on the factor inputs of various industries. In many an actual situation, say in Nigeria, one could not work through an input-output table because none existed.[7] Moreover, the general relevance of inter-industry economics does not necessarily mean that input-output tables are the best planning tools in the African or Asian context. It is important to realize, however, that—once more the problem of shadow pricing apart—profitability calculations do in fact allow for complicated interactions without requiring the planner to do the inter-industry calculations. The market will in fact perform these latter calculations. Imperfect though the market is, profit reckonings based on it are initially more reliable than any factor-intensity criterion.

As with the various factor-proportion arguments, so also with import substitution as an investment criterion: it is not as operational as it seems. Only when import substitutes are economically profitable on an honest accounting can one be sure that there really has been an import saving. In addition, the logical validity of the abstract arguments for import substitution and foreign-exchange savings as an investment criterion is one thing, and its translation into planning practice another. An import substitution that is not viable but requires permanent subsidies, directly or by means of tariffs or quantitative import restrictions, is likely just to shift imports from relatively efficient to relatively inefficient uses.

This really should not be surprising. Subsidies for inefficient industries are a charge on the budget. Either the pressures generated will reduce consumption permanently—hardly a proper

7. The appendix prepared by Nicholas G. Carter for this book is the first attempt to construct a Nigerian input-output table.

developmental object—and forestall efficient investments, or, if not financed by additional taxation, they will generate inflationary pressures that will create the very balance-of-payments difficulties which the import substitution was intended to relieve. In all cases, permanent subsidies to inefficient industries must reduce savings ratios and thus increase balance-of-payments pressures.[8]

The notion that it is inherently desirable to replace imports by home production wherever physically possible undoubtedly antedates even mercantilism. Only the misnamed infant-industry argument gave it some respectability. The argument (which is really an infant-country argument) recognizes the virtues of eventual free trade, and says that only between countries at different stages of economic development are tariffs justifiable to give a backward country a chance to catch up with the more developed ones. When the argument—as distinct from the protective practice—was developed, America and Germany were the underdeveloped countries, and, as is well known, German economic thought from the forerunners of Friedrich List to Arthur Spiethoff and his theory of "economic styles" has tried to come to grips with economic development through a theory of stages, a theoretical trend recently revived and expanded in certain directions by W. W. Rostow. The arguments are old and respectable. They can be used to defend, for example, a practice permitted by the rules of the Common Market—the practice of allowing the weaker partner protection against the stronger.

The argument has intellectual respectability, but, as is also well known, what happens in practice has more to do with the equally ancient art of logrolling than with the ancient theory of the stages of economic development. So much so that one might characterize the theorist as a man who will admit there is

8. For an analysis of various "gaps," see H. B. Chenery and M. Bruno, "Development Alternatives in an Open Economy: The Case of Israel," *Economic Journal*, LXXII (March 1962), 79-103.

something to be said for protection *in abstracto* but not in reality, and the practical man as one who believes free trade to be all right in theory but not in practice.

Now obviously tariffs will play a major role in Nigeria as in all underdeveloped countries. They are the major tax-collection device; they affect consumption and wage levels; they influence the balance of payments and the composition of imports; and they give protection. Furthermore, no matter what experts say, logrolling will affect the final outcome of events. All of this is not unduly disturbing. What is important is that tariffs and other import restrictions be consistent with optimizing the amount and allocation of resources, including foreign exchange.

However, neither the theory of stages, including its latest Rostow version, nor the previous reincarnation of Spiethoff's extremely interesting theory of economic styles offers any operational guidance to the planner or policy maker. The planner still needs to know whether a particular type of protection for a particular plant or industry is economically justifiable, and this brings the whole discussion back to profitability calculations. The infant-country argument visualizes that eventually an industry will be able to stand on its own feet. The only known test for that is profitability. To refer to such "non-economic" benefits as that businessmen will learn their business is only of limited relevance. The test of whether an entrepreneur has learned his business is whether he can compete successfully within a reasonable time, whether he can make profits by his efficiency. In practice, therefore, the only guidelines for planners arise from a proper analysis of the use of funds. If a project requires subsidies for fifty years before it has a chance of paying for itself, it is a waste of resources. The time horizon is too long. The subsidy should be calculated as part of the cost of investment against which future income streams are to be offset. Calculating a discounted flow of revenues and costs will show whether a project is justifiable or not. If the profitable moment comes too late, the industry should not be started at all or should be launched at some future time. The use of resources as subsidies will slow growth. Expecting the growth of a market and allowing for a period of shaking down the plant are legitimate reasons for protection. But eventually there must be a profit, and the sooner the better. Whatever intellectual aura the theory of educational tariffs may lend to general policy pronouncements, when it comes to an operational version one is pushed back to the problem of economic profitability, which alone can determine in which direction it is reasonable to apply these generalities.

The ideas developed by W. A. Lewis, Albert O. Hirschman, and other writers are much more useful than generalizations about import substitution. In his justly celebrated *Report on the Industrialization of the Gold Coast*, Lewis makes most imaginative use of import statistics, location theory, and industry analysis to arrive at a selection of industries the establishment of which might be further considered. Import statistics give an important clue to the size of the market, and imports can develop a market to the size needed for efficient domestic production. Import projections can be used for forward planning. To extend Lewis' argument, the imports of neighboring countries will suggest a potential market which allows for exports, particularly when, as in the case of Nigeria or Ghana, the potential producer can count on the advantages of cheap sea freight, while neighboring countries such as Upper Volta, Niger, and Chad depend on expensive overland routes. But finally, investment decisions will still need to be made on the basis of eventual profitability within a reasonable time horizon. Where to invest, where to try to save foreign exchange, and exactly when to invest are the key questions.

As in the case of any factor-proportion argument, one cannot be sure what the final demand for a factor—this time foreign exchange—will be unless the whole input-output matrix is worked through. Suppose the production of iron requires substantial protection to make it viable or at least to avoid financial losses. This will immediately raise the cost of all iron and steel inputs into the development program. In addition, making a basic industry "viable" by making it expensive uses more domestic and probably also more foreign resources. There are two effects. As imports are shifted from iron and steel products for development, to machinery to produce the iron and steel products less efficiently, imports will increase in the short run, though it is, of course, hoped that imports will decrease once the imported machinery starts producing. If the efficiency of the new industry cannot be increased, however, imports will not decrease in the long run, and the balance of payments will not right itself. The less efficient industry will tend to increase wage payments and will have cost-raising effects throughout the economy. This will simply shift import demand toward increased consumption and in other directions, and balance-of-payments troubles will persist. If tariffs and other import restrictions are employed widely, not as a tax device to reduce consumption and real wages (which is quite a different and legitimate thing), but to protect industries, in effect imported resources are being misused. If the iron and steel industry becomes viable sooner or later, the question to be answered is whether the timing was right. Perhaps the potential market for domestic steel products would have grown faster if investment in iron and steel production had been postponed for a few years and in the meantime the resources invested in something else.

If subsidies in the form of a tariff go on forever, this may be entirely the result of introducing the industry too early. Subsidies are resources that could have had alternative uses which would have raised income, hence increased both savings and consumption, hence increased the market, hence made the industry viable at a later stage. Increasing subsidies in an economy will slow the rate of growth. Profits are simply not the same as losses.

If shifts in import demand are dealt with by additional restrictions of imports elsewhere in the economy, the subsidies (and tariffs) simply will reduce real wages. This may be desirable. But one should not pretend that the reduction in real wages is somehow an increase.

The argument can proceed along other lines. The import component of protected industries, taking into account repercussions throughout the economy, are likely to be greater than the import component of the final bill of goods in the absence of protected production. For example, a calculation of the estimated import component of 1 million deutsche marks of East German import substitutes (after eliminating commodities such as coffee or cocoa that could not be produced in East Germany) reveals it to be greater than the import component of 1 million deutsche marks of East German exports.[9] A simultaneous reduction of exports and imports with an accompanying shift in production toward import substitutes raises import requirements relatively. Therefore, if imports were held constant, less could be produced with than without import substitution. The conclusion is that a substitute for imports will not save imports or improve growth if it requires protection. (To repeat, the use of tariffs for other purposes is a different matter altogether.)

If a project eventually becomes self-supporting, the nature of the problem shifts, as already indicated, to one of timing. If, however, protection is needed permanently, domestic resources that could have been used elsewhere are perpetually employed,

9. See W. F. Stolper and K. W. Roskamp, "An Input-Output Table for East Germany with Applications to Foreign Trade," *Bulletin of the Oxford University Institute of Statistics,* XXIII (November 1961); W. F. Stolper, "East Germany's Foreign Trade and the Structure of Her Economy," in *Guest Lectures in Economics,* ed. Elizabeth Henderson and Luigi Spaventa (Milan: Dott. A. Giuffrè, 1962), pp. 213-229. As far as I am aware, this article is the only attempt to measure the gains from trade in a manner consistent with modern theory—that is, to measure them by comparing factor allocations and outputs.

not to increase either consumption or the productive apparatus of the economy, but just to maintain an operation that continues to require more resources than it produces.

Only if the employed resources would otherwise lie idle can some argument for protection be made. Even then the argument has little to do with import savings or import substitution. There is a factual question as to whether the complementary factors needed with foreign exchange have really been unemployed. There is the second and equally relevant question as whether they could not be employed in other and less damaging directions.

The question of shadow pricing—whether, in economic calculations, to value foreign exchange above the official rate—can be left aside for the moment. The point that deserves emphasis here is that separating any one factor from others and treating it as especially scarce is mistaken because it neglects the interactions in the economy. If more domestic resources are needed in one direction because subsidies are required, they will be missed elsewhere in the economy. If the subsidies to iron and steel come from taxes, they will affect consumption and/or savings elsewhere. This may react seriously on production in the agricultural sector and thus affect export earnings. For example, increased taxes on palm-oil exports may affect the supply of palm kernels for export and hence aggravate any "shortage" of foreign exchange. If savings are adversely affected, the repercussions on capital requirements will be shifted to the balance of payments. It has been pointed out that in Nigeria domestic savings fell short of domestic investments. This is characteristic of many underdeveloped countries. If an "import substitution" is not profitable, it is virtually certain to shift import needs and raise requirements for capital imports.[10]

10. Brazil and Pakistan are sometimes mentioned as countries where import substitution has been successful. Both have suffered from very serious and continuing balance-of-payments troubles which have been alleviated by very generous foreign aid. It is possible that the continuation of generous aid for a few years more will eventually allow the countries to

All the arguments in favor of using economic profitability as the overriding criterion amount to a plea that what matters is the allocation of many factors in such a manner that more factors become available for allocation in the next period in which decisions can be made. Statements about an economy's being a complicated network of interrelationships cannot be made too often even if they sound commonplace. Any interference in one part of the economy will have effects elsewhere, sometimes in unexpected places. With perfect knowledge of an economy, one could calculate effects by working through an input-output table or by tracing the effects of changes through some model. As it is, our knowledge is less than perfect in several ways: we do not always know elementary facts; we do not know some parameters; and sometimes we do not even know whether we have all the equations we need or what the functional form of the equations is.

This discussion has indicated that any "development strategy" that neglects economic payoff is likely to be self-defeating. Just

---

grow successfully into their import substitution. Yet lingering doubts remain, and some questions must be answered.

For example, excess capacity in Pakistan industry is said to average 50 percent. The plants are said to be profitable even at so low a rate of utilization. The low rate of utilization is said to result from lack of foreign exchange for spare parts and raw materials. All this may well be true. It is difficult to see, however, that imports which were employed to install twice as much capacity as could be used saved any foreign exchange at all. Surely, if half as much had been used for plant and, say, another 25 percent had been used for spare parts, etc., output, employment, and growth would have been bigger with less foreign exchange. Here is a clear case of a smaller investment program leading to greater growth.

Nor is it, *a priori*, very convincing to be told that more foreign exchange will solve the problem, because if plants are profitable at 50 percent capacity, they ought to be even more profitable at 100 percent. Unfortunately, the apparent reason for the profitability is the restriction of output, and it is not clear whether *all* the plants built would be profitable at full capacity.

Obviously, much more study is needed to answer these and related questions. The existence of persistent balance-of-payments troubles coupled with generous aid does not suggest *a priori* that import substitution has saved foreign exchange.

as an economy *in abstracto* consists of interrelated elements which can be sorted out and classified according to one's specific needs and problems, so the development program consists of interrelated projects and policies which for purposes of presentation can be grouped into sectors. The question whether social-overhead expenditures should come first or whether one should lead with direct payoff sectors is not really meaningful in the form of a choice, though it is frequently posed in this form. One has to push ahead all along the front in interrelated efforts.

One might answer: "Naturally. No one thought anything else." Unfortunately this is not quite true. The problem confronting the planner is essentially marginal in nature in the sense that he is dealing with "more or less" questions and not with "either-or" questions. The moment this proposition is granted, the problem ceases to be one of sector priorities and becomes a question of reckoning: "If I push further along a particular line, what is the economic result, what do I get for it, and what does it cost me in terms of real resources and hence in terms of alternative uses?" Once the question is put in this manner, the criterion of economic profitability becomes central.

C. INTERACTIONS IN THE ECONOMY

Growth is of course not the only aim of developing countries. Equity considerations will play a role when it comes to deciding who should pay the taxes; how the resources needed for development should be raised; where in the country the new investments should be located; whether to consider the provision of all goods equally desirable if only their production is profitable; and so forth. All these considerations are important.

Yet, first things come first; redistribution requires something to be redistributed. Equity considerations become self-defeating if they prevent growth altogether. Geographic dispersal of new investments so as to benefit different parts of the country is a worthy aim. But surely, whatever is dispersed must be worth having when received. And surely, geographic dispersal becomes self-defeating if it involves additional transport requirements, the provision of which eats up resources that could otherwise be profitably invested, and if it means losses that require subsidies which could have been either profitably invested or used to increase the standard of living directly.

It is, moreover, by no means self-evident that economic profitability is inconsistent with the other social and political considerations when the facts of the case are considered. The facts suggest that subsidies are in fact inequitable and interfere with both the mobilization and the allocation of resources.

Some of the statements made in the preceding section are undoubtedly somewhat overdone. Yet one does not kill an ox with a surgeon's knife; subtlety has its place after fundamental issues are settled. The stress on "economic" profits has several implications. The word "economic" is meant to indicate that any particular investment must be seen in the general context of the economy and that demand and cost must be realistically assessed.

The distinction made here is between those investments for which economic calculations can be and those for which they cannot be made, rather than between social and economic overhead or between infrastructure and superstructure. The latter distinction is only too likely in practice to lead to wrong policies. "Infrastructure" suggests a foundation for an "economic" superstructure which could not function without it. The connotation of the term "infrastructure" is that it lies outside the money and market nexus and that in fact it would be wrong to apply to it the same criteria of economic efficiency as the "superstructure."

Yet many economic services such as telecommunications, electricity, and transportation are no more and no less social than are steel and food production. They are essential parts of the other economic services, and they definitely enter into the market. This being so, they must meet the test of economic profitability.

Questions about the appropriate rate structure for electricity or telephone services, say, reflect only in part problems of equity. They are to a considerable extent straightforward economic questions of mobilizing and allocating resources.

The realm of economic calculation extends further: sewerage systems and water supplies are also suitable for economic calculations and in fact have been so treated in the Nigerian Plan. The calculations serve to determine, first, whether a particular investment should be undertaken, and, second, in case subsidies become necessary, who should pay for the investment, how much, and why. On principle, the people benefitting from an economic service or good should pay for it. The principle establishes merely a burden of proof: the advocates of subsidies must get a fair hearing, but it is they who must make the case for the subsidy. Subsidies are resources that might have been used elsewhere in the economy as investment or consumption. Clearly they are justified only if they will either eventually spur growth or if they redistribute income in a clearly desirable way.

The cases of water and sewerage illustrate perfectly the impermissibility of considering subsidies as automatically equitable or politically justifiable. Water in urban areas is essential for industrialization. But both water and sewerage are at present provided only in the few urban centers. It would cause great political difficulties as well as severe inequities to use taxes from farmers to subsidize urban water supplies for people who, on the whole, are already better off than the farmers. Water supplies in rural areas are quite a different matter. But even there the supply of water can be made to increase resources.[11]

If the alternative to subsidies is a profitable investment, the growth rate will be higher with a different allocation of resources. If the alternative to the subsidy of an unprofitable investment

11. Cf. W. F. Stolper, "Social Factors in Economic Planning with Special Reference to Nigeria," *East African Economics Review*, XI (June 1964), 1-17.

is greater consumption, either the growth rates will not be affected or an incentive might increase them. Certainly, the level of current production will be higher, since losses, by definition, mean that the resources generated by production are less than the resources required for it.

Moreover, it cannot be stressed enough that in underdeveloped countries subsidies are more likely to flow from the poor to the rich than vice versa, and they are likely to increase consumption rather than savings. Taxes collected through Marketing Boards from cocoa and groundnut farmers, say, to be used on heavily unprofitable jet airlines, or to subsidize interest rates on civil-service housing, or even to subsidize an expensive road system without regard to the likelihood of opening up new productive areas or improving the evacuation of crops, represent rather obviously a redistribution of income from the poor to the rich and toward increased consumption.

The case for making honest calculations thus becomes overwhelming even from an equity standpoint and even when the decision is eventually reached to subsidize. It may be decided in the case of an economically profitable investment that the beneficiaries of the project should not pay for it; or it may be decided that a project which is not currently profitable will later repay the subsidy in terms of higher income to society.

It would be foolish, however, to increase the use of fertilizer unless it would eventually increase the net value of agricultural output. The question of whether farmers should pay for it or should be subsidized requires a separate and independent decision.

Profits depend on cost and the amount of sales and prices received—that is, on demand. The demand itself already reflects a great deal of interaction in the economy. How big the demand will be for the services of, say, a port authority depends on what is likely to happen to agricultural production of export products, to investment proposals requiring machinery and raw material imports, and so forth. Thus demand projections become one of the focal points of analysis. In many cases such demand projections cannot be made without allowing for considerable interactions within the economy.

Suppose one wishes to analyze the ports program or a proposed iron and steel complex. The first question (aside from technical feasibility, which will be discussed when the cost aspects are considered) is: what demand do you expect and why?

In the case of ports this means: what tonnage do you expect to move in and out? In the case of a steel mill, it means: how much do you hope to sell and at precisely what product mix and at what price?[12] It is obviously impossible to answer either question without fairly detailed projections of the economy. These projections themselves will become conjectural at various stages. It is not too difficult to project what is likely to happen one or two years hence, because the gestation period for any major change will be at least that long. In a sense, the immediate future has already happened. As the future recedes, however, one allows for more and more contingencies: if A happens, the program is P; but if B happens, it is Q. This means that a plan is seen, not as a blueprint fixed once and for all, but as a method of organizing facts as they come along so as to make rational decisions possible as events occur. These rational decisions may be adaptations of plans already formulated or originations of new ideas that become feasible, but they always ought to relate to what happens in the economy as a whole.

The Nigerian Ports Authority already had a well-thought-out

12. In Nigeria the iron and steel complex was analyzed in great detail. In the Plan there is a table giving 1960 imports and expected demand in 1967 and 1975 for the four groups of iron and steel products which it was considered feasible to produce in the foreseeable future in Nigeria. There is clearly no sense in projecting a demand for, say, seamless tubes and expect the production of such an extremely difficult product in the near future. See Federation of Nigeria, *National Development Plan, 1962–68* (Lagos: Federal Ministry of Economic Development, 1962), para. 46.

ten-year development program when the formulation of the National Development Plan started. A beginning had been made, then, on analyzing the demand for dock space and port equipment in terms of the requirements of the economy. The original analysis, of course, had to be revised in the light of the Plan. Initially, a projection of exports and imports in terms of tonnages rather than values was required. Such projections had already been made in as great detail as was feasible for purposes of balance-of-payments projections.[13] Most of this detail was essential to arrive at a rational port program.

Exports and imports had to be treated separately, because from the standpoint of the Ports Authority they presented different problems. Exports were on the whole commodities that could be shipped in bulk. Imports consisted of a great variety of miscellaneous commodities requiring different dock equipment, different sheds, and so forth.

The exports themselves consisted of a great variety of products, some (for example, cocoa) with distinct seasonal fluctuations, others (such as oil-palm products) with a more or less constant stream to the ports, as the market dictated. The specialized port at Bonny through which petroleum went out had to be dealt with separately from the more conventional port facilities.

The projection of the major bulk items required a closer look at the plans of the individual Regions and of the expected production of the major export goods.[14] What was known at research stations about promoting production? How fast could the knowledge at research stations be transmitted to farmers and be put into practice?

In the case of cotton, for example, distribution of better seed strains was relatively simple. Since farmers brought the raw cot-

13. For a description of the methods used, see Chapter IV.
14. The export projections were made for twenty individual export products which in 1960 accounted for well over 90 percent of total exports by value. See Chapter IV.

ton to the ginnery and received the seeds for the next crop there, it would be easy to hand out improved seeds. In the case of cocoa, improved seedlings were available at subsidized cost. This might induce farmers to purchase them, but no direct control could be exercised either on how many seedlings would be purchased or on the specific method of planting so that they would yield the best returns. An informed guess had to be made as to what farmers were likely to do.

For oil palms, an indigenous plant, matters were even more difficult. Most of the oil-palm products came from wild palms. What were the Regional programs of substituting new and better-yielding varieties? How fast would palm-grove rehabilitation proceed? How many seedlings could be produced at the West African Institute for Oil Palm Research at Benin? What about increases in acreage? What about possible domestic uses of export products? This required judgments on the effect of industrialization programs using domestic raw materials, and on possible increased uses of export products by domestic consumers. As stated in another context, most Nigerian exports—groundnuts, palm oil, cotton, cattle hides, goat skins, tin ore—have important domestic uses.

How dependent were crop yields on weather, and what average allowances should be made for weather over the next six years? This required some research on past weather, its pattern and likely effect on crops, which was done in a most impressive fashion by the economists and agricultural experts of the Northern Region. What would be the likely expansion of acreages? This required some consideration of the feeder-road program. And so forth.

From the questions, it can be seen that a great part of the development program as a whole—including the private sector —relates directly to the analysis of the demand for port services. In formal terms, the fact-finding that has to be and largely has been undertaken is equivalent to finding the transport content of a great number of cells in an input-output table.

Yet there is an important difference. The programs that are undertaken to affect the production of export products are themselves subject to both technical and economic analysis. The long-run prices likely to be received for individual export products must be estimated as best they can. The problem has been discussed in Chapter IV and will not be taken up again here.

In order to arrive at a reasonable estimate of the demand for port services, it becomes necessary, as pointed out, to estimate the probable domestic uses of export products. How much cotton will be domestically used? How many groundnuts will be domestically expressed into oil, and how much of that oil is likely to be exported? The Nigerian industrial programs that used domestic raw materials which would otherwise have been exported had to be analyzed for their direct effect on export tonnages. The domestic use of cotton depends on the establishment of new cotton mills, their profitability, the timing of the investments, and the speed with which they get into operation. New or expanding mills may, of course, depend on subsidies. Are these subsidies to be given directly through the budget or indirectly through tariffs or tax benefits? In effect, expected developments of the private sector enter into the estimation of export tonnages of a particular crop. Thus the ministries of commerce and finance and the agencies responsible for the development of private production outside of agriculture must be consulted.

The expected extension of acreage will partly depend on the railway program and on the road-building program. These two come into the picture also in another context: Nigeria, like some other countries, has several possible means of evacuating export crops. Therefore the question arises as to which of the possible alternatives is likely to be developed and which one should be used. This, in turn, requires some consideration of: railway-rate schedules, development of inland waterways, road traffic, marketing-board policies as to choice of evacuation routes, and so forth. Estimates were required of what would happen to inland waterways as the Niger dams project matured. What would happen to transshipments from neighboring territories in general and as a result of the high priority given in the Plan to international road links?

I stop here and refer to the published *National Development Plan, 1962–68*, as well as to a more detailed account by L. M. Hansen.[15] The Nigerian Plan embodies economic-profitability calculations in addition to financial calculations. Professor Hansen's article contains more information on procedures and on the reasoning underlying the formulation of the Nigerian Plan, as well as more calculations than are published in the Plan. The calculations of transport demand, as has been indicated, allow for a very considerable amount of interaction in the economy—the forward and backward linkages, in the terminology of A. O. Hirschman. They allow for honest profitability calculations in other areas affecting demand for port services. Thus they are integrated into the general picture of resource allocation. They are linked as firmly as is possible to forecast demand.

However, since the planner knows the future no more than does anyone else, a maximum of flexibility is required. In Chapter III it has been argued that a plan should be viewed essentially as a sequence of short-run decisions designed to open up further possibilities. This flexibility finds expression in the Plan in the proposed timing of the new structures and in such statements as: "Consideration will be given by 1966 as to whether the Customs Quay at Lagos should be replaced or renovated" (paragraph 103). Similarly, with respect to inland waterways, the Plan states:

15. *National Development Plan, 1962–68* (cited in note 12); L. M. Hansen, "Methods of Economic Programming and Analysis of the Plan," *Nigerian Journal of Economic and Social Studies*, IV (July 1962), 92-109.

86. . . . The development of the navigation facilities will, however, be related to the expected expansion of traffic. At present, excess capacity exists in the river fleets, and considerably increased traffic could be carried without additional investment. When, however, a steel mill and other industrial developments mature on the Niger, the picture will change radically.

87. River traffic is expected to develop as follows:—

Table XIV
Niger and Benue Traffic and Cost

	1962–3	1964–5	1967–8	1971–2
Traffic based on known projects (million ton miles)	120	135	160	240
Traffic if potential developments mature (million ton miles)	120	156	243	293
Total cost per ton mile (pence) known projects	2.08	2.17	2.05	1.66
If potential developments mature	2.08	1.92	1.68	1.10

88. For these reasons, the Department's programme will be implemented in two stages. During the years 1962–5, £1.447 million will be invested for the improvement and expansion of the buoyage system and for patrolling the river to Kainji (the site of the proposed Niger dam).

. . . .

90. In 1965, the programme will be re-evaluated. If traffic developments warrant, £534,000 will be allocated for the implementation of the second stage . . .

To return to the example of the Ports Authority's development programs, the cost side becomes equally important. I am quoting at length from Hansen's description of what was done, as follows:

We then had estimates of total [traffic] through Lagos and Port Harcourt by commodity, direction and year.

The next step was to determine . . . [if] existing facilities could handle the projected traffic and what new facilities would be required with what economic and financial implications. The former is a question of the characteristics of the traffic, and the efficiency and potential improvement in use of existing ports . . . With Ports, the evaluation of past performance was of immense assistance in focusing on obstacles to efficiency as well as a way of measuring efficiency.

Statistics revealed that ship delays . . . to load or discharge, and average ship turn-around times were constantly reducing over past years. This was confirmed by an increase in tons moved over the quays per year and month, and especially per lineal foot of quay . . . the economist must depend on . . . technical people for [efficiency measurements] . . . The conclusion was that the harbour operation and movement over the quays was highly efficient . . . and . . . it was agreed that there was little room for improvement on the quays themselves.

Like most ports, however, access to, and evacuation of, port storage sheds and space leaves much room for improvement. Unlike many ports, custom clearance was judged to be relatively efficient. The problem was *inter alia* limitations in access roads . . . and especially the institutional practice whereby importers and, therefore, lorry operators work on an eight to twelve hour day whereas the ports could work twenty-four hours . . . [After exploring] the possibilities of quicker clearance, . . . first priority given to the Second Mainland Bridge . . . another planning linkage.

N.P.A. [Nigerian Ports Authority] also agreed to review their storage fees schedule as the old system contained a possible inducement not to clear storage up to two weeks . . . However, there was a limit to increasing fees to induce quicker clearance. We had to enquire into what would be the implications of increased storage fees to lorry operators, importers, wholesalers, retailers, and ultimately the consumer . . . N.P.A. is still exploring these possibilities as an entire institutional complex is involved in any changes.

. . . .

The N.P.A. then prepared a capital construction and cost schedule, and a financing forecast showing the results of anticipated operations. [For] the accuracy of construction costs, an economist can only rely on the technical people . . . We . . . attempted to isolate the effect of price inflation, but not uniformly as the composition of project costs varies too much . . . [The] staff and materials for construction and operation [were] analyzed in order . . . to assess the import component for foreign trade and aid calculations; to assess demand for standard commodities like cement and steel construction rods for industrial planning; and to measure the employment effect of the investment . . .

divided into net increase by type of staff, and net increase in Nigerian staff. We attempted a foreign exchange cost and benefit analysis, but with less success due to the difficulty in tracing ultimate source of payment. All are links in the Plan inter-relationships.[16]

Similar calculations were made for the proposed iron and steel industry—with the result that a final decision was postponed. The transport system as a whole was analyzed in a Stanford Research Institute report.[17] The plans for electric power were analyzed on the basis of calculations of the Electricity Corporation of Nigeria, the Niger Dams reports, and other studies. In every case, all available information was collected and co-ordinated, so that the evaluation of every single proposed project proceeded as far as possible in the context of the whole program, including the private sector.

It is sometimes asserted that one cannot plan for the private sector, and there is much truth in this assertion. Yet it is exaggerated. Agriculture, the most important "industry" in most countries (including socialist countries), is in the private sector. To be sure, it is difficult, if not impossible, to set definite targets for the private sector, and any targets set cannot be enforced by the usual means. Nevertheless, reasonable projections can be made for imports and for the consumption of some major products such as gasoline and construction steel and cement. One of the purposes of planning is precisely to disseminate through the economy a knowledge of what is likely to happen throughout it, and a national plan takes, to some extent, the place of a signaling

16. Hansen, pp. 99-100, 102. Dr. Hansen, together with the experts of the Ports Authority, carried the major burden of scrutinizing port costs. Dr. Hansen expects to publish details on the calculations; it is therefore inappropriate for me to go into details of work for which the major credit should go to him. See also L. M. Hansen, *Comprehensive Economic Planning in Nigeria*, E/CN.14/CP/7 (Addis Ababa: Economic Commission for Africa, 1962).

17. H. Robinson, S. Smith, and K. Clare, *The Economic Coordination of Transport Development in Nigeria*, Stanford Research Institute Project no. 1-3280 (Lagos: Federal Ministry of Economic Development, 1961).

device for the private sector that is normally provided in advanced countries by the price system.

As has been mentioned, the projections of demand must be made both in physical terms (where applicable) and in value terms, to allow for economic calculations and hence proper resource allocation. As has also been pointed out, it is not necessary to put only one price into the calculations for the entire plan period. For one Nigerian export good, for example, two prices were used to project proceeds for different subperiods. The table for inland waterways (Table XIV in the quotation from the Plan, above) shows several costs—and by implication prices—for the period it projects. This means in effect that in the evaluation of any individual project the future implications of a plan as a whole are made explicit and allowed for.

When it comes to the private sector, the implications of the plan for, say, cement needs or steel needs can be worked out.[18] When the projected private investment requires no government action, the question of resource allocation resolves itself. But this is a most unlikely event in Nigeria, where land cannot be held by non-Africans outside of Lagos and the old Colony and where therefore location either in or outside an industrial estate must be negotiated by any expatriate firm; it is equally unlikely for indigenous modern enterprise because water and electricity are normally not available except in industrial estates. For that matter, complete freedom of capital movements, investments, and production exists hardly anywhere. Government influence works through general tax and tariff policies that reflect—or ought to reflect—the aims of development and that most certainly reflect the scarcity of resources and the attempts to overcome them as well as to channel them into particular directions. Where government is involved, problems of projecting demand and cost

18. See n. 12.

arise, as do questions of subsidies in one form or another—income-tax exemption, special grants, etc. In this case all that has been said on public investment becomes applicable.

The case for proper calculations and for making people pay for the benefits they receive rests on grounds both of efficiency and of equity. There always exists a problem of shifting, of course. More on this subject will be said in Chapter VI. It must be pointed out, however, first, that it may be impossible to trace the ultimate impact not only of any cost or tax but also of any subsidy that might be contemplated. In planning it is therefore clearly preferable to put the initial impact of the costs where the benefits are and to let the market work out the rest.

Thus a ports authority must be required to increase rates (if it is not already doing so, as in the case of the very efficient Nigerian Ports Authority) so as to speed the clearance of sheds and so as to obtain funds for internal financing, while paying competitive wages in line with internal productivity. A telephone system should at least pay for itself and should be expected through a revised rate structure to begin to contribute to its own growth. A road system as a whole should not require the taxpayer at large to subsidize road users; for a transport subsidy in underdeveloped countries is likely to be very substantial. The principle that road users should contribute to the road system at least its current expenses would require that they pay, through licenses, taxes, import duties, and so forth, at least for the maintenance of the road system, including an imputed rate of interest. This principle, adopted in Nigeria as the result of the Stanford report already mentioned, led to a rise of gasoline import duties in the budget of 1962–63. Road users still pay only a part of the recurrent cost of the road system as defined. The principle, if fully executed, is equivalent to leasing the road system to the users for the cost of maintaining it, without charging a repayment of original capital.

Without such calculations, at least in rudimentary form, it would be impossible to allocate funds as between different means of transport. Nor would it be possible to decide on the allocations of funds to the transport system as a whole compared to electricity and all the other uses. For all funds allocated must come from the total of resources to be raised, whether through the budget and taxation or through the domestic or foreign capital market.

It is important to be fully aware of any discrepancy between the real cost of a transport system and the transportation charges paid by users. Whether one likes it or not, the prices actually charged affect the economy and resource use. Charging less than cost has the effect of increasing the demand for transport services. Reducing transport cost to users below the real cost to the economy interferes with an efficient location pattern and, by absorbing resources that would have been used in other ways, slows growth all around. It is difficult to see who can ultimately gain by this.[19]

Clearly, the burden of proving the need for a subsidy must rest on the proponent of the subsidy, and it is extremely dangerous to rely on unspecified non-economic benefits. Even if such benefits can be demonstrated to exist—which is by no means self-evident—it remains true that their achievements require real economic resources, whose alternative uses are likely to have been preferable. This in turn means that their achievements will have involved not only real economic cost but probably also non-economic benefits foregone elsewhere in the economy. In all such cases, subsidies are not true subsidies at all but investment allocations of a particularly inefficient kind.

---

19. For a discussion of these problems in the Indian context, see Louis Lefeber, "Indian Transport Problems," *Economic Weekly,* Annual Number (February 1962), 203-205. The Stanford report (see n. 17) deals with these problems in the Nigerian context.

D. INSUFFICIENT DEMAND?

Suppose that even with all interactions taken into account and even after allowing for all contingent developments, demand still falls short of what is needed for a profitable operation. It then becomes necessary to analyze, as best the available facts permit, why this should be so. Without such an analysis, it is impossible to make the proper policy decisions. For insufficient demand may mean a number of diverse things, and policy prescriptions suitable for dealing with one kind will be inconsistent with prescriptions that will be right for another kind. Insufficient demand may mean simply low income; it may mean that incentives are needed for increased aspirations and efforts. It may even mean what it usually means in an advanced economy in a state of depression: that there is insufficient purchasing power.

It is all too easy to overstate one's case. It has been stressed repeatedly that the proper allocation of resources is at least as important as their mobilization. A proper allocation of resources will, for any given amount of resources, maximize growth rates and hence future resources for further allocation. In addition, the mobilization and allocation of resources are interrelated in such a manner that the better the allocation the more resources can be mobilized at any one moment of time.

This incentive effect cannot be belittled merely because, in an advanced economy, the incentive effect of taxation on investments and effort is said to be of only marginal importance. One of the major development problems consists in drawing more people and more production into the money nexus. There is an extensive literature on backward-sloping supply curves of labor in underdeveloped countries and on the difficulties of making "traditional" farmers adopt better methods. More recent investigations suggest that the problems are not what they were thought to be. These problems will be discussed later in greater detail. Here it suffices to stress that a rational allocation itself is the strongest possible incentive to increase the available resources.[20]

Finally, in any economy, factors of production are not merely substitutes for each other but quickly become complementary. The fact of complementarity means that the problem of insufficient demand cannot be the Keynesian one which presupposes that *all* resources are in infinitely elastic supply. There may be a case for inflationary financing as a resource-mobilization device, but its limits are clearly set, not only by a balance-of-payments problem that arises with frightening speed, but by scarcity of almost all factors except unskilled labor.

If capital, foreign exchange, skilled labor, and entrepreneurs are scarce and fully employed, simply to increase monetary demand has no effect at best and leads at worst to a shift from more to less desirable production through the distortions that inflation is likely to induce. If these scarce complementary factors are not

20. I consider this fact so important that I do not apologize for discussing it in several contexts. In an advanced economy we are by now accustomed to considering any tax proposals in a general equilibrium context, that is, in the context of both the tax and expenditure side of the budget. The *locus classicus* of the theory is R. A. Musgrave, *The Theory of Public Finance: A Study in Public Economy* (New York: McGraw-Hill, 1959). Is it not an extremely dangerous procedure for advisers to propose taxes without considering the purposes for which such taxes are to be used, and indeed to propose the taxes while considering the level and composition of expenditures as given? Surely it is within the competence of an a-political technical adviser to point out to the political leaders that a given set of priorities not only will not produce the desired growth but will seriously interfere with the desired mobilization of resources.

It should also be stressed that Nigeria does not present the picture of a dual economy with a subsistence sector and a modern sector which do not meet. There is subsistence production and production for the market. But the same goods may be used either way, and the same people produce both. This means that the incentive problem is of overwhelming importance. On this point, see also Ojetunji Aboyade, *Foundations of an African Economy: A Study of Investment and Growth in Nigeria* (New York: Frederick A. Praeger, 1966). John Adler made the same point many years ago in "The Economic Development of Nigeria: Comment," *Journal of Political Economy,* LXIV (October 1956), 432.

fully employed, an increase in monetary demand will, of course, lead to more imports and output all around, but whether or not this is desirable depends on whether the increased monetary demand can be maintained once the complementary factors have been brought into production. This in turn will to a large extent depend upon the profitability of the new production and particularly upon its effect on the future supply of complementary factors.

This problem becomes particularly relevant when there are accumulations of foreign reserves that can be drawn down. As is well known, India, Latin America, the Gold Coast, and Nigeria all came out of the last war with substantial accumulated reserves. The accumulation of sterling reserves in the English-speaking countries of West Africa continued even until 1954. The rate of utilization of accumulated foreign-exchange assets becomes an important economic as well as political issue.

Suppose the foreign-exchange reserves are being drawn down. This will undoubtedly raise employment, output, consumption standards, and even tax revenues without any increase in taxable capacity, since customs duties are a major source of government income. There is a limit to the speed with which the foreign resources can be utilized, if clear waste is eliminated. (It is always possible to buy such things as ships, supersonic airliners, complicated medical equipment, and machinery of all kinds; but, although such purchases appear in the national accounts as investments, their effect on growth in the medium and long run is questionable.) Presumably, however, foreign-exchange resources are not unlimited, nor can foreign aid be obtained to cover every imbalance.

As reserves are being drawn down, therefore, it becomes essential, in order to sustain demand in the future, to increase exports or otherwise earn additional foreign exchange or to find domestic substitutes for the previously imported factors. This can be done only if the increased production resulting from increased monetary demand meets certain minimum productivity conditions: the production must, within a reasonable time, add to resources at least as much as it absorbs, including enough foreign exchange to keep itself going. At the very least, it must create a substitute for the foreign exchange. Otherwise the limits to fruitful monetary expansion are again met, and, as reserves are used up, increased monetary demand cannot even sustain employment. If, as the result of balance-of-payments difficulties, imports have to be restricted, real demand cannot be expanded as long as imported goods are essential complementary factors. What is expanded with one hand is restricted with the other. The employment created while foreign reserves are used up will necessarily fall again if the investments have not met these minimum productivity conditions. There has simply been a temporary dole to the economy, a capital consumption that has come to an end with the disappearance of foreign assets. Similarly, if the "expanded" demand, say, by government is financed out of taxation, there is simply a shift in the direction of demand and no net increase.[21]

The basic fact is that underdeveloped countries lack the internal flexibility of production which makes monetary expansion in advanced countries so important a tool of economic policy. In developed countries, to prohibit the importation of a good cheap machine may lead to the substitution of a slightly inferior and slightly more expensive domestically produced machine.[22] In un-

21. The importance of pursuing proper policies when running down foreign reserves is discussed by Sir Donald MacDougall, "The Government Financing of Development: Bold or Cautious?" *Social and Economic Studies,* VII (September 1958), 75-84 (published by the Institute of Social and Economic Research, University College of the West Indies, Jamaica). In Appendix II to this article (pp. 83-84) Sir Donald explains "How Reserve Building May be a Good Investment" by enabling a country to avoid devaluation, exchange controls, and deflationary policies.

22. Even in India, which is capable of producing a wide variety of machines, albeit not always at competitive cost, the capacity of industry would quickly be exhausted and could not be quickly enlarged without substantial imports. Similar comments apply also probably to most under-

derdeveloped countries, no machine can be substituted at any price. Restricting imports in developed countries is a hidden method to lower real wages and the standard of living. It will have the same effect in underdeveloped countries and in addition produce an absolute limit to employment and output.[23]

A policy of increasing monetary demand (particularly if it is so simple-minded as to encourage demand for existing capacities that on any honest accounting are unprofitable) will not even add flexibility to the economy, since it will of necessity be directed toward what the economy can produce already with available local factors at low productivity and without being able to compete with imports. These are not loaded words used to prejudge a case. If there were not low productivity and if production were competitive, the balance-of-payments problem would not be so serious and the demand would have been present to start with.[24]

Thus in underdeveloped countries the limits of monetary policy and of the effectiveness of expanding monetary demand by government action (including, of course, the central bank if one exists) are quickly reached. Both are important, but they cannot do in underdeveloped countries what they are expected to do in advanced economies. On the contrary, it is precisely one of the purposes of development to increase the effectiveness of monetary policy, that is, to increase the internal flexibility of the economy. If the expansion of spending with the concomitant

developed countries that have already begun to build up a sophisticated industrial structure.

23. The same limit to employment was found in post-war Europe and was one major reason for the Marshall Plan. I have discussed the phenomenon of employment's depending on imports rather than on aggregate spending in "Notes on the Dollar Shortage," *American Economic Review,* XL (June 1950), 285-300, using a Keynesian framework to discuss an essentially classical problem.

24. These problems are discussed at greater length in the specific Nigerian context in W. F. Stolper, "How Bad Is the Plan?" *Nigerian Journal of Economics and Social Studies,* VI (November 1964), 261-276.

absorption of the foreign-exchange reserves leads to a self-sustaining operation, the case will come under the general profitability criterion stressed in the preceding section. If it does not, it will lead at best to some internal redistribution of income and at worst to a waste of a very scarce resource. But internal redistribution is not being considered here (and it is very questionable whether the redistribution will tend in a politically or socially acceptable direction), and the other result—waste—must be avoided. It is even questionable whether a mere expansion of monetary demand will increase the mobilization of resources, because of the lack of internal flexibility. Moreover monetary expansion and import demand in the African setting—and probably not only there—are virtually identical phenomena requiring no intervening variables.

This analysis bears an obvious relationship to the writings of the so-called structuralist school. The policy conclusions drawn seem to be quite different, however. I suspect that the difference results from my insistence on economic profitability as the primary development criterion in place of import substitution, even though development will, as pointed out, inevitably lead to import substitution. More generally, the policy conclusions probably differ because the idea of profitability involves a very disaggregated micro-economic approach, while the concept of import substitution in the structuralist sense appears to be derived from an aggregative analysis of the balance of payments. I share with the structuralists the preference for attacking a problem directly. A disaggregated micro-economic approach, however, identifies the problem as one of productivity and profitability and *not* primarily as a balance-of-payments problem. Questions about the structure of an economy arise in the course of asking which specific investment would make sense.

It is interesting that West German economic policy makers also have come to the conclusion that when bottlenecks appear in an economy, they must be broken by rather specific means. But the

Germans, too, have rejected either inflation or withdrawal from the world economy as suitable means of overcoming structural handicaps to growth. Some of the actions have been outlined before. Since West Germany was spectacularly successful whereas Argentina and Brazil were not, perhaps underdeveloped countries may look for ideas in this direction.[25]

To press the point, even if factories with excess capacity exist, this only proves that resources were wasted in the past.[26] If the factories could have earned even their running cost, they would have been used. To guarantee them sufficient demand amounts to throwing good money after bad. Resources are used as subsidies when they could have been used to raise income; and if these resources are raised by taxation rather than inflation, consumption is shifted from more to less desirable channels.

So the evidence points to the conclusion that simply raising monetary demand cannot be the remedy for an underdeveloped economy. Nevertheless it is argued by some people that demand must be induced by the government before development can take place. One reason given is that the people lack demand because they have no ambitions. Another reason given is that there is a clear "social" need for goods which somehow is not translated into effective demand. These poor people—I have heard this argued passionately and in all seriousness—obviously need and want shoes and other things they could produce. Why does the government not stand ready to buy things from them at a price that will guarantee a profit and then distribute the shoes and the like to the people? Welfare and product would "obviously" be increased; there would be "no" cost, since these peo-

25. For a detailed discussion of German policy, see Karl W. Roskamp, *Capital Formation in West Germany* (Detroit: Wayne State University Press, 1965). The subject is also dealt with in W. F. Stolper and K. W. Roskamp, "Planning a Free Economy: Germany since 1945," in a forthcoming book edited by Henry Kissinger at the Center for International Affairs, Harvard University.

26. The case of profitable excess capacities is mentioned in another context in footnote 10.

ple are underemployed; the social value of the goods would clearly be greater than their price, and so on. The obvious sloppiness of this formulation does not change the fact that it is actually put forward; and its very sloppiness makes it difficult to deal with it effectively.

The first of these problems, namely the absence of ambitions, is real. The second, namely the absence of effective demand despite an urgent need, is not only spurious but, in the formulation in which it is met, dangerous.

In many countries, it *is* difficult to get going. There *is* a problem of insufficient ambitions, not dissimilar to the problems that advertising tries to cure in highly advanced economies. The creation of wants may present problems. There may be societies so primitive as to have no desire to break out of the narrow circle of their traditions. There may be numerous societies which would like the benefits of development without giving up traditions inconsistent with it. In all these cases the problem is to create or utilize incentives for change. Yet I find it hard to believe that a Yoruba mother is any less upset over the death of her child than an American mother would be. There is a passionate desire to see one's child educated. There are demands for roads to go to the market more easily, for better clothing.

Obviously it is not easy to teach farmers who have lived by picking bunches of oil-palm fruit off wild trees something about crop rotation and fertilizer use, even where such programs might work technically (which is by no means always the case). There are all too many cases in which social organization has defeated otherwise quite feasible programs. Land-reform programs have been defeated because traditional peasants could not be transformed overnight into efficient farm managers. But there have been significant successes, and the key to them was that the new techniques lay within the horizon of the farmer, that they worked, and that they made him better off. I am convinced that in many cases resistance by farmers to modern methods, including, for example, the use of fertilizers or irrigation, results from quite rational causes: the methods do not work, or they do not pay.[27] Only when new methods work both technically and economically are they likely to be adopted. When people want something, they will work for it—that is, they will increase effort and production.[28] In too many agricultural programs that are technologically feasible, the question is not asked: will it pay?

"Will it pay?" is a question that can be put into monetary terms only with difficulty if there is inflation and if the people want disparate goods and services. These goods may be "investment" goods, such as roads or schools or dispensaries; they may be consumer goods such as textiles. But they must be *real* goods and not pieces of paper. If farmers are to be drawn increasingly into the money nexus, they have to be persuaded that money is somehow desirable. It may be necessary to shift the internal terms of trade in favor of peasants and the subsistence sector.[29] But again, this means providing real goods cheaper than before.

Thus, at every turn, one comes back to raising productivity and using resources profitably. The need to provide real incentives puts a limitation on tax policy and on the degree of austerity that is economically desirable—to say nothing of the political implications which taxation and austerity inevitably have.

27. See in this connection Montague Yudelman, *Africans on the Land* (Cambridge, Mass.: Harvard University Press, 1964). The effective use of fertilizer requires delivery when needed and water available at the proper time. Resistance of farmers to the use of fertilizers can be traced in some cases to irregularities of supplies, etc. There are, of course, also other cases in which fertilizers were used to whitewash walls.

28. The adoption of new techniques may cause new problems no matter how much one wishes that new problems would not always arise. The bore-hole program in Bornu province of Nigeria has been highly successful in stabilizing the cattle population by providing water, but it also threatens to lead to sheet erosion. Such unexpected consequences of success are not unknown elsewhere.

29. See on this subject the various writings of Hla Myint, including "An Interpretation of Economic Backwardness," *Oxford Economic Papers*, VI, N.S., (June 1954), 132-163.

If taxation is raised so much that incentive goods become too expensive relative to agricultural production, the latter will not increase. It may even be difficult to persuade people to leave subsistence production and to supply more goods to the market and less to their own consumption.[30]

Finally, one must deal with the confusion that exists in practice among insufficient demand, the "need" for some particular good (say shoes), and low productivity—a confusion that is by no means easy to disentangle. It is, of course, true that Nigerians could use more shoes and indeed would want them if shoes were cheaper and their incomes higher. It is also true that there are shoemakers, including some factories, that could produce more shoes and could sell them if they got a higher price and/or they could reduce cost. The provisos, however, tell the story. Productivity is low—hence prices of shoes are high and incomes of the workers are low. Productivity may be low for various reasons. A description of a visit to an inefficient shoe factory having an expatriate manager may serve to illustrate the theoretical points already made and still to be made.

The shoe factory in question made two kinds of products: a sneaker with a rubber sole and canvas uppers, and a plastic sandal made by an extrusion process. Output was small. There was some internal division of labor which seemed to make sense.

The manager complained that he could not compete with shoes imported from Hong Kong and shoes "dumped"—his expression—by Czechoslovakia. He claimed that regardless of the price he could offer, the Czechs were willing to undercut him, and there was no reason to doubt the truth of his statement.

Yet even a casual inspection of the production line showed inefficiencies. The molds of the sandal-making machine were

30. There is some evidence that the taxation of oil palm products has reached a level where it becomes self-defeating, in that it not only leads to no increase in supplies but interferes with the planting of the new high-yielding oil palm varieties developed by the West African Institute for Oil Palm Research (WAIFOR) at Benin.

worn, and so rejects were numerous, and the sandals had considerable excess plastic hanging on them as they came off the mold, which in turn required labor for trimming. The workers who cut rubber soles out of sheets worked quickly but not to the best advantage. With a little care and working a little more slowly, they could have got one or two more soles out of each sheet. The sheets themselves were of domestic manufacture, of good quality, standardized as to their thickness, but not uniform in size and shape. No such waste was apparent in the cutting of the canvas uppers; the canvas, coming in standard sheets, could be stacked and pressed, and a non-European expatriate foreman cut out the pattern with a saw as is usual in developed countries (including Hong Kong).

When the attention of the manager (who, of course, wanted protection from foreign competition, on which he blamed all his woes) was drawn to the inefficiencies, he insisted that there really was no waste. Labor was abundant, so why should he not use the old molds instead of replacing them and let labor trim the excess plastic by hand? He pointed out the fine equipment to recondition scrap rubber and the excess plastic shorn from the imperfect sandals. But the reconditioned plastic could not be dyed as easily as the new, and this was a limitation on re-use. And worse, it had obviously not occurred to the manager that waste is an economic rather than a physical concept in the context relevant to him. Replacement of the molds would probably have been cheaper than the running cost of the reconditioning machine. This was certainly true of rubber reconditioning, for the process required large amounts of electricity that was expensive to begin with and came through a system which broke down so frequently as to raise costs still further. In many industrial operations, particularly those involving heat, when electricity goes off for even ten minutes, it is not possible to resume at the point where the process broke off. A day's production may be lost and machinery may be damaged.

When, in such a case, requests for subsidies, government purchases, or tariff protection are granted, low productivity and low income are perpetuated, and foreign exchange is wasted in the form of machinery inputs, plastic raw materials, coal and oil to generate electricity, and so on. The infant-industry argument is simply irrelevant. Protection will not remedy the situation; the provision of industrial extension services will. Cash subsidies financed from taxation in the name of providing sufficient demand amount to a redistribution of income from productive to unproductive uses. Aggregate demand is not raised; the shoes are purchased too expensively. If the shoes are purchased with newly created money, a balance-of-payments problem is bound to arise, as was discussed before.

All this, unfortunately, has to be spelled out. Suppose the shoe production has not been as unnecessarily inefficient as it was in the actual case described. How far does the argument go that there is need for shoes (a need which everyone approves of) which comes to nothing because of insufficient demand? One answer is clearly that the problem will be solved when efficiency and thereby income are increased. This is, after all, the rationale of providing for technical education, training, establishment of small-industry centers, and the like. This seems to be the logical approach.

Another approach is to inquire why, with their given income, people do not buy the shoes which they presumably need. It is, of course, possible that people insist on spending the money on imported liquor or local palm wine. The argument becomes then one of channeling demand into directions that are socially beneficial. *In abstracto* one can say that it is not the business of planners to tell people how they should spend their money. *In concreto,* there will be a consensus that expenditures on liquor are not conducive to growth and that this perhaps justifies an intervention. Even if this is granted, the logical steps still seem to be to increase taxes on liquor and spend the proceeds to raise productivity and thus income, leaving consumers free to decide how much they want to spend on shoes and how much on other things.

What cannot be argued is that because shoes are higher in the scale of values of the policy makers than liquor and because there is usually a political consensus which allows one to translate what might otherwise be a planners' prejudice into political action, "the social value of shoes is higher than their price." Nor is it acceptable to argue that a subsidy to shoe production and free distribution by the government will therefore necessarily enhance welfare and, indeed, social product. Yet this kind of argument is precisely what the planner is frequently confronted with, in exactly these words, and not only in Africa.

If the subsidies that go to the purchase of shoes come from newly created money, the problems discussed before arise: the balance of payments will be immediately affected, requiring some sort of exchange control or tariffs or import quotas (or, of course, increased capital inflows or further depletion of external reserves). Controls mean not merely a possible redistribution of income but a cut in real wages. Government is forcing people to spend money on shoes that they would have spent in other ways. There is, in effect, no over-all increase in effective demand. Government spends more money on shoes. It then taxes the money away again as it is spent and gives the shoes to the people. In the meantime complementary factors have been used to produce shoes that no one wants at the given income level and with existing relative prices, complementary factors that would have been available to raise productivity in the production of shoes or elsewhere in the economy. There may be a perfectly good case for subsidizing the use of shoes to combat, say, hookworm. But this is quite a different issue from maintaining employment, and it does not justify using methods of subsidization that perpetuate inefficiencies in production.

Subsidies financed out of taxation will redistribute income, though the problem of shifting makes the final result of the combined tax-expenditure pattern not always predictable. But aside from the question of whether this redistribution is equitable, government is reducing the income of some to finance inefficient production, when the same tax revenue could and might have been used either for increasing productivity or for social purposes much higher in the scale of values (such as schools or hospitals). Or the thought might even have been entertained of *not* collecting quite as much taxes and leaving consumption at a higher level; this might have had an incentive effect on production and would, at the worst, have been neutral as far as growth was concerned, whereas subsidized inefficiencies reduce the rate of growth.

If the preceding paragraphs read somewhat like a harangue, this is because one meets in practice all too often a refusal to analyze a particular situation and to look facts in the face—or to become conscious of a void in the absence of facts—while basing policy conclusions on hypothetical examples in which the real problems are assumed away. There is, inevitably, something personal in this account. It is not pleasant to be accused of having no heart, to be told that life consists of more than economics and factor allocations, and that it matters whether shoes or cosmetics or liquor are produced. With all this one can only sympathize. But the planner, whose job it is to get the best allocation of resources, cannot avoid going behind generalities to the facts in each situation. Particular "social" subsidies will affect balance of payments, budget, incentives, and the rate of growth no matter what intention lies behind them. Nor can the planner, faced with alternative policies, avoid choosing those that will achieve the results desired with the least cost. He cannot avoid such considerations even if he starts merely with the problem of investment criteria and factor allocation. When implications are traced through and when the cases in which "social" values are asserted to be greater than private values are analyzed, it will frequently be found that the real problem is low productivity, not insufficient demand; that, therefore, the policy requirements are different; and that an inefficient allocation of scarce funds will backfire, making it impossible to achieve the very social goals so ardently espoused.

E. SHADOW PRICES

Throughout I have insisted on economic or social profitability as the only operational investment criterion applicable to the allocation of resources to all those uses for which economic calculations can be made. I have suggested how, in the calculation of profitability, interactions in the economy may be allowed for. It is now necessary to deal briefly with the problem of inapplicable prices generated by imperfect markets for goods and factors.

For a number of interrelated reasons, true shadow pricing was not used in Nigeria. Actual accounting practice in many cases did not allow for depreciation or else gratuitously assumed subsidized rates of interest. This was shadow pricing of the wrong sort. Therefore, just to keep accounts on the basis of interest rates which actually had to be paid was already a step in the right direction.

As discussed in Chapter III, the budgetary implications and the dangers of inconsistency that creep into shadow pricing, particularly if applied on an *ad hoc* basis, discouraged the planners from any attempt to apply shadow prices. That shadow prices would not be stable—and that information with which to arrive at them was hard to come by—also weighed in the planners' minds.

An unsuccessful attempt was made to limit government investments in economic enterprises to cases with a projected payoff of 15 percent or so. No shadow pricing or belief that the "true" marginal efficiency of capital was this high lay behind the attempted limitation, however. Rather, if a growth rate of 4 percent or more was to be achieved, and since a large proportion of existing projects had no foreseeable payoff, more-than-average return was needed from additional projects.

Legitimate shadow pricing requires the solution of a complex set of interrelated equations, interrelationships that indeed should allow also for intertemporal changes. In theory, when factors are technically substitutes for each other, and unless one or more factors are absolutely redundant, proper pricing will induce their employment in the economy in the proportions in which the factors exist. Chakravarty has suggested a shortcut for arriving at various factor prices.[31]

In practice, lack of data makes both the complete and the shortcut method inapplicable in most countries, including Nigeria. Moreover, the manner in which shadow prices are applied when they can be determined does not as a rule accomplish their theoretical purpose. Ideally, the planners of individual projects ought to be confronted with one or more sets of shadow prices. The engineer-economist ought then to construct different proposals corresponding to the different sets of shadow prices, such that, for example, a lower shadow price for labor and a higher one for capital should lead to the use of a more labor-intensive method of producing a given output. Something like this happens in practice when, for instance, a hydroelectric proj-

31. See A. Qayum, *Theory and Policy of Accounting Prices,* Contributions to Economic Analysis, no. 20 (Amsterdam: North Holland Co., 1960); Gustav F. Papanek and Moeen A. Qureshi, "The Use of Accounting Prices in Planning," in *Organization, Planning, and Programming for Economic Development,* United Nations Conference on the Application of Science and Technology for the Benefit of the Less Developed Areas, vol. VIII (Washington, D.C.: G.P.O., n.d.), pp. 95-105. I wish someone would reprint the superb article by H. B. Chenery, "Development Policies and Programmes," *Economic Bulletin for Latin America,* III (March 1958). For the Chakravarty shortcut see S. Chakravarty, "The Use of Shadow Prices in Programme Evaluation" (mimeo., M.I.T. Center for International Studies, 1960), now published as chap. iv of P.N. Rosenstein—Rodan (ed.), *Capital Formation and Economic Development* (Cambridge, Mass.: M.I.T. Press, 1964).

ect is compared with a thermo project producing an identical output of electricity. This, however, is not the usual procedure. More often—because it really is the only feasible procedure—a number of projects are designed by engineers without reference to shadow prices and are then evaluated at shadow prices by the economists, whereupon those that do not meet the test of profitability at the shadow prices are eliminated. Under such a procedure, shadow prices do not affect the factor proportions in individual projects at all. Factor proportions in the economy are, however, somewhat affected by a change of the project mix—provided that shadow pricing will result in such a change.

Such a change is not certain, however. Alternative calculations made for farm settlements and other agricultural projects in Nigeria indicate that different shadow rates for labor and capital affect profitability reckonings for suggested projects only marginally.[32] Similar results appear to have been obtained elsewhere. To the extent that shadow pricing will not affect even the profitability of individual projects, factor proportions in the economy are not affected by different shadow rates. The projects stand with their original factor proportions, and the project mix is not affected. In such a situation the application of shadow prices would simply create a budgetary problem without changing the employment of factors. It should be noted, however, that even at best the application of shadow prices leads to the substitution of one problem, the budget, for another one, an imperfect market.

The problem of correct prices nevertheless remains a serious one in many countries. In setting a price on labor, capital, and foreign exchange, questions of fact as well as of feasibility remain. As far as labor is concerned, it cannot be argued that in

32. See Jerome Wells, "An Appraisal of Agricultural Investment Projects in the 1962–68 Nigerian Development Program" (unpublished Ph.D. dissertation, University of Michigan, 1964). Professor Wells is now expanding his analysis.

most countries labor in general is abundant. Skills are scarce everywhere. The abundance or redundance applies primarily to unskilled labor which can be substituted for other factors only within limits. Other factors quickly become complements.[33] There is evidence that as long as wages of unskilled workers are very low, entrepreneurs will employ them simply because the wage bill is negligible. Once wages are raised, however, efficiency becomes important. In East Africa, for example, manufacturing production has risen with falling employment, as wages rose.[34] To maintain employment by shadow rates requires subsidies which lead the problem back to the budget.

Moreover, when evaluating an actual project, one is confronted with a bewildering array of factor requirements. A ports authority requires not merely sweepers and stevedores but also accountants and bookkeepers, supervisors, messengers, mechanics to run the workshops, maintenance crews, crane operators, and so forth. Dock construction and the like cannot be carried out with unskilled labor alone. Take any example you care to choose, an involved operation such as a ports authority or a simple one such as the shoe and sandal factory mentioned previously: the number of people without skills whose employment could justifiably be reckoned at wages below the market in an evaluation of a project seems limited. Considering that most modern operations require intricate interrelationships and smooth flows of processes, it becomes doubly doubtful whether a substitution of labor for machine pays beyond a certain point

33. See in this context the pathbreaking article of R. S. Eckaus, "The Factor-proportions Problem in Underdeveloped Areas," *American Economic Review*, XLV (September 1955), 539-566. Reprinted in A. N. Agarwala and S. P. Singh (eds.), *The Economics of Underdevelopment* (Bombay: Oxford University Press, 1958), pp. 348-378. This book in turn has been reprinted in the Galaxy Books paperback series (New York: Oxford University Press, 1963).

34. I am indebted to Mr. Emil Rado, formerly at Kampala, Uganda, now at Glasgow University, for the fact and its interpretation.

even at zero wages.[35] This consideration is likely to be important in all but agricultural operations.

Interest rates raise different problems. In a perfect market there would be a uniform rate structure varying with maturities. Reality has imperfections. Some of them can be eliminated by institutional changes that create or improve a money market (see the next chapter) and make funds available to increasing numbers of potential borrowers. Others, however, are inherent in the nature of the world, such as, for example, that it has extent, whereas most theory assumes it to be a point without extension. Even in the U.S., interest rates vary substantially by locality and type of borrower, reflecting not only location patterns but differences in risks. Thus Richard Youngdahl has shown that types of loans and rates differ according to location, industry, size of loan, etc., although here too institutional changes that improve the interregional flow of funds will reduce the spatial spread of interest rates.[36] In countries where fiscal institutions are not well developed, interregional interest-rate differentials may fulfill an

35. A very detailed analysis using shadow prices is Hollis B. Chenery, George E. Brandow, and Edwin J. Cohn, Jr., *Turkish Investment and Economic Development* (Ankara: U.S. Operations Mission to Turkey, Foreign Operations Administration, 1953). The authors explicitly state that, in determining the social return on investment, "It would also be desirable to make allowances for the degree of skill required of labor as suggested above, but we have been unable to develop reliable measures of this factor" (p. 73n2). On the other hand, farm labor was apparently evaluated at zero wages: "In practice it is very difficult to evaluate the 'opportunity cost' of resources, but in a few cases we have applied this correction. It is particularly important in investments such as farm mechanization, where equipment 'saves' on labor which has no alternative employment. In this case the saving to the private investor is greater than that to the economy" (pp. 57-58).

36. Richard Youngdahl, "The Structure of Interest Rates on Business Loans at Member Banks," *Federal Reserve Bulletin* (July 1947), pp. 803-819; Youngdahl, "New Statistics of Interest Rates on Business Loans," *Federal Reserve Bulletin* (March 1949), pp. 222-237; A. Lösch, *The Economics of Location* (New Haven: Yale University Press, 1954); E. M. Hoover, *The Location of Economic Activity* (New York: McGraw-Hill, 1948).

economic function. This means, first, that the "true" marginal productivity of capital is hard to assess. It means, secondly, that it is not necessary to apply a uniform shadow rate to all projects.

The "true" marginal productivity of capital is assumed to be high in underdeveloped countries. Yet in Nigeria it was extraordinarily difficult to find a great number of projects that could pay even 6 percent, let alone the 10 percent or 15 percent often suggested. The same is undoubtedly true in many other countries. The IBRD finds it difficult to channel sufficient capital into underdeveloped countries without abandoning the lending criteria originally adhered to. The productivity of capital remains a question of fact to be investigated at intervals in each country. In India, or Pakistan, absorptive capacity is perhaps no problem, and given a few years it may not be one in Nigeria.[37]

In practice it appears that higher accounting rates are seldom used to influence factor proportions but are often used to restrict the number of projects in accordance with the available capital. Close attention should be paid to this practice, for at the same time at which market interest rates are neglected in favor of higher shadow rates, an attempt is made to "accelerate" growth by subsidizing interest rates. I have never run across an investment that could be economically sound but not financially so. I have met many proposals that have been made financially pre-

---

37. Chenery, Brandow, and Cohn state: "We have found a considerable volume of investment in agriculture and industry where both the private and the social returns are above 25 per cent. From the sample of investment opportunities which we have studied, we have concluded that priority should only be given to investments showing a social return of 20 per cent or more. This yield can be used to evaluate government as well as private sectors" (p. xvi). If this high rate of returns were insisted upon in Nigeria, not many government investments would be undertaken. Also, something went obviously wrong in Turkey soon after Chenery, Brandow, and Cohn had made their study. They wrote: "The annual return on the combined investment in agriculture and transportation as measured by the increased national income per unit of investment may be estimated at 60 per cent" (p. xii), a remarkably high yield. See L. M. Hansen, "Methods of Economic Programming and Analysis of the Plan" (my n. 15), pp. 103-104, for what was done in Nigeria and why.

sentable by such crude devices as forgetting about depreciation charges, not charging any interest on capital at all or charging a lower rate than the lender himself has to pay, and deliberately assuming higher prices for the final output and lower cost of material inputs than is realistic. Compared to such methods, it is already an achievement to insist on realistic pricing and costing, to insist on depreciation charges, and to charge—as was done in Nigeria—a uniform rate of 6 percent for capital as the rate that government had to pay when borrowing on the domestic market, so that at least budgetary repercussions are avoided.

A case can be made for charging a rate equal to the borrowing rate of government to all capital projects undertaken by government or in which government is indirectly involved through subsidies, investment allowances, income-tax holidays, tariff exemptions, and the like. This has the advantage of being uniform, hence unambiguous to apply, and it does reflect the actual alternative uses of these resources, at least as long as the borrowing rate of government is not rigged in any way and the government can in fact borrow freely for all projects with a prospective yield of the borrowing rate. Such a rate of, say, 6 percent would be applied also to funds obtained through the International Development Association (IDA) at much lower rates. It is justifiable to treat the borrowing of IDA funds and their use asymmetrically. Soft loans are justifiable as a subsidy to an underdeveloped country, for example, in order to avoid an unbearable strain on the balance of payments. But as long as soft loans are limited in amount, the internal allocation must still allow for their scarcity.[38]

Because any development program will contain a large number of projects with no foreseeable payoff, the achievement of any specified growth rate for the economy as a whole requires a

38. There is generally an asymmetry between the provision of aid and its use. It can be argued that the rich countries have a moral duty to help the poor ones but that the poor countries have no moral right to such help. It can be argued that the help given by rich countries should be in the form of grants but that the recipients should nevertheless charge a cost.

sufficient number of investments that pay more than the average rate of growth. However, the less resources are used for enlarging the directly productive capacity, the more resources are available for the social overhead; and, through the buildup of recurrent cost, projects in the latter area will affect adversely the future availability of resources for all purposes. This must affect future shadow rates of interest adversely, as well as growth and employment prospects. The instability of shadow prices over time has been considered in Chapter III. Here it should be noted that this instability could easily become "explosive" in the theoretical sense: shadow rates of interest rising and wages falling over time.

The danger is very real that the composition of the investment program may, as the result of a decision designed to save resources, become slanted toward those projects that do not contribute directly to growth. It follows that the total size of the program must be considered and that it may be desirable to include projects that yield 6 percent rather than eliminate them in favor of non-payoff investments. This is all the more important if the number of projects with *any* positive return above cost is limited. Thus the attempt to influence factor proportions becomes entangled immediately with the size of investment expenditures.

If this is the case, a number of problems arise. If only investments with a return of, say, 10 percent or more are undertaken, should the whole program of economic and non-economic projects be reduced? Should less resources be raised internally and a higher level of consumption be allowed? Should the reduction in the program be absorbed entirely by a reduction in the anticipated balance-of-payments deficit financed, presumably, by foreign aid?

Or should resources be put into non-economic investments which are not directly productive? Should calculations on the basis of 10 percent for capital be disregarded when actual investments are being decided upon, and are the investments to be subsidized? If so, why make the calculations at the higher rates

in the first place? In any case, it appears once more that allocation and mobilization of resources are not independent of each
other.

It is sometimes argued that as long as a project has any positive
return, it should be undertaken. But this appears to imply that
a shadow rate of interest should be lower, not higher, than the
rate at which one can actually get funds. If the program is limited
by any interest rate, market or higher, there are implications for
tax policy. Putting too many resources in non-payoff projects
will increase requirements and is likely to slow the rate of growth.
If, on the other hand, the rate of growth is to be raised, then
any project paying at least the desired rate of growth will be
desirable. In this case, what becomes of the higher shadow interest rate?

Someone might argue that the preceding discussion misses the
whole point of shadow pricing; that the decision on the size of
the program and the projects to be executed is different from the
decision as to the factor proportions to be employed within individual projects; and that the calculations of a project's profitability with shadow rates of interest will not decide whether it is
undertaken or not. But these arguments are not effective. The
truth is that the calculation involving higher interest rates and
lower wage rates is a particular way of making a profitability
reckoning so as to determine simultaneously the best methods
of using resources and the size of the program. If it is now argued
that an investment should be undertaken even though the calculations show a loss—the discussion still refers only to projects
for which an economic calculation is possible—then the whole
purpose of the calculations is lost. If the resources are available
to subsidize loss enterprises, why is the higher rate of interest
put in? If the additional resources are not available at the lower
interest rates, where are the funds required for subsidies coming
from?

Thus a shadow rate of interest higher than the one at which

funds are actually available makes sense only if there is in practice another rationing device besides the price of funds (as indeed there frequently is) and if one seeks to restrict the size of the development program. A good case can be made out, however, that since in many cases investment opportunities with a positive payoff are limited at any moment of time, resources in the largest possible amounts should be pushed into uses that will stimulate growth directly. In this case the limitation on investment is most appropriately the interest rate that government has to pay marginally on international markets.[39]

Just as the shadow-price problem as applied to labor is usually discussed in the context of a country like India, so the problem of saving foreign exchange is usually discussed in the context of a balance-of-payments crisis. Thus in one study Hollis Chenery, George Brandow, and Edwin Cohn make an allowance for the unrealistic Turkish exchange rate.[40] Shadow-price calculations involving exchange rates appear also to have been made in India and Pakistan. None were made in Nigeria. When imports have to be restricted by quantitative controls or foreign-exchange allocations, the exchange rate is obviously not an equilibrium rate by any definition one wishes to choose.

Nigeria, at the time when the Plan was made, had ample foreign-exchange reserves. The emergence of a balance-of-payments crisis was conceivable. But it could probably be prevented by proper policies. The demand for foreign exchange depends not only on relative prices but also on the level of income (and some other parameters which are of secondary interest in the present context). A currency may therefore be overvalued even

---

39. It may be interesting once more to refer to the German experience. In order to safeguard growth, the capital market was split, with low interest rates being charged for investments in the bottleneck sectors such as steel, power, shipping, and coal; with housing being subsidized; and with high market rates being charged for other investments. See book by Roskamp and article by Stolper and Roskamp, both cited in n. 25.

40. Cited in n. 35.

if prices at the exchange rate are the same abroad and at home.

Exchange control, devaluation, and shadow pricing of foreign exchange are all methods of restricting as well as redirecting demand. To the extent to which a balance-of-payments crisis is caused by an excessive level of spending rather than by relatively high domestic prices, cutting planned and actual spending directly seems preferable to depreciating the exchange rate or setting high shadow rates. The basic advantage of either shadow pricing or exchange depreciation is that it shifts demand in favor of using more domestic and less foreign resources. It will do so, however, only if a project that has passed the profitability test with a shadow rate of foreign exchange (which normally implies a devaluation of the currency) actually gets the necessary foreign-exchange allocation at the shadow rate of exchange. Using a shadow rate for evaluating a project without making the recipient of the foreign exchange pay that rate gives him a double windfall: he gets a profit from an exchange allocation and a profit from higher prices, and in both cases is sheltered from competition from the unfortunates who are left without foreign-exchange allocations.

If the investment receiving the exchange allocation is a government plant, the profits go to government, and it is possible that savings will thereby increase, although this really depends on the whole expenditure pattern. If the allocation goes to a private plant, particularly one making consumer goods, the windfall profits are more likely to be consumed, especially because in this case the other economic controls which are usually part of the syndrome of a balance-of-payments crisis militate against expansion.

Shadow prices have so far been discussed here in terms of factor prices. There are two reasons why the prices of final goods have not been mentioned. First, although a project must be evaluated at a price for the finished goods that excludes any tariffs, the temptation in reality is to put into the calculation much too high a price. Second, estimating particular prices is mixed up with considerations of equity and income distribution. Prices of shoes are too low because, given the income distribution, people cannot buy shoes. But it is not clear how evaluation in higher shadow prices can help. A "solution" to the problem by means of high shadow prices which then would be accompanied by low real prices leads into the problem of budgetary repercussions which have already been discussed at length.

F. NON-ECONOMIC INVESTMENTS AND THE BUDGET

Profitability criteria with or without shadow pricing are obviously not applicable to so-called "social" expenditures without modification. Yet such expenditures require as much scarce real resources as the directly productive investments do. Economic considerations therefore cannot be avoided, and the economist cannot withdraw from the scene and leave the decision on, say, health measures and education entirely to the political authorities.

Economic considerations enter any given project on health and education in several ways. Once it has been decided to go ahead with a project, the economist must ask whether the project in question is being executed in the most economic possible manner. The purpose is not merely to save scarce resources. The questioning of every step has the purpose of making sure, first, whether the general aims expressed—improvement of this or that aspect of health considerations or education—are sufficiently specific to be executed; second, whether the proposed means are suitable to achieve the given ends; third, whether the means proposed can be improved upon; and fourth (not entirely unconnected with the other three), whether the projects, once started, can be staffed.

One essential product of these searching questions is the discovery of new targets—either targets that should be executed instead of the original proposals or targets that should be added to them. In Nigeria, although initially the Economic Planning Unit of the Federal Ministry of Economic Development in Lagos merely collected and collated outlines of what the individual executive ministries and agencies wanted to do, the process of analysis led to considerable changes and—it is hoped—improvements.

Consider the aims of education or measures for health. It is, of course, true that only a healthy and educated people will be able to lead full and productive lives. Moreover, without an educated and healthy population the more narrowly economic projects cannot be executed or can be executed only with difficulty. But it is not entirely relevant to state that "ultimately" it is people who produce everything. For it is equally true that resources are scarce and that one must take one step at a time. To calculate the returns on investment in education in the manner of advanced countries may be misleading.[41]

In advanced countries, such as the United States, attempts have been made to calculate the value of investment in education. But the problems with which underdeveloped countries are faced are rather different in two respects from those faced in advanced countries.

First, the economies of underdeveloped countries are not yet going concerns, and, as has been stated before, they lack the flexibility which enables advanced countries to shift resources quickly into desired uses. It cannot be taken for granted that educated people coming out of schools will find the necessary resources to enable them to be productive. For reasons which have already been discussed and which will be outlined further in Chapter VI, increasing aggregate spending cannot be relied upon to create the necessary jobs. Thus the question of how much education and what type becomes more important in

41. The Western discussion of investment in human capital seems at times a capitalist version of the labor theory of value!

underdeveloped than in developed countries, and the proper timing of sequences become crucial.

Second, the general level of literacy is low, and illiteracy has to be eradicated. The purpose is partly political, partly economic in the sense that a pool of people must be created out of which the next generation of leaders can come. There obviously cannot be higher education without a pool of generally literate primary-school graduates. Yet one of the problems met with in under-developed countries is that primary education, which is the essential basis of advanced education but has itself little economic value, is often looked upon as professional training. When one starts with zero, even a simple knowledge of reading and writing does give one economic power to escape from the drudgery of subsistence farming.[42] But the stage in which a simple primary education has by itself great economic value is quickly passed, so quickly that the recipients of primary education seem to find it difficult to understand what happened to the promise of education. In the industrial countries at the time they were developing, many students could hardly wait to get out of school and earn money as farmers or workers. The African almost always wants to get away from farming, and few factory or office jobs exist.

The problem of determining the optimal—or at least a reasonable—amount of resources that should go into education is more difficult to solve in underdeveloped than in developed countries even though the logic of the approach needed to solve the

---

42. A superb study by Samuel S. Bowles indicates that in Northern Nigeria even an elementary education has a substantial return. This study is important for methodological reasons even though probably not all its conclusions can be generalized to Nigeria as a whole. See Samuel S. Bowles, "The Efficient Allocation of Resources in Education: A Planning Model with Applications to Northern Nigeria," unpublished doctoral thesis, Harvard University, September 1965. Dr. Bowles also presented a brief discussion at the annual meeting of the American Economic Association in December 1965 which was scheduled to appear in the Proceedings of the American Economic Association, *American Economic Review*, May 1966.

problem may be the same in the two kinds of countries. It seems to me there are two different sets of reasons for the difficulty.

The first is emotionally charged, though I make no apologies for this fact. Pre-professional education is really part of the social framework of society within which the economy can work. To have educated people is an end of economic development. To make the ends of society subject to economic tests is repugnant. It is, one feels, also very likely to become self-defeating. For we deal here with a rather distant future which no one can possibly foresee with any degree of certainty. To be sure, growth in an advanced society depends on technological change. Yet it would be extremely difficult to predict what kind of education would bring about the biggest change and the fastest increase in available resources. This is certainly true for the fundamental discoveries which have radically changed the course of a science or of some technological application. It is only slightly less true of the education of advanced engineers or chemists or computer men. Everyone knows the difficulties in determining the right amount and the criteria for the allocation of funds for research and development.

The second set of reasons for being rather hesitant about the methods used to determine the amount and distribution of resources for education is much more economic and straightforward. The problem of training for fundamental discoveries discussed in the preceding paragraph is hardly relevant to underdeveloped countries as yet. At the same time it cannot be denied that the creation of the extra-economic framework of society, without which it cannot live and develop, is an essential task. And education and training remain, of course, essential also from a narrow economic point of view. The problem is to find a method of limiting the resources to be allocated to education. This limitation is urgent because education is a voracious devourer of scarce economic resources; in effect the demands of education are limitless.

In advanced countries economists have tried to make cost-benefit calculations for expenditures in education. Even in advanced countries the application of their analysis is difficult. In underdeveloped countries the difficulties are compounded because they lack the flexibility of the economy and the abundance of entrepreneurial talent which in advanced economies permit the analyst to assume that, given the proper stabilization policies of the government and the central bank, the educated and trained people who will come on the market will in fact be absorbed at the calculated rates. Such an assumption in underdeveloped countries could not be taken for granted but would have to be justified in each specific case. Some of the difficulties of pursuing stabilization policies will be discussed in the next chapter. Here it may suffice to say somewhat blandly that the benefits of education depend on the profitability of the enterprises in which the educated labor will be employed; and that the provision of educated manpower gives no assurance that the number of profitable enterprises can be increased sufficiently quickly to absorb all the new educated people coming into the labor market, because lack of trained manpower is only one constraint on increasing the number of profitable investments.

The traditional manpower planning approach for the economy as a whole depends essentially on a series of fixed technical coefficients, frequently derived from other countries, to get at the *number* of people to which education and training should be given. These numbers are then translated into money terms by costing the programs envisaged. The major shortcoming of the manpower planning approach lies in its assumption of fixed coefficients independent of the prices of the various factors of production and that it does not link the cost to the benefits of various education programs. The method of using coefficients found in another economy is a shortcut which necessarily fails when the numbers in that other economy are not optimal—that is, if these coefficients themselves do not satisfy reasonable cost-benefit criteria. Thus coefficients derived from Egypt—simply because Egyptian data permit their calculation—may lead to quite unrealistic targets because for various reasons Egypt has apparently more Ph.D's per square inch of arable land than any other country in the world!

It seems best, therefore, to approach the planning of social investments in the following manner, which combines aspects of both the cost-benefit and the traditional manpower planning approach and which, I believe, makes both operational.

First, as much resources as possible should be pushed into directly productive uses. This is feasible because the amount of resources that can be so employed is limited by absorptive capacity, and it is necessary because a threatening Malthusian problem can be averted only by the speedy creation of a productive and adaptable economy.

Second, the implications of the productive program for social expenditures must be worked out. This means that the planning of education, for example, is approached initially by way of manpower planning, with the aim of breaking bottlenecks in the way of absorptive capacity. It will be found, however, that the amount of training that can be justified by direct economic reasoning is quite limited. It will be found also that when the manpower planning approach is applied to specific projects rather than to the economy as a whole it surmounts the basic criticism that cost-benefit calculations are not allowed for and that fixed factor proportions are assumed. By considering what might be practically involved it can be seen why this is so.

Suppose the planners are instructed to find projects which are profitable on reasonable assumptions regarding demand, price, and cost, but specifically excluding the question of where the necessary skilled labor is to come from. Suppose next that the manpower requirements are worked out realistically and specifically and are brought to the planners, who will immediately want to know whether the required labor will be available and what is done about training. The planners will next want to know whether the labor requirement can, in fact, be modified without raising the cost too much. This means that in the process of evaluation they introduce variable factor proportions into the traditional manpower approach. Since they deal only with projects with a reasonable prospect of profits, they already have introduced cost-benefit considerations into the manpower planning approach.

Third, over and above direct investment and manpower planning, the health and education programs should be as large as the economy can afford. This recommendation is made operational by carefully working out what it will cost to run facilities established by capital expenditures. The recurrent budget becomes the link between the allocation of resources to directly productive investments and to other expenditures. Through the recurrent budget the criteria applying to investments in social expenditures can be linked to ordinary investment criteria. But, as preceding sections of this chapter have indicated, the whole point is to get away from narrow investment criteria and to arrive at the wider concept of resource allocation.

The amount of resources to be pushed into directly productive uses depends on the profitability of the uses. The manpower implications can be worked out in detail once the composition of the development program is known in reasonable detail. In addition, a manpower board can utilize such studies as the one made by W. A. Lewis to plan for the necessary personnel for the private sector.[43] Nevertheless, the manpower-planning approach

43. W. A. Lewis, "Education and Economic Development," *Social and Economic Studies*, X (June 1961), 113-127. Lewis uses the formula $x = n \dfrac{(a + b + c)}{m}$ to determine the percentage of the age cohort which should receive secondary education. The symbols denote: $x =$ proportion of age cohort to be recruited; $n =$ ratio of number of secondary-type jobs to adult population; $m =$ ratio of number in age cohort to adult population; $a =$ normal percentage wastage of nationals of the country; $b =$ abnormal

does not come to grips with the final problem of providing health facilities and education independently of the immediate economic benefits. This final problem raises the question of the amount of resources that can be spared and in particular of the proper time sequences with which Chapter III has dealt. Staffing, recurrent costs, and the kind of services to be provided must all be fitted into a timetable.

I have suggested that there should be as much primary education as it is economically and technically possible to provide in order to establish the pool out of which students for the higher skills will be taken. This statement is made with the full realization that universal primary education by itself and without follow-up is more likely to leave its graduates unemployable than to meet a demand for more skilled workers and farmers. Yet no planner can take it upon himself to decide which children should get a primary education. For the child who does not is, in fact, condemned to a marginal life; he is excluded from education, not on the proper grounds that he is incapable of being educated, but because of a sheer arbitrary decision.

Everyone knows this. It may account for the willingness of parents to undergo any sacrifice to permit their children to attend school. It is a fact that villages will pool resources to send the brightest children to school and that civil servants with comparatively high incomes will educate three or four children not

---

wastage resulting from replacement of expatriates; c = percentage rate of growth of the number of secondary-type jobs. For Nigeria as a whole, Professor Lewis guesses x to be:

$$x = \frac{0.01\,(0.025 + 0.005 + 0.08)}{0.045} = 2.4 \text{ percent}$$

Professor Fred Harbison has made a valiant attempt to guess at the Nigerian manpower requirements in his contribution to Sir Eric Ashby *et al.*, *Investment in Education: The Report of the Commission on Post-School Certificate and Higher Education in Nigeria* (Lagos: Federal Government Printer), Part II, chap. I, pp. 50-72. See also the dissertation by Samuel Bowles cited in the preceding footnote.

their own. This incentive can be utilized. The issue is not whether education is consumption or investment—it is obviously both— but how to maximize resource mobilization and how to get education going without interfering with economic growth.

The provision of secondary education should not wait for the achievement of universal primary education. As soon as enough students are available, high schools can be started. As soon as high schools produce qualified graduates, the next levels can be planned—if staff and resources are available.

The burden of constructing elementary schools can be almost entirely shifted to local communities, as has been done successfully in the Eastern Region of Nigeria. The problems of constructing elementary schools can be handled locally. The equipment needed is uncomplicated: there are no laboratories, only chairs and benches and tables. The real limitations arise from the recurrent budget and from staffing problems.

The planning of educational expenditures requires answers to three questions: How much resources can the budget spare? Where are the teachers and students coming from? Are the targets achieved at minimum cost?

Teachers can for a while come from such foreign agencies as the Peace Corps and church missions, but it is clear that teacher training will need high priority if the school program is to get off the ground and if the foreign assistance is eventually to become unnecessary. Here again one meets the timing problem. First comes the teacher training. Paced behind it comes the expansion of schools.

Common sense should prevail when the expansion begins. Recurrent cost can be substantially reduced by increasing the ratio of students to teachers. Even in the rich countries it is often impossible to reach desirable ratios of thirty to forty students per teacher in elementary schools. For underdeveloped countries such ratios are quite unrealistic. The teachers are simply not available. Buildings have to be suitable for their purposes and as cheap as possible. There is no point to building universities which cannot be staffed and whose student bodies cannot meet minimum requirements.

In countries such as Nigeria, the limitation of the recurrent budget is very real. It is relatively easy to shift much of the construction onto local communities.[44] But it is exceedingly difficult to get foreign aid for recurrent cost. Moreover, foreign teachers require substantial local expenses. Their housing, medical care, and the like put a strain on the budget and affect the balance of payments if what they require has a substantial import content.

The training of teachers and of students, obviously, has to go in a certain sequence if the program is to work at all. Only if the schools provide the necessary minimum quantity of directly productive manpower to the economy can the growth in resources be generated that is required to widen and lengthen the streams of education.

Thus initially—that is, until the economy is a going concern— extra emphasis has to be put on realism of targets in physical terms, economy in achieving the targets, and sound judgment as to the taxation that can be spared for education without interfering with growth. This means essentially a limitation on the resources to be allocated to education from the side of the recurrent budget with the proviso that more can be done if—and only if—communities and individuals will generate the additional resources required.

For all these reasons, the planning of education must start with the recurrent budget. Only after the recurrent budgetary implications of the capital expenditures have been worked out

44. In post-war Germany, students were admitted to study at universities only after they had helped to rebuild them with their own hands. There seems to be no reason why this example could not be imitated elsewhere. All it would need is some professional supervision and possibly some construction machinery which a ministry of local affairs or a ministry of community development could supply at little cost.

can the capital budget as a whole be determined. Only after the size of the capital budget has been fixed can it be distributed in such a manner as to produce, on the one hand, the maximum number possible of the types of trainees needed for development and, on the other hand, working backward, the number of elementary students that can be accommodated. After these requirements have been determined, perhaps additional resources will become available for widening the streams and increasing the targets. If the targets are set too high initially, the recurrent budgets will become so tight that the developmental effort proper will have to be curtailed.

No formula can be given to every country such that x percent of total development expenditures should always be allocated to education or y percent to health measures.[45] Situations in different countries will differ. The amount of foreign aid that can be expected will vary. The possibilities of getting foreign aid for local cost is not always excluded. In French-speaking African countries, foreign aid to defray recurrent cost is considered normal, though in English-speaking African countries such aid to ordinary budgets is looked upon as an interference with sovereignty.

With all qualifications duly made, it still remains true that the central problem in planning education is the recurrent budget. Within that budget, a consistent time sequence of training must be designed so as to produce the necessary minimum manpower for the economic program proper. The effectiveness of that program will allow a further expansion of education for reasons other than economic rationality.

When social overhead is approached in this manner, definite economic limitations to political decisions on the rate of expansion

45. This is not necessarily a handicap. Since one deals with a continuing problem of resource allocation rather than with once-and-for-all decisions, it is important to be clear what the real issues are: the budgetary burdens and the availability of teachers and staff.

of education will emerge. Taxation to provide the funds for economic expansion cannot be allowed to grow into a disincentive. And if education absorbs so much resources that too little is left to employ the educated and train them, further education is indeed consumption, and conspicuous consumption at that.

The problem of planning health measures is essentially similar. Public health, like education, is something that one feels strongly should be outside the economic nexus. Here, too, one will certainly not wish to limit the provision of health facilities to only those who can pay. Here, too, as much resources as possible should be devoted to the care of the health of the people, not because it improves productivity but because a society is judged by how it treats those who cannot take care of themselves.

Yet, as always, resources are scarce, and one starts with a given situation. There is no doubt that in Africa, as elsewhere, provision of health has high priority in the value judgments of the individual, so high that he is willing to pay for it and make productive efforts to get it. As with education, it is not so much the capital expenditures but the recurrent cost and the staffing problems that soon set the limit to what can be done. There just are not enough doctors, nurses, pharmacologists, radiologists, physical therapists, and so on, for rapid expansion.

Pushing as much resources as possible into directly productive enterprises becomes all the more necessary when preventive health measures in particular accelerate an already rapid growth of population. Hence even where no population problem exists now, it will arise in the near future unless the economic base for the rapidly growing economy is created. Because the absorptive capacity for economic projects is certain to be limited, some resources for non-economic projects will be available. As with education, it is the eventual recurrent cost that will define a limit. The bigger the recurrent cost, the smaller the budgetary surpluses that can be generated with any given level of taxation.

The smaller the surpluses, the less is available for the capital program. Since foreign aid is normally available only for capital expenditures, and since it requires, as a rule, matching domestic resources, the capital program will be expanded or contracted by more than any available increase or decrease in the ordinary budget surplus. Once the surpluses vanish or become so low as to threaten the execution of even profitable investment projects, the limits of the expansion of the non-economic sectors have been passed.

The parallelism between education and health continues all down the line. Just as in education it is essential to create a base for further training, so in health it is only sensible to start with preventive measures. The people to be helped are already born. Keeping them well is likely not only to cost less resources but to permit them to be more productive. Curative measures must, of course, be available, not only to heal the sick but to backstop preventive measures. But curative measures are likely to be more expensive than preventive ones, and it makes obvious sense to prevent sickness in the first place.

Most preventive health measures do not entail strictly medical projects but engineering ones—e.g., good water supply or sewage disposal. These are not only easy to introduce; they can be made to pay for themselves. Anyone who has been in the bush can understand why villagers, with help and encouragement, will work for a pure water supply. Since the provision of public health does require economic resources, this fact is not unimportant. Someone has to pay in any case. It is therefore fortunate that the provision of public health facilities at a cost can be used to increase productive effort and to mobilize additional resources. In urban areas, it should be quite easy to make a water system pay for itself, particularly when such a system becomes essential also for planned and expected commercial and industrial growth.

There is no point in building hospitals that cannot be staffed and in buying equipment that cannot be operated. The training of doctors must have highest priority. This requires pre-clinical training and must therefore be integrated with the educational program. There is a limit to which a doctor-training program can be pushed. It is good to push to the limit but senseless to go beyond.

Doctors are not able to practice widely without supporting staffs of nurses and assistants. And nurses can't be trained without nurses' hostels. In general, the rule "if you can staff it, you can have it" will eliminate a substantial number of plans for capital expenditures. It will also suggest proper time sequences for expanding the program in a sensible manner without wasting scarce resources.[46]

Thus the planning of the non-economic sectors becomes, on the one hand, a technical exercise of designing a program for schools or health and of working out the proper sequences for introducing it. The planning becomes, on the other hand, part of a general exercise in resource allocation and budgetary implications. Through the recurrent budget, non-economic programs are linked directly with the economic ones. The effectiveness of the economic expenditures will affect the taxable capacity and the recurrent revenues. It is the recurrent cost that will affect the re-

46. The *National Development Plan, 1962–68* shows that the provision of sewerage, water, and markets can be designed in such a manner that its maintenance becomes self-supporting. Even a low-cost housing program could be designed without subsidies by developing the land and by turning out "by mass-production methods shell houses at a cost which will allow individuals to purchase them at a price which is lower than the (frequently subsidized) rent paid at present" (p. 94). The Eastern Region Plan envisages that "fifty per cent of the recurrent costs of these pumped and piped (rural water) schemes and the full cost of maintaining simple water points will be a charge on local communities" (*National Development Plan*, p. 245).

A fuller discussion of the issues involved in planning the social sectors is found in W. F. Stolper, *Social Factors in Economic Planning, with Special Reference to Nigeria*, E/CN.14/SPD/3 (Addis Ababa: Economic Commission for Africa, 1963). Reprinted in *East African Economics Review*, XI (June 1964), 1-17.

sources that can be mobilized for the expansion of the productive apparatus and the social capital of the country, after the day-to-day running of the government has been taken care of.

Foreign aid can help over the humps. It may last for decades. Nevertheless, a country must look to the moment when it can take over its own day-to-day expenses. From the recipient country's standpoint, dependence on another country's good will for the running of its daily affairs is hardly palatable.

The crucial problems of economic development lie in finding profitable investments in increasing numbers and producing manageable *recurrent* budgets. The neglect of the implications of capital expenditures on recurrent cost and revenues causes economic trouble. In a consideration of investment in the social sectors, the ordinary recurrent budget takes the place of the profitability calculations of a private or economic investment. Neglect of the recurrent-cost implications of capital investment may underlie much of the political tension that accompanies foreign aid. No donor can give money for ordinary expenses without exercising some control, and no self-respecting recipient can be happy with such control. But this is another story.

VI

Economic Policies from a Planning Standpoint: Money, Taxes, and the Balance of Payments

FINANCE may be humbug and money a veil. Nevertheless, the development of good financial institutions and credit facilities plays a useful role in the development of the "real" economy. At the same time, the manner in which policies can in fact be executed depends not merely upon the institutions developed but also upon the structure of the economy. If it is true, as is generally and not unreasonably claimed, that the expansion of the money economy is a prime problem of economic development, it surely follows that establishing a solid monetary base and executing rational monetary policies are essential to achieving the purposes of economic development.

In the Western world, the development of the economy, of the money and banking system, and of central banking have gone hand in hand—institutions growing up as the real problems required. To some extent this has also been true of development in Africa. The Nigerian Central Bank was not established until 1959. The West African Currency Board, which had much more restricted functions than a central bank, dated back only to 1912.[1] But money and bank credit supplied by expatriate banks existed

1. Central Bank of Nigeria, *Annual Report* for 1960, p. 3; W. T. Newlyn and D. C. Rowan, *Money and Banking in British Colonial Africa* (Oxford: Clarendon Press, 1954), chaps. ii-iii.

before, and so did "manillas" and non-British coins. The monetary development might, therefore, be considered by a historian taking the long view as following the economic development of the territories, starting with capital movements supplied by expatriate banks and traders to finance foreign trade and ending up with the mobilization of domestic resources for economic development. In this, the development would not be essentially different from what happened in Europe when the modern economy was developed.

From the planning standpoint, monetary, fiscal, and balance-of-payments policies are part of an interlocking system for the purpose of mobilizing more resources and aiding in their allocation. Certain inherent features of an underdeveloped economy limit the effectiveness of all such policies, and often institutions through which to carry them out are lacking. The two aspects of the matter are logically separate, though they affect each other as a matter of course.

Monetary and fiscal problems come up, in the first instance, when the financing of any plan is considered, in particular the question of whether to raise resources by inflationary finance and forced savings. When in the process of monetization of the economy the money supply must be enlarged, such an increase becomes legitimately a source of development finance. But when countries distinguish administratively between recurrent and capital budgets and when the raising of resources for development requires substantial surpluses in the ordinary recurrent budget, it cannot be argued too strongly that deficit finance for the ordinary budget would play havoc with any economic development. Internal financing of any substantial portion of the development plan by credit creation also rapidly runs into objective limitations that cannot be eliminated by what one may call institutional tricks. In that sense finance is humbug. However, the issue is rarely posed in the either-or manner suggested, but really becomes one of how many long-term government bonds or short-term treasury bills it is safe to circulate. What volume of reserves is needed abroad? In monetary and fiscal matters, as in all economic issues, the problem is normally one of "how much."

A. LIMITS TO INFLATIONARY FINANCE AND EXCHANGE CONTROL

Monetary policy is usually discussed under the double heading of (1) mobilizing domestic resources and (2) stabilizing an economy that depends to a very large extent on foreign trade and that has, at the same time, a substantial amount of non-monetary production. It is commonly assumed that domestic monetary circulation depends primarily on foreign trade. The stabilization aspects of monetary policies then are naturally linked, on the one hand, with stabilizing foreign-exchange proceeds and export prices and, on the other hand, with widening the scope of the domestic money economy so as to allow compensatory domestic action. The stabilization and mobilization aims of monetary and fiscal policy join at that point.

It is questionable to what extent foreign trade does in fact determine monetary circulation and money income within an economy. The facts do not bear out a very close relation, and Ida Greaves' study of the question indicates why not too close a relation should be expected.[2] Moreover, where Marketing Boards are interposed between the foreign-exchange earnings and the

2. The interested reader is referred to Ida Greaves, *Colonial Monetary Conditions,* Colonial Research Studies, no. 10 (London: Colonial Office, 1953); and the already cited study by Newlyn and Rowan, *Money and Banking.* The two studies disagree violently about some effects of Currency Boards and the accumulation of sterling balances in London by West African territories, but these disagreements are of no concern in the present context. Alasdair I. MacBean, in his forthcoming *Export Instability and Economic Development,* to be published at London by Allen & Unwin and at Cambridge, Mass., by Harvard University Press, concludes that there is very little connection between the growth of economies and the instability of their export earnings.

domestic income paid out to farmers, the direct link is cut in any case.

The problems inherent in making monetary and fiscal policies serve the purposes of development are most clearly brought out when it is considered how they can be made more effective. Deficit financing in one form or another plays a positive role in both the Schumpeterian and the Keynesian system. Many other writers have of course treated money in a cyclical context, from R. G. Hawtrey's ancient discussion of the business cycle as a monetary phenomenon to the discussion of neutral money. But the views of writers other than Joseph Schumpeter and John Maynard Keynes are of only limited interest in the present context.

In the Schumpeterian system inflationary credit creation is an essential part of financing investments of the growth-inducing kind—that is, those that are new, those that disrupt the equilibrium of the economy and set it going on a path to a higher equilibrium level. The ideas contained in the Schumpeterian theory are obviously attractive to economists concerned with the development of underdeveloped areas even though Schumpeter meant them to apply primarily to growth in developed areas.

A brief analysis of the process of forced savings, however, indicates the difficulties of applying the ideas to underdeveloped countries. In the Schumpeterian case, entrepreneurs with new ideas go to banks for credit because there are no other ways of breaking into a self-contained circular flow. As they spend the money, wages will rise as entrepreneurs bid workers (and other factors whose prices also will rise) away from existing industries; consumer goods prices will rise as their supply falls—workers having moved to the production of new goods, which are typically investment goods—and as monetary demand rises. Thus consumers are forced to consume less than anticipated.

The essential mechanism of forced savings is a shift of resources from whatever they were doing before the new production. It is precisely this essential condition for the mobilization of resources by inflation that is lacking in underdeveloped countries. To be effective, inflationary finance requires that factors of production be internally mobile among different types of production. This is not the same as stating that the elasticity of supply of individual goods must be high, since this elasticity also depends upon the degree of employment. The internal flexibility needed is largely technological. Farm laborers cannot often be shifted easily to, say, the generation of electricity.

But even this example does not yet do full justice to the difficulty. It is possible, after all, to train unskilled workers into semiskilled ones and to import—at a price—skilled and managerial labor. Germany and Switzerland absorb hundreds of thousands of foreign workers into their booming economies. Many of them have no previous skills; yet they are converted rapidly into a skilled labor force. Both Germany and Switzerland illustrate, however, what is necessary for success. Both confront the immigrants with an institutional framework in which they are quickly forced to behave in a "modern" and productive way. Both are comparatively rich in capital and hence can afford the resources necessary for training large numbers. Both have the supervisory personnel required. In short, both are highly advanced economies.

In a modern economy, the internal bottlenecks of manufacturing are minor and can be broken quickly. Developed countries have machinery and machine-tool industries. Even where important industries are lacking, the necessary manpower exists to create them rapidly. Thus the complementary factors necessary for employment and capital formation can be quickly produced. The absence of a flexible industrial structure capable of turning out all sorts of goods and capable of quick shifts in its output mix is the real limitation to the mobilization of resources by inflationary means.

In an African context, extensive deficit financing would primarily raise domestic prices and wages. Some of these increases would spill over into the domestic monetary sector and might possibly enlarge it by making it, at least temporarily, more attractive than subsistence production. But most of the increases inevitably would spill over into imports.

If the increased import demand can be met from foreign-exchange reserves, imports will rise, and domestic prices will not rise much. But what has then happened is simply a drawing down of foreign assets, and this is economically justifiable only if it results in a permanent rise in employment and if the foreign resources are profitably employed so as to raise income permanently. Otherwise the rise in spending cannot be self-sustaining.

If the increased import demand cannot be met out of previously accumulated foreign assets or from new capital imports, prices will rise. If the necessary import restriction is brought about by increasing import duties, at least government revenues will increase and the import duties will act as a "stabilizer." If, however, imports are restricted by physical controls, imports will not be forthcoming either, but private profits will have been substituted for public revenues—even if everything goes reasonably well otherwise.

Other consequences will be downright harmful. If imports do not become available, neither do real resources. Hence the complementary factors necessary to employ additional people do not become available either. Consequently the only results are inflation and balance-of-payments troubles, with no benefits to resource mobilization and employment. Worse still, to the extent that wages rise, the cost of investment will rise further. This in turn means that the marginal efficiency of capital—the expected profitability of investment—is bound to fall as the result of inflation. It is no accident that in all underdeveloped countries, which, in any case, have strong preferences for land and buildings, such investments become even more desirable with rapid inflation.

Some may object that the case against inflation has been overdrawn. Undoubtedly the composition of imports can be affected so that complementary goods necessary for investment and to create employment can come in freely while consumer goods are kept out. The point is well taken. Yet, the quicker the "unnecessary" imports are eliminated, the less leeway remains for future action, and in any case it is not quite clear what the change in the structure of imports has to do with inflation. Such a change in the structure of imports may become necessary if a country wants to develop, but if it does become necessary this is independent of whether resources are mobilized by inflationary or by non-inflationary means.

The case against inflation as a method of resource mobilization thus rests basically upon the insufficient internal flexibility of underdeveloped economies and upon their dependence on resources and technology from outside. Obviously monetary measures can be important in mobilizing resources. They must be used with caution, however, for they are limited by the inflexibility of the economy, and the development of a money and capital market must be seen as part of developing the internal flexibility required.

The Keynesian case can be viewed as a variant of the Schumpeterian case. The internal flexibility necessary for the effectiveness of inflationary policies arises in the Keynesian case from the fact that unemployment of all resources is assumed. The problem of complementary factors theoretically does not exist. Yet in reality bottlenecks quickly arise; imported machinery is needed; there are no excess capacities in the few investment goods that are being manufactured, such as cement. In short, the conditions under which the Keynesian approach in its naive form would be useful are not given. Yet it is the naive form that is invariably met with.

The lack of internal flexibility of the economy not only makes an inflationary policy virtually useless but defines the basic limits against which monetary and fiscal policies have to struggle.

Initially, there is very little that monetary policy can do. Among the inflexibilities of the economy, however, are many that immobilize funds, and the creation of money and capital-market instruments can substantially ease this problem. Basically, the problem becomes one of increasing the internal mobility of factors and the internal adaptability of the economy by any means open to the Central Bank and the Ministry of Finance.

It may be well to safeguard against misunderstandings about the remarks just made. I do not suggest that without basic industries no country can achieve the necessary economic structure upon which economic policies can play effectively, or that a country should strive to build up as full a complement of industries as is physically possible. Some such notion undoubtedly underlies the desire of many countries to have a steel industry, which is not only prestigious but is seen as the key to freedom of action. And the same notion may be a reason—not the only one, to be sure—for the Russian insistence upon the priority given to heavy industry. But, as argued before, international integration makes it obviously unnecessary to have a full complement of industries, indeed makes it foolish, and may even retard growth and make economies less adaptable, if the scale of industries becomes too small for the market. The degree of specialization does, after all, depend upon the size of the markets.[3]

Flexibility, though largely a technological problem, has also a considerable economic component. It is often possible to break technological rigidities only at excessive economic cost. The solution of the real problem quickly requires the consideration of the conditions of economic competitiveness. It depends on the ability of businessmen to grasp opportunities quickly, to shift labor quickly, to learn quickly how to produce and market new goods. It also requires a banking system that can move funds

3. This appears to have led to the witticism in Hungary that "socialism in one country" was all right but that it was rather difficult to achieve in one city.

quickly from location to location and between industries. It requires, in short, a well-organized and well-developed economy with educated, knowledgeable people and a network of economic interrelationships. The creation of such a network is precisely the task of economic development.

The major long-run solution to this problem lies clearly in education and capital accumulation. But this end cannot be achieved if the economy develops increasingly on noncompetitive lines. For these reasons stress has to be laid, not indeed on fiscal and monetary orthodoxy, but upon policies that will force businessmen to behave competitively and efficiently. Inflation is a sign of trying to use more resources than are available. If used deliberately as a method of shifting resources from consumption to investment, it is likely to be unsuccessful in underdeveloped countries and, worse yet, to make it more difficult for them to achieve the necessary flexibility, insofar as it misdirects savings and teaches businessmen the virtue of being noncompetitive.

For the same reasons exchange control and physical import restrictions are likely to be catastrophic and must be used exceedingly sparingly and only as a last resort. Obviously, a country must continuously watch its balance of payments. There are perfectly good reasons for changing the composition of imports away from luxury goods to investment goods. It can be convincingly argued, however, that all the legitimate aims of balance-of-payments policies can be achieved much more easily by other and better means and that quantitative import controls and exchange control have side effects which undo the effects on the composition of imports.

Exchange control like inflation is a sign of failure. The failure may be imposed from the outside: a war, a sudden catastrophic worsening of the terms of trade. Or it may be the consequence of policies that are within the control of the country. In either case both inflation and exchange control are means of restricting real demand to a feasible level. Advocates of exchange control argue either as if it could somehow increase the available resources to the economy; or as if it were the only means to keep out "luxuries"; or as if it were the only or the best means to insulate domestic policies from foreign influences; or as if it were costless.

Now, clearly, any feeling that exchange control can somehow increase the amount of resources available to an economy must logically depend upon the proposition that a country can influence its terms of trade by its own action and that the elasticities are right. In the context of a developed country it may be sufficient that the terms of trade improve. Even if as a result of improved terms of trade total imports and exports fall, the internal flexibility of the advanced economy ensures that, since *relatively* less resources are needed for exports to buy the imports than before, the fall in imports will be compensated by an even greater fall in exports and thus by an increase in domestically available resources.

Unfortunately, in the case of an underdeveloped country, imports are essential complementary goods. An improvement in the terms of trade—even if a country could achieve it by its own action, which, of course, is hardly plausible for a country such as Nigeria or even India with its much more advanced status— will do the country no good unless the demand for its exports is inelastic. Simply importing *relatively* more compared to exports will *reduce* available resources, precisely because the resources are hard to shift internally. To the extent to which they can be shifted, they will increase consumption, not investment, as will be argued presently. If changed terms of trade are to do a developing country any good, it is necessary that the volume of imports increase absolutely as the result of the change, for imports are essentially complementary to the employment of domestic factors, and exports frequently have no alternative domestic uses.

Although the elasticity of demand for the export products of underdeveloped countries is said to be less than unity, the countries cannot, acting in isolation, affect their own trading conditions. In "Nigerian" circumstances, the controls will, however, tend to minimize the available resources. (I am using "Nigerian" as a generic term to refer to all countries in a similar position.)

How much can be imported depends on the availability of foreign exchange. This in turn depends upon export earnings, capital imports, and previously accumulated foreign assets. Previously accumulated assets are a stock that is available only once. In the present context, the flows rather than the stocks are of primary interest. All countries with development plans expect capital imports. They hope, of course, for a large proportion of gifts and soft loans which do not raise unpleasant problems of repayment and balance-of-payment adjustment.

Conventional loans, however, do raise problems. When conventional loans are expected, exchange control must necessarily be shot through with exceptions. Obviously, the repatriation of profits and capital must be permitted on principle, and any restrictions on their repatriation must meet the wishes of the potential investors if the capital imports are to materialize in the first place. If repatriation on mutually agreeable conditions is not permitted, capital will not flow in, or, if some does, risk premiums will raise its cost, and other capital cost too.

In discussing exchange control from a planning standpoint— that is, from the standpoint of an actual situation in which specific decisions have to be made, rather than from a purely theoretical standpoint which might allow one to neglect the probable side effects of exchange control—one cannot escape the possibility of administrative inefficiency. Administering exchange control is a negative task for which it seems a pity to use extremely scarce administrative talent. Moreover, it is all too easy to avoid exchange controls, and the temptations of corruption are enormous. No mere economist can hope to match the ingenuity of lawyers and businessmen. In most underdeveloped countries, exchange control is bound to degenerate into a device to organize capital flight for the powerful and the rich.

On paper, exchange control has the advantage of being selective. But this advantage can be had also by tariffs and taxes. Using a direct administrative measure when an indirect will do puts additional strains on the civil servant and subjects him to almost unbearable political pressures.

But matters are actually much worse. Exchange control is almost certain to cause the composition of capital imports to shift in undesirable directions, and therefore exchange control is most unlikely to achieve its purposes. The favorite textbook case of exchange control assumes, of course, that it will eliminate undesirable luxury imports. But, in reality, luxury imports are not likely to be very significant and are much better eliminated by tariffs together with domestic excise taxes. In addition, the side effects of exchange control are really what must make the planner determined to avoid it if he can.

One just has to visualize a concrete case to see what side effects of exchange controls are likely to arise. A particular project requires machinery imports. Because of exchange restrictions, the machinery cannot automatically be purchased in the cheapest market. If suppliers are asked to put up some equity or other financing, respectable firms will quickly decline and less respectable ones increasingly come in. The price of machinery will increase by a substantial risk premium. Any equity acquired will be at best a part of the profits to be made on the sale. Since supplier firms work with substantial margins of gross profit, say 20 to 30 percent—a figure that invariably comes as a shock to people who feel that already 6 percent is high—these firms can acquire a substantial equity without risk and without making available any real resources. Even governments are not beyond this kind of exploitation, as the venomous debates in the United Nations at the time of the Soviet-Yugoslav break indicate.

Thus exchange control: (1) is likely to mean that capital imports will come from less desirable suppliers; (2) will almost certainly require the importing country to devote more of its resources to essential imports than need be the case; (3) is likely to reduce the volume of foreign capital so urgently needed; (4) will almost certainly burden future balances of payments with unnecessarily high debt repayments. Whatever can be said for exchange control when these side effects can be legitimately neglected, nothing speaks for it when the controls are yet unnecessary, when alternative methods of control without these undesirable side effects are available, and when it is still possible to plan for the avoidance of emergencies in which exchange control becomes inevitable.

Nigeria has no active exchange control—only standby legislation for emergency use—but examples elsewhere are embarrassingly easy to find.[4]

Once a country has maneuvered itself into a situation in which exchange control becomes inevitable—or once exchange restrictions become necessary for reasons beyond the country's power to avoid—controls must, of course, be used. But one should be clear about the very high cost and essential inefficiency of the system. There are cases in which direct controls are both legitimate and feasible; the total prohibition of transfer of monies from Nigeria to England for football pools is an instance. So would be the total prohibition of the imports of certain goods, say trucks

---

4. Excess capacities in Pakistan throughout industry are said to average 50 percent because of lack of raw-material imports and spare parts. It is easy to say that this is a sign of faulty planning. So it is. Nevertheless, all administrative pressures are in the direction of permitting imports of machinery and not of materials and spare parts. In New Delhi, a major power failure in 1962 resulting from breakdown of a generator could not be made good without hardship, because the emergency equipment that had burned out several months before had not been repaired, exchange authorities having refused to give top priority to the necessary imports. One can hardly blame the administrators for such decisions, since circumstances work against them. One can, however, blame theorists who refuse to see the economic consequences of non-economic aspects of an administrative limitation of imports.

of more than five-ton capacity, which chew up roads and rapidly raise the cost of building adequate roads beyond the financial powers of a country. But this is a very different matter from raising domestic money incomes and then attempting to deal with the consequences by direct controls.

Nor does exchange control fare much better as a device for shifting the uses of income from consumption to investment. Importers lucky enough to get allocations will make windfall profits which may or may not be taxed away. There is no guarantee whatsoever that the profits will be saved and invested. They are as likely to lead to conspicuous consumption or, when exchange control can be evaded, to capital exports. The production of consumers' goods may be stimulated if it becomes more profitable as the result of reduced imports. This may or may not be a good thing, but it does not necessarily increase investment; moreover it could be achieved by a tariff.

Exchange control will make incipient industrialization more difficult by isolating the price structure of the economy from that of the rest of the world. It will simultaneously raise the cost of production for the economy (though not necessarily for individual producers) and it will induce producers to turn increasingly to the domestic market rather than to exports. It will thus make any except traditional raw material exports increasingly difficult and may decrease even those. This will in turn more and more preclude the imports of goods needed for development. It will therefore make the aims of development—rising production and increased productivity—increasingly difficult to achieve.

The conclusion seems inevitable that whatever can be said for exchange control in some situations, it is likely to be self-defeating in circumstances in which an economy lacks internal flexibility and administrative capacity and depends on imports of capital goods and intermediate goods. Increasing balance-of-payments deficits as well as inefficiency, corruption, and poverty will be made chronic by exchange control. All plan priorities quickly will become distorted, and development will at least be slowed below what it could be, and might be halted or even reversed. The political implications need not be stressed here but they, too, are serious. Examples abound.

In circumstances where inflation and exchange control do not yet exist, the aim of planning and of monetary and fiscal policies must be to mobilize resources to the maximum possible without crossing the fine line beyond which there will be a self-defeating reaction. This suggests that the best fiscal policies and monetary institutions are those that will increasingly produce the desired outlets for local funds, make them available for local businesses, and allow, through the development of a local capital market, increasing domestic control over the economy.

To create an increasingly productive economy is the main thing. The development of financial institutions has an obvious high priority.[5] But the best bond market will not work without a productive economy. It is hardly sufficient to issue treasury bills or government bonds if the interest on them cannot be paid out of increased taxable capacity. If it must be paid out of increased taxation without an increased tax base, the creation of a "capital market" is of dubious value. Nor will it do to create development corporations to issue private stocks and bonds if there are no real outlets for these securities at home and if there is no real prospect of income from them. What has been said earlier about investment criteria, economic profits, and optimum size of a plan is therefore of crucial importance also in the context of monetary and fiscal policies.

5. Professor Torsten Gårdlund has, however, pointed out to me in a letter that the importance of financial institutions can be exaggerated: "I made, years ago, a study of the financial records of 27 large Swedish industrial firms, going back to about 1850 . . . For the first thirty or forty years, industrial take off went on very nicely with a financial structure almost altogether lacking commercial bank credits and bonds . . . So during the *Swedish* take off financial institutional form did not matter very much."

B. THE DEVELOPMENT OF A MONEY AND CAPITAL MARKET

The Problems

Under advanced economic conditions we have become used to thinking of the monetary system as consisting of a number of institutions which form a spectrum from the issuance of cash to the issuance of various types of credit to equity and long-term indebtedness; from gold to central bank money. We think of money, a money market, and a capital market as a continuum. We may think in terms of a closed economy in which there is no limit on the control which the various institutions—commercial banks, central banks, treasuries and so forth—in combination can exercise. Or, if we postulate that we deal with one economy among many, we tend to think of the balance of payments as the only objective limit on what the set of institutions can do. Thus we take it for granted that the "real" economy will react to the stimuli or constraints emanating from the "money" side, and we have every reason to do so.

Even in advanced countries, the money and capital markets are far from perfect. Banking funds in the United States have had near-perfect mobility among locations for a long time, but the mobility of mortgage funds, for example, is of much more recent date. In Europe, the markets for different types of funds are not as closely interwoven as in the United States; and the United States, unlike Europe, has legislation that prohibits the same institution from providing commercial banking and long-term investment funds.

In underdeveloped countries it cannot be assumed that the "real" economy will react to stimuli and restraints as it does in developed countries. To take over institutions from developed and dump them into underdeveloped countries without the awareness that one has to worry about the relation of the institution to the "real" economy will therefore not necessarily achieve the aims that one has set for oneself. In addition, in many underdeveloped countries, particularly but not only those with a colonial past, such institutions as have developed have tended to be branches of banks and other businesses in the metropolitan country. The monetary policies applied to the underdeveloped territories, whether independent or not, have therefore tended to emanate from, and to be determined by the needs of, the metropolitan country. Therefore it becomes the aim of monetary policy both to develop the "real" economy and to give increasing weight to the needs of the domestic rather than the foreign economy.

Even the issuing of money and the increasing monetization of an economy which has large amounts of nonmonetary production, and which even physically is but a loose network of interrelationships, must be related to the "real" economy. Everyone knows that money transactions are more efficient than barter. But introducing money does no good if there are no potential transactions for money to bring about.

The issue of money is but the first step in achieving control over the domestic economy. The development of the monetary system, including commercial banks and a central bank, is intended to provide the policy instruments for the development of a more flexible "real" economy, to give increasing cohesion to an economy, and to permit the execution of policies that will bear a close relation to the needs of this economy.

Laws to create banking institutions are easy to pass and institutions are easily set up. What these institutions can *do* and *should* do is more difficult to determine and depends on the situation that exists where they are set up. Institutions will remain largely window dressing unless they can be made tools of raising resources, and of improving the productivity of the economy and the allocation of investments.

Nigeria's financial institutions are comparatively recent, and they illustrate the problems and possible solutions relevant also to other parts of the world. The first important injection of modern money started with the importation of British shillings by expatriate banks in the nineteenth century to meet the needs of export trade. When the West African Currency Board was set up, it simply issued West African money against a deposit of sterling in London. Though the issuing of money was thus linked with foreign trade, it was a function of the balance of payments, including capital movements, rather than merchandise exports. Thus it cannot be argued that the availability of funds in Nigeria depends upon exports, much less upon an export surplus. Unquestionably, however, until the establishment of the Central Bank, the control of money was largely dependent upon forces centered in London.

Banking, too, has in the past been dependent essentially upon Great Britain. Until the early nineteen-thirties, the only banks were expatriate banks interested primarily in financing trade. This is not meant as a criticism: there was not much else to finance for a long time, and the banks undoubtedly performed a useful service. The flow of funds to and from Nigeria was determined basically from London and depended upon both trade and the cost of transfer. This meant, however, that the banks provided needed capital: funds flowed into Nigeria for a purpose and were sent back to London when not needed.

The oldest indigenous bank that still exists is the National Bank of Nigeria, which was established in Lagos in February 1933 with a nominal capital of £10,000.[6] The other important Nigerian bank still in existence is the African Continental Bank, which was founded in 1948. Both are occasionally referred to as "political" banks, the former being associated with the Action Group of the Western Region, the latter with the National

6. Newlyn and Rowan, *Money and Banking,* p. 99. In the *Report of the Coker Commission of Inquiry into the Affairs of Certain Statutory Corporations in Western Nigeria* (Lagos: Federal Ministry of Information, 1962), II, 1-18, is a detailed discussion of the National Bank of Nigeria, the Agbonmagbe Bank, and the Merchants' Bank. See also Charles V. Brown, *Government and Banking in Western Nigeria: A Case Study in Economic Policy,* Nigerian Social and Economic Studies, no. 5 (Ibadan: Oxford University Press, 1964).

Council of Nigerian Citizens. But there were (and are) other Nigerian banks among the licensed banks, though their importance was relatively small. Thus bank credit has been known for some time in Nigeria, in addition to coin, though most of it originated abroad when the system was established.

In Nigeria, as in other countries with a Marketing Board system, the demand for domestic credit and cash is not directly linked to the value of exports but is related to the *domestic cost* of exports. This includes the producer price set by the Marketing Boards; these boards in this context should be seen not merely as a device to stabilize producer incomes by manipulating the local price but also as a tax device and a part of the monetary system.

The problem of how to make the supply of currency and deposits dependent as much as possible on Nigerian rather than English conditions becomes one of providing outlets for funds which might have gone to London—of reducing the flows back and forth while at the same time raising the supply of funds in the Nigerian economy. Repatriation of Nigerian funds, a widening of choices available to Nigerian investors, and a widening of the circle of credit takers are all parts of the problem.

Centralization of Sterling Assets

Sterling and other assets held abroad by some Nigerians have been centralized in the hands of the Central Bank of Nigeria, and this centralization serves a fourfold purpose. It allows the Central Bank to gauge its domestic policies by the state of the balance of payments, including the reserves. It also frees reserves for imports of goods for development. It creates a market for domestic government paper. And it allows a tighter control over the spending of various former holders of foreign assets.

The last point deserves, perhaps, a few more words. In most countries, the foreign-exchange assets of an official and semi-official nature are concentrated in the central bank or a similar institution (such as an exchange equilization account). But, unless there is strict exchange control, private banks and businesses may hold funds abroad on their own account. Nigerian enterprises have this freedom.

In most underdeveloped countries, however, not only is there an actual or potential balance-of-payments problem, but government through its various agencies plays a substantial, if not a dominant, role in investment decisions. Over-all control over spending can be immeasurably eased if the control over assets held abroad can be centralized.

In Nigeria the method of centralization consists simply of requiring certain Nigerian holders of assets abroad to hand them to the Central Bank which exchanges them against Nigerian bonds. If the previous owners wish to spend *either* at home or abroad, they must acquire the necessary cash by selling their bonds to the public or to the banks. For the public to buy bonds means savings. For banks to buy them may or may not be inflationary, but in either case the Central Bank gains considerable control. Thus the decision made at the time of the Plan to centralize reserves was not merely an attempt to free sterling assets for development. It was also intended to build a local capital market and get increasing control over domestic spending as well and thus to help mobilize additional domestic resources.

Treasury Bills

Historically, the money and capital market in most countries arose with the issuance of various types of government paper. In British West African colonial territories it appears that the traditional function of short-term paper was, following English ideas of propriety, the financing of government expenditures in anticipation of tax revenues. The Ministry of Finance of the Federation of Nigeria started to issue treasury bills in April 1960, half a year before independence but several years after self-government. The total amount was originally limited to 10 percent of anticipated government revenues, and the first issue was £4 million worth of 91-day bills, at 4 5/8 percent. By the end of 1960, £9 million worth of 91-day treasury bills was outstanding, which approximately corresponded to the 10 percent limit initially imposed.

During 1961 the limit of treasury-bill issues was extended to 20 percent of the anticipated government revenues, and during 1962 it was further extended to 40 percent, which allowed the issue of up to roughly £50 million worth of short-term paper. At the same time, the frequency of issuing the bills was increased from monthly during 1960 to fortnightly in 1962 and weekly in 1963. During 1962 the bill market was supplemented by a call-money market.

The gradual establishment of a successful bill market over three years not only reduced sharply the seasonal movement of surplus funds out of and into Nigeria but allowed the Central Bank to exercise considerable control over bank liquidity. By the end of 1962, £24 million of treasury bills had been issued in all. The issue rate (which is linked to the London rate) was 4 percent, and the rediscount rate was 4½ percent. As of 1964, the maximum amount of treasury bills that had been held by the Central Bank was £15,452,000 (in November 1963), but its normal holdings fluctuated between £3 million and £5 million.[7]

The Fiduciary Issue of Money and the Supply of Money

The centralization of official sterling reserves and the creation of a domestic market for short-term paper, successfully started with the establishment of a Treasury Bill market, raises the question of how to establish a long-term capital market and—on the other end of the scale—the question of fiduciary issue of the currency. Under the Currency Board system, the Nigerian pound was simply another name for the English pound. To state that it

7. Central Bank of Nigeria, *Economic and Financial Review*, December 1964, p. 20.

was backed 100 percent by sterling is formally correct but makes the issuance of Nigerian pounds sound more complicated than it was. Already under the Currency Board system there was a substantial amount of bank money in circulation. In 1951, the year before the Banking Ordinance of 1952 put some control on banks, net currency in circulation (currency held outside banks) was £36,579,000, and demand, time, and savings deposits were £22,422,000.[8] Demand deposits alone were £18,430,000. Although they are the only kind of deposit customarily included in the money supply—the annual report of the Central Bank conforms to this practice—there is evidence that in Nigeria the common man considers time and savings deposits to be equivalent to cash, as well as deposits in the Post Office Savings Bank, which amounted to another £3,239,000.[9]

By the first quarter of 1959, when the Central Bank was established, net currency in circulation had increased to £53,534,000, and total bank deposits to £65,294,000, of which £40,168,000 were demand deposits. Deposits accumulated in the Post Office Savings Bank had increased only to £3,615,000, and the rate of increase had been falling since 1956 because customers apparently had shifted their funds to the commercial banks where they were more easily available as cash, even when put in a time-deposit account. Demand deposits, which in 1951 had been only half as big as net currency in circulation, in 1959 were about three fourths. By the end of 1963, total bank deposits had risen to £95,908,000, of which demand deposits were £49,853,000, and net currency in circulation amounted to £84,492,000.[10]

These figures reflect in part the Nigerianization of the money issue and the development of a local credit market. The ex-

8. Figures for net currency in circulation refer to March 31, 1951; those for total deposits to December 31. Nigeria, *Annual Abstract of Statistics, 1960* (Lagos: Federal Government Printer), pp. 17, 12.

9. *Ibid.*, p. 15. Refers to March 31, 1951.

10. Central Bank, *Economic and Financial Review*, December 1964, pp. 29, 25.

patriate banks which originally held most of the deposits not only were branches of English banks but had sterling assets of their own. After the establishment of the Central Bank, banking legislation was changed in 1962 to give the Central Bank more control over the domestic money supply. Central banking, however, raised in a new form the question of foreign-exchange reserves. Actually two separate questions were involved. What should be the amount of fiduciary money? What should be the minimum average level of foreign and gold reserves to be aimed at?

When the Central Bank was established in 1959 the Minister of Finance answered the first question by stressing that a certain amount of money had to be in circulation at all times, but that regard for establishing confidence in the new Nigerian pound required that the permissible level of money not backed by foreign-exchange assets and gold be increased only gradually. The original Central Bank legislation of 1959 provided a minimum cover of 40 percent in sterling. In 1962, the law was amended to include other currencies and gold besides sterling. The definition of the Nigerian pound was changed from sterling to gold, and thus a change in the par value became possible independently of any action the British government might take. The foreign-exchange and gold backing of the currency was expected to fall gradually to the legal minimum of 40 percent.

The question of what kind of assets the Central Bank should hold for the other 60 percent is related to the problem of inflation, which in turn depends upon the domestic real resources that can be mobilized and upon the development of additional means of Central Bank action to mobilize and control resources. The level of desirable foreign-exchange reserves hinges on the amounts needed to guarantee a smooth flow of imports at all times for development purposes.

The required amount of international resources is rationally linked to the amount of imports needed and to the expected flow of exports, i.e., the seasonal pattern as well as the long-term prospects of foreign-exchange proceeds. If there is no doubt about convertibility, short-term capital flows can be counted upon to smooth out the seasonal demands for imports. The decision finally made was to maintain minimum foreign-exchange reserves at a level equal to at least four months' value of imports. This of course is an arbitrary compromise between various figures, but three months seemed the minimum needed, and four months seemed to provide an adequate safety margin. Imports during 1962 were about £200 million; so this meant an official reserve of about £70 million, almost 90 percent of the *currency* in circulation and well below the actual reserves of more than £87 million.[11]

In the usual textbook discussion, which it is perhaps not entirely fair to cite, international reserves are closely linked to the domestic money supply. It might seem that, with an anticipated money supply of, say, £100 million, the sterling and other foreign-exchange reserves could be drawn down to £40 million, thus setting free substantial additional sterling assets for the financing of the Development Plan. But, as has been argued before, *one* major problem confronting the planners was that domestic savings had not increased enough. If the foreign reserves were drawn down too quickly, before the economy had grown, and particularly if they substituted for rather than supplemented an effort to increase the domestic mobilization of resources, the economy would be built up to a level where it depended upon the continuance of a level of capital imports which could not then be maintained.

It would, therefore, be dangerous to forget that the present Plan is presumably the first of a series and that indeed the de-

11. Imports during 1963 are provisionally given as £207.6 million. Total overseas assets of "banking and official" and "semiofficial" institutions in September 1964 were £80.4 million. *Ibid.*, pp. 45-46; and Nigeria, *Digest of Statistics* (Lagos: Federal Office of Statistics), July 1964, pp. 16, 19.

velopment of any economy, whether planned or not, is a continuing process. Obviously reserves could be drawn down in the short run. But this would be a once-and-for-all affair, justifiable only if the export capacity of the nation increased or if there was evidence that future import requirements would decrease. This was certainly not the case in Nigeria, nor is it likely to be the case elsewhere in the underdeveloped world. There was one more reason why the planning had to proceed so as to raise taxable capacity and export capacity, and why it was essential to stress profitability. Unless this were done, Nigeria would end the present Plan at best at a higher level of income but with insufficient resources and, worse, with insufficient capacity to mobilize further resources for the next Plan.

Although the discussion has been put in terms of Nigeria the problem is general, and more examples from the underdeveloped world can be found. Latin American countries have depleted their reserves and have depended on aid to make up for lack of domestic savings. Tunisia has used up its reserves without raising taxable capacity and domestic savings adequately through the uses to which the reserves were put. In most cases, capital imports are needed not only for the future enlargement of capacities but to keep the existing capacities in production.

In advanced economies the problem of monetary and fiscal policy presents itself as one of achieving domestic autonomy without having to worry about the balance of payments. In the simplest textbook case, a fall in reserves leads to deflationary policies which will raise exports, lower imports, cause some unemployment (as an unwanted by-product), and in the process lead to an adjustment of the economy. When the cause of the trouble has been a depression abroad, the problem is then seen as one of insulating the economy from the effects of other countries' policies. The shocks from abroad have, on the whole, been fairly small in the postwar world. With full employment policies everywhere and with advanced flexible economies, it should therefore be possible to achieve the adjustments with modest reserves which are reasonably linked to the speed with which adjustments can take place and to the amount of foreign transactions that must be financed.

In underdeveloped countries domestic flexibility must first be established. The creation of a money and capital market is part of the process. The manner in which investments take place is important in completing it. The faster exports and *economic* import substitution can be built up, the faster it is possible to raise domestic savings and the domestic financing of transactions— and the more long-term government bonds the central bank can afford to hold permanently. By absorbing such bonds, it will have mobilized domestic resources permanently and without danger of balance-of-payments repercussions. If the holding of long-term government paper by the central bank is *not* linked to domestic resource mobilization and to the growth of the economy, at best a once-and-for-all boom will have been achieved, soon to come to a halt, and possibly deflation will have to be imposed later. Exchange depreciation will of course reduce the need for domestic deflation, but it will not make domestic spending less dependent on import possibilities. Exchange depreciation cannot bring back reserves that have been unwisely spent.

Thus the development of the local capital market becomes the major aim of monetary policy, in order to provide increasing outlets for domestic funds and increasingly shift the financing of domestic investment to domestic sources—two sides of the same coin. This in itself will allow increasing Central Bank control over domestic circulation and the balance of payments.

Control of the Banking System

The short-term and medium-term market is closely related to the control of the banking system and the local financing of local businesses. This involves the creation of bill finance and rediscounting, and it involves various other measures to give a central bank effective control over commerical banks.

Certain technical aspects of controlling the banks require legislation. In Nigeria, banking operations were restricted to licensed banks in 1958. The 1962 revision of the banking ordinance of 1958 raised the minimum capital requirements of new banks from £12,500 to £250,000 and gave the Central Bank control over expatriate banks by requiring them "to maintain funds in Nigeria in amounts no less than the prescribed minimum capital." The 1962 legislation also required the "commercial banks to link their interest charges to the Central Bank's minimum rediscount rate."[12] Further provisions are being sought to enable the Central Bank to control the amount and cost of credit, which is "undeniably high . . . in Nigeria—a cost which is, quite frankly, seriously influenced by the very high incidence of frauds and bad debts."[13]

Fraud, bad debts, and a high cost for credit are, of course, not characteristic merely of Nigeria. American economic history

12. Central Bank, *Annual Report* for 1962, p. 24. "Banks already in operation, whose capital falls short of the new requirements, are given seven years to comply" (*ibid.*). The Budget Speech of 1964 promised further unspecified amendments "with a view of providing better control and supervision of banks and other related financial institutions"—*Approved Estimates of the Government of the Federal Republic of Nigeria 1964–65* (Lagos: Federal Ministry of Information, 1964), p. 316.

There has been a small relevant literature about the problems discussed. See particularly: H. M. A. Onitiri, "The Central Bank of Nigeria and the Problem of Domestic Monetary Stability," in Nigerian Institute of Social and Economic Research, *Conference Proceedings* (Ibadan, 1958), pp. 80-90; J. O. W. Olakampo, "Monetary Management in Dependent Economies," *Economica* (November 1961), pp. 395-408; C. V. Brown, "The Recent Nigerian Banking Amendments: A Tentative Appraisal," *Nigerian Journal of Economics and Social Studies,* IV (July 1962), 156-164.

13. Budget Speech 1963, p. 41; the reference is to "The Modernization Budget 1963–64," Budget Speech by Chief Festus Sam Okotie-Eboh, Federal Minister of Finance, April 2, 1963 (Lagos: Federal Ministry of Information, 1963). This and the five preceding budget speeches are printed in *The Six Budget Speeches made by the Hon. Minister of Finance Chief Festus Sam Okotie-Eboh during the Period 1958–63* (Lagos: Federal Ministry of Finance).

can give many examples. But the control of banks and the elimination of anything that would interfere with their growth becomes particularly important when the banking habit must be developed and domestic savings are to be raised.

Nigeria, nevertheless, has been better off than most countries. Alone among West African countries, it developed indigenous banks.[14] Ghana, formerly the Gold Coast, would most likely have developed banks had there not been until 1950 an outright prohibition on their incorporation.[15] By 1960 in Nigeria, thirteen banks held licenses, six of which were Nigerian, three British, two American, one French, and one Lebanese. During 1962 four more banks were licensed, two Nigerian, one Indian, and the Arab Bank, whose nationality was not clear. In addition, a Japanese Bank established a representation. During 1963, "no new banks were licensed, but nine branch offices were opened, bringing the total number of offices and branches to 218."[16] The financial growth of the banking system is shown in Table 10.

The Central Bank has been a success in terms of monetizing the economy and internal mobilization of resources. Total assets grew rapidly throughout the period, the drop in 1962 being statistical. Loans and advances rose continuously from about a quarter to over half of total assets, and advances of more than

14. The term "bank" is ambiguous, however, and until the enactment of the Banking Ordinance of 1958, amended in 1962, it covered quite literally a multitude of sins. Newlyn and Rowan, in their *Money and Banking in British Colonial Africa*, pp. 107 ff., discuss this "spate of bank formations" in the early 1950's and give a list of eleven "banks" about which little more was known at the time of their writing than that they called themselves "banks" and were "in an embryonic stage." The fraudulent operation of these "banks," which should of course not be confused with the respectable National or African Continental Banks or the banks now licensed under the Banking Ordinance, was described graphically and amusingly by an all-Nigerian committee under the chairmanship of Chief H. O. Davies. Federal Ministry of Commerce and Industry, *Report of the Advisory Committee on Aids to African Businessmen* (Lagos: Government Printer, 1959), pp. 38-39.

15. Greaves, *Colonial Monetary Conditions*, p. 22.

16. Central Bank, *Annual Report* for 1963, p. 18.

Table 10. *Consolidated assets and liabilities of licensed banks*
in Nigeria, 1952, 1956, 1959–1964
(£ thousand)

| December of | Total assets and liabilities | Cash | Loans and advances[a] | | Investments | |
			Up to 1 year	Over 1 year	In Nigeria	Abroad
1952	36,039	3,856	9,150	—	322	30
1956	67,652	6,810	25,511	—	380	56
1959	100,529	9,121	39,039	1,785	738	579
1960	117,918	9,415[b]	54,635	2,365	2,676	179
1961	147,327	10,998[b]	57,085	2,905	4,300	29
1962	142,616[c]	12,348[b]	77,036		4,972	29
1963	162,582	11,663[b]	89,486		2,313	29
1964	197,991	14,421[b]	122,408		6,960	29

| December of | Capital issued and paid up[d] | Deposits | | | |
		Demand	Time	Savings	Total
1952	197	22,230	3,325	2,289	27,844
1956	2,181	35,352	4,131	6,525	46,008
1959	2,594	40,168	10,846	14,280	65,294
1960	2,966	41,117	8,954	18,441	68,512
1961	10,209	41,658	14,068	21,188	76,914
1962	13,060	45,296	17,420	24,224	86,940
1963	11,363[e]	48,773	18,948	28,187	95,908
1964	11,547	57,831	23,083	34,131	115,045

a. Includes call loans and bills discounted. After July 1962, excludes call money at the Central Bank.

b. "Cash holdings, balances with Central Bank, and beginning in July 1962, call money at the Central Bank" (*Economic and Financial Review*, June 1964, p. 27).

c. "Adjustments in inter-branch accounts of some banks in July reduced the system's total assets by approximately £ 16.4 million" (Central Bank, *Annual Report* for 1962, p. 29).

d. This column applies only to banks with head offices in Nigeria.

e. ". . . As a consequence of an adjustment of the capital accounts of two banks during October, the capital and reserve funds of indigenous commercial banks fell to £ 11.3 million and remained at that level for the rest of the year" (*Annual Report* for 1963, p. 28).

SOURCES: Central Bank, *Annual Report*, 1961, 1962, 1963; Central Bank, *Economic and Financial Review*, June 1964, pp. 26-29, and June 1965, pp. 27-30. Data for back years in *Annual Abstract of Statistics, 1963* (Lagos: Federal Government Printer), p. 38 (tables 26, 27).

one year came into existence. Investments held abroad were repatriated. Total deposits and total capital rose substantially.

For 1962, the Central Bank showed for the first time the amount of treasury bills held by the commercial banks.[17] For the first time also, consolidated figures on the details of loans and advances are being published, and these show the increasing domestic financing of agriculture, manufacturing, and commerce. The figures, given in Table 11, reflect not only the general growth of the economy but "also the gradual withdrawal of the large expatriate firms from retail trade and from the agricultural marketing field as produce buying agents . . . [which] has reduced the volume of self-generated resources which provided the major source of finance in these areas in the past."[18]

Thus the shift from foreign to domestic financing has created outlets for domestic funds. Whether it has increased the total of domestic and foreign short-term funds to the Nigerian economy is, however, not certain. Very likely it has. International transfer of funds from and to West Africa are extremely expensive. The very cost of the transfer must have restricted the flow. But even if there has been merely a substitution of domestic for foreign short-term funds, the shift is, of course, important in creating domestic conditions for expansion.

Although there is no government policy to limit the activities of expatriate business to manufacturing, the Federal Minister of Economic Development suggested in a 1961 speech that most trade and transport should be a Nigerian preserve.[19] As the

17. Central Bank, *Economic and Financial Review*, August 1963, and later issues.

18. "The expansion of manufacturing and construction activity has also led to greater demands for bank credit; in particular, the large expatriate firms, in shifting their operations away from trade toward industry, have over the past two years tended to look to banks in Nigeria for their working capital, rather than to overseas sources." Central Bank, *Annual Report* for 1962, pp. 28, 30.

19. *Ministerial Statement of Nigeria's Economic Planning Policy and Its Relationship with Distributive Trades and Road Transportation Made in the House of Representatives during the Supplementary Budget Session, 22nd November, 1961* (Lagos: Federal Printing Division, 1961).

Table 11. Consolidated loans and advances of commercial banks in Nigeria, by type of borrower, 1959–1964

(£ thousand; calendar years)

	1959	1960	1961	1962	1963	1964
Governments	596	1,276	1,483	737	694	933
Native Administrations	306	1,061	851	—	—	—
Local Authorities	290	215	632	—	—	—
Utilities	—	522	102	178	980	779
Financial Institutions	3,391	2,927	2,432	868	1,324	3,648
Agriculture (direct loans)	9,360	11,281	12,614	18,039	19,672	30,223
Cocoa	2,581	2,658	2,834	4,700	—	—
Groundnuts	3,376	5,210	5,922	8,583	—	—
Palm Produce	824	759	1,144	765	—	—
Other export crops	1,623	2,246	2,284	3,340	—	—
Other agriculture	956	408	430	651	—	—
Mining	409	543	474	526	577	577
Tin	326	419	248	259	—	—
Other	83	124	227	267	—	—
Manufacturing	1,649	2,429	3,296	5,857	8,933	13,131
Textiles, leather, clothing	486	594	672	740	—	—
Wood products and furniture	46	90	125	334	—	—
Detergents, soaps, and oils	666	675	1,008	1,658	—	—
Stone, cement, brick, glass, ceramics, pottery	158	314	601	3,125	—	—
Other	293	756	889	—	—	—
Construction	3,086	3,595	5,541	5,185	6,444	5,740
General commerce (direct loans)	13,554	21,017	19,435	27,736	30,684	33,467
Miscellaneous, incl. call loans	8,481	12,354	14,128	14,811	12,716	18,837
Bills discounted	606	1,271	1,117	3,098	7,444	15,052
Agriculture	n.a.	n.a.	n.a.	n.a.	4,650	12,304
General commerce	n.a.	n.a.	n.a.	n.a.	2,794	2,747
Totals	40,824	57,000	59,990	77,036	89,486	122,407

SOURCES: Central Bank, *Annual Report*, 1960, p. 7; 1961, p. 14; 1962, p. 27; 1963, p. 30; and 1964, p. 35; Central Bank, *Economic and Financial Review*, August 1963, p. 24; December 1964, p. 1; and July 1965, p. 31.   n.a. = not available.

figures in Table 12 indicate, there was actually a substantial out-flow of foreign capital from trading in 1962. But during 1963, foreign capital flowed again into all sectors of the Nigerian economy.

Control of Producer Prices

The figures in Table 11, particularly those on bills discounted, reflect yet another point of policy, foreshadowed in the 1962 budget speech of the Federal Minister of Finance. In advanced countries, the typical traditional method of monetary control centers around discounting operations. In underdeveloped countries, the conditions for an effective monetary policy have to be created.

Since the bulk of the population makes its living off the land, a large part of its money income is derived from export crops. Monetary circulation is, in this case, influenced by the size of the crop and the producer price of the export crop. The majority of the export crops is sold through Marketing Boards. In order to make monetary policy effective, the Marketing Boards, which started as a device to stabilize producer incomes and then were transformed into a tax device for purposes of economic development, now have to undergo yet another metamorphosis and become part of the monetary system.

This transformation of Marketing Board functions started in 1962 with the financing by the Central Bank of up to £13 million of Northern Nigeria Marketing Board crops.[20] In 1963, the financial support was extended to "the produce in the Eastern and Western Regions."[21] The success of the operations

20. Budget Speech 1963, p. 7.
21. Budget Speech 1964, p. 313 (for full citation see my note 12). The Federal Minister of Finance continued: "The invitation to the Eastern Nigeria Marketing Board to join the scheme is still open. The basic arrangement of the scheme is that a marketing board, on the basis of a contract for the sale of its produce, draws a 90-day bill of exchange on the Nigerian Produce Marketing Company Limited. When the company accepts his bill the marketing board then discounts it with a bank or acceptance

*Table 12.   Total foreign investment, net flow of foreign business
capital by type of activity, and total earnings, 1961–1963*
(£ million)

		1961	1962	1963
A.	TOTAL FOREIGN INVESTMENT IN NIGERIA	n.a.	218.1	256.0
	Mining	n.a.	80.5	93.1
	Manufacturing and processing	n.a.	36.7	47.8
	Agriculture, forestry, fishing	n.a.	4.3	4.8
	Transport and communications	n.a.	2.4	2.5
	Trading and services	n.a.	85.7	96.3
	Building and construction	n.a.	7.6	10.7
	Other activities	n.a.	0.9	1.1
B.	NET FLOW OF FOREIGN BUSINESS CAPITAL	+27.3	+17.7	+37.9
	Mining	+6.9	+7.5	+12.5
	Manufacturing and processing	+5.9	+20.5	+11.0
	Agriculture, forestry, fishing	−1.1	−0.2	+0.5
	Transport and communications	+0.3	+0.2	+0.1
	Trading and business services	+14.6	−15.4	+10.5
	Building and construction	+0.7	+4.6	+3.1
	Other activities	—	+0.5	+0.2
C.	EARNINGS OF FOREIGN INVESTMENT			
	Total earnings	7.0	11.5	18.0
	Total retained earnings	2.7	7.9	13.4

Note: The data are company returns for either calendar years or the nearest company fiscal year. Plus mark means net inflow of capital into Nigeria.   n.a. = not available.

SOURCE: Central Bank, *Economic and Financial Review*, July 1965, pp. 8, 10, 11. "There are reasons to expect as much as 25 percent increase in the inflow of private capital in 1964. Important factors underlying this expected increase of private foreign investment include the establishment of the Nigerian Industrial Development Bank, Ltd., in January 1964" (p. 11).

led the Central Bank to consider the rediscounting of import bills, a procedure which can be used not only to influence the quantity of funds but, through the imposition of varying eligibility requirements relating to the nature of imports, also to influence the composition of imports.[22]

The general point involved in this method of establishing bill financing and rediscounting is perhaps worth expanding. In the past, Marketing Boards have determined producer prices primarily on the basis of the expected world market prices and the fiscal needs of the government. The injection of the Central Bank introduces consideration of stabilization of the economy as a whole. By making a crop forecast and influencing producer prices, the Central Bank is in a position to declare to what extent it will rediscount crop financing bills. In this way the Central Bank not only creates outlets for Nigerian funds, but, by standing ready to rediscount Marketing Board paper originally handled by the commercial banks and by fixing the amount of paper it will rediscount for them, acquires an additional effective instrument of control over the banking system. The banking system thereby is induced to seek deposits more actively in order to

house participating in the scheme . . . The bank or acceptance house which has discounted the bill can either hold it until maturity or refinance it at the Central Bank. The support of the Central Bank is essential to the success of the scheme and it is one of the schemes designed to ensure that most of the finance needed to meet the short-term needs of Nigeria's growing industry and commerce are provided locally. At the peak of the current season last December, the Central Bank held nearly £15 million of Marketing Board bills."

22. Budget Speech 1963, p. 9. In 1964, the Federal Minister of Finance pointed out that "the Central Bank has also agreed to offer rediscount facilities within limits to bills of exchange drawn on banks and acceptance houses by reputable licensed buying agents with substantial paid-up capital in respect of produce bought on behalf of marketing boards. During the current season, facilities totaling nearly £2 million were approved under this arrangement. The Central Bank is also prepared to grant rediscount facilities within limits to other bills of exchange drawn in respect of other exports and essential imports strictly defined, provided they meet its other reasonable requirements as to maturity and names." Budget Speech 1964, p. 313.

avoid Central Bank control. This in turn tends to raise the savings ratio—a step urgently needed to finance economic development.

In his budget speech of 1962, the Federal Minister of Finance made these points plainly:

It is one thing to welcome foreign capital for our development, but it is quite another to rely upon such capital to finance our day-to-day trade and commerce. The Central Bank will, therefore, increasingly stand behind the commercial banking system and itself provide the seasonal expansion of credit required by re-discounting bills of exchange held by the commercial banks and particularly bills related to Marketing Board crops . . . This "Nigerianization" of our credit base will enable our economy to expand or contract according to our own needs rather than be forced to accept changes dictated by the needs of some other money market . . .

I am aware that this will necessitate some changes in the techniques and procedures both of the commercial banks and also in the Marketing Boards and other borrowers . . .

There must be effective co-ordination and consultation between the various authorities whose activities have a major bearing upon the supply of money and credit in the economy. Paramount in this field are the Regional Marketing Boards, whose producer price policies have a major and direct bearing upon the supply of money within the economy—indeed their impact upon the overall economy is probably the greatest of all monetary factors operating in Nigeria today. Without wishing to derogate from the ultimate responsibility of the Regional authorities to determine produce prices, it is clearly in the national interest that these prices should be fixed only after consultation with the national monetary authorities and in the light of the overall monetary situation prevailing. A steep increase in producer prices for a major crop in only one Region could, in unfavorable circumstances, add overwhelming weight to inflationary pressures in the economy. The converse is, of course, equally true. I am glad to say that the Regional authorities are sharing increased awareness of this danger, and I trust that they will continue to maintain the closest co-ordination with the Central Bank in this field. I need not perhaps stress that the ability of the Central Bank to provide the short-term credit required by the Marketing Boards, a factor to which I have already referred, will be governed to a large extent by the prevailing pressures in the economy.[23]

The creation of a short-term and medium-term money market was facilitated by the establishment of an acceptance house in 1960, a Lagos Clearing House in 1962, and a Kano Branch of the Central Bank as well as of a Kano Clearing House in 1962. The size of the operations has increased with surprising rapidity. The speed of the development is, of course, linked with the fact that the Nigerian economy had in its export crops a substantial base for maneuver. Providing banks with profitable domestic outlets does increase the possibility of their appealing to ordinary people to put money on deposit. Though at first domestic funds simply take the place of previously imported short-term capital, there can be little doubt that this substitution provides the base for a more durable and increasing mobilization of domestic resources and a gradual shift to the financing of other domestic activities.

An increasing volume of funds at reasonable interest rates is the probable outcome of these activities. Information on rates goes back only to 1961, when First Class Advances were available at 8 percent, as compared to 7 percent in 1964. The most important Produce Advance cost the borrower 7–8 percent in 1964, compared to 8–9 percent before the Central Bank financed Marketing Board paper. The cost of other Advances remained unchanged at 7½–10 percent.[24]

Long-Term Capital

The creation of a domestic long-term capital market has gone hand in hand with the development of a bill market, as it should. The experience of Nigeria and other countries indicates

23. Budget Speech 1962, pp. 7, 11. The full citation is "The Mobilization Budget," Budget Speech by Chief Festus Sam Okotie-Eboh, Federal Minister of Finance (Lagos: Federal Ministry of Information, 1962).

24. Information on "Selected Predominant Interest Rates" is published for the first time in Central Bank, *Economic and Financial Review*, December 1964, p. 32.

that despite their low per-capita income, substantial domestic funds can be mobilized for public and private investments provided the investor can be ensured safety and a reasonable return and a certain degree of liquidity even for long-term investments. These conditions can be provided by an organized market and a Central Bank that stands ready as a buyer of last resort.

How many long-term government bonds can be issued depends, as stated before, on the manner in which taxable capacity rises, which ultimately depends on the composition of the development program. As long as the great bulk of economic activity and the value added are agricultural, the weather and the prices of export crops determined on world markets and outside the control of Nigeria will necessarily play a dominant role. Nevertheless, the point made previously stands. No matter how favorably export proceeds mount up for reasons that have nothing to do with the development program, if the composition of the development program leads to rapidly rising recurrent cost and no growth in taxable capacity, the financing by long-term bonds taken up by the banks or the Central Bank rapidly becomes inflationary, rapidly leads to balance-of-payments trouble, and spells the end of any hope of gaining control over the economy by making it more viable. The interest payments will rapidly become mere redistribution of income which has not grown adequately, and this raises political as well as economic problems. In such circumstances, the creation of a market for government bonds becomes self-defeating.[25]

25. That there is some reason for concern on this point is indicated by the fact that the Central Bank, in the second year of the Plan, helped finance the Plan to the extent of £20 million, out of a total expected financing of £40 million long-term government bonds which the Central Bank was expected to purchase over the whole Plan period. (Budget Speech 1964, p. 313). This undesirable development is the consequence of the distortions in the Plan which in turn are linked to the initially unrealistic size. Since Nigeria is well aware of the problem, there is, of course, every expectation that it will be dealt with successfully.

The nature of the development program will itself determine the inflationary pressures. Aside from its other uses, a market for government bonds as well as private issues is needed if the government wishes to roll over its holdings in successful development projects. As will be argued later, a policy of selling off successful government investments to private investors will in fact help to create a capital market, to mobilize resources, and to increase the savings ratio as well as the absolute size of both the private *and* the public sector.[26]

The point is that the market for long-term capital can be created once the economy is going, and can add substantially to the ease with which domestic resources can be mobilized and increased. Once created, it also can add considerably to the manner in which both the Central Bank and the government can influence the course of the economy, even when investments are mostly private.

When Nigeria became independent on October 1, 1960, the internal Federal Government debt was very small: a £300,000, 3¾ percent Nigeria Registered Government Stock falling due in 1961 and an offer of originally £2 million which carried interest of 5 to 6 percent depending on maturity and which as the result of being substantially oversubscribed was raised to £2,355,000. By March 31, 1961, the total internal funded debt had risen to £12,650,000; the unfunded debt stood at £12,350,000. Table 13 shows the development of the Nigerian public debt.

26. In some parts of the world, "privatizing" public utilities may be the only way in which private funds can be initially mobilized. A case in point may be Malta, an island of very limited resources, with substantial investments abroad. The best way to create domestic outlets for savings may be to sell part of the utilities and use the money thus raised for further development. See W. F. Stolper, Rune Hellberg, and Sten Ove Callander, *Economic Problems of Adaptation and Development in Malta* (New York: United Nations, Commissioner for Technical Assistance, Department of Economic and Social Affairs, 1964). When one of the policy problems is to raise the savings ratio, and when increased taxation is difficult, rolling over government capital may stimulate the desired savings. Not to create outlets for private savings may discourage production and virtually force potential savers into consumption. Egypt may be a case in point.

From the standpoint of developing the market and raising domestic savings, three questions are of major importance: at what rates were the securities issued? who subscribed? who held the issues at a given time? The first and second questions can be easily answered. The third one cannot be answered fully.

Table 13. *Public debt of the Nigerian Federal Government, 1960–1964*
(£ million; March 31 of each year)

Type of debt	1960	1961	1962	1963	1964
Internal loans					
Funded	2.65	12.65	19.35	34.35	54.36
Unfunded	12.84	12.35	11.84	11.78	11.76
Treasury bills (special issue)	2.00	2.00	1.23	0.45	—
External loans					
Funded	16.75	16.75	16.75	16.75	11.05
Unfunded	9.00	18.04	26.19	29.37	29.63
Floating debt	4.48	9.00	17.00	21.00	30.00
Totals	47.72	70.79	92.36	113.70	136.80

SOURCES: Central Bank, *Economic and Financial Review*, August 1963, p. 30; June 1964, p. 37; December 1964, p. 40.

The issues were gradually increased. The First Development Loan in 1959 was £2 million, raised to £2.3 million as stated. The Second and Third Development Loans of 1961 and 1962 were £10 million and £7 million, respectively. The Fourth Loan of February 1963 was £15 million.

The first loan was issued at 5 percent for five years, 5½ percent for ten years, and 6 percent for twenty years, half the issues offered maturing in twenty years. The second loan carried 5 percent for a six-year maturity, 5½ percent for a sixteen-year maturity, and 6 percent for a twenty-four-year maturity, 40 percent of the issue being of the longest maturity. The third loan earned 5 percent for four years and 6 percent for twenty-four years, the long maturities being £5 million out of £7 million. The fourth loan earned 5 percent for a five-year maturity, 5¼ percent for ten years, and 5¾ percent for twenty-four years.

Thus interest rates have remained roughly constant, maturities have lengthened, and the successive issues have been used to allow investors a wider spread of maturities. Under the title of Federal Republic of Nigeria First Development Loan, a fifth loan was floated in January 1964. Of a total of £20 million, public subscription amounted to £2.4 million, the rest being taken up by the Central Bank for sale through the Lagos Stock Exchange as in the past. It can be taken for granted that creating a wider range of maturities has been part of the purpose of the new issues.

The Central Bank, which did not have to buy any of the first loan in 1959, had to buy initially 36.9 percent of the second, 34.8 percent of the third, 61.7 percent of the fourth, and 90 percent of the fifth. Yet by the end of 1962 the Central Bank had sold all of its holdings "to meet investment demand arising, in large part, from the repatriation of overseas assets,"[27] and by the end of 1963 it had sold off two thirds of its holdings of the fourth loan.

Table 14 shows the holders of Federal securities at various dates. The long-term issues meet the needs of institutional buyers and the more wealthy groups. To raise resources and reach the small savers, other devices are needed, but savings certificates and premium bonds have not had a big success thus far.[28]

As important as the gradual provision of issues of varying maturities, however, is the establishment of a stock exchange that can provide liquidity for long-term investors and can develop into a means of raising new issues particularly when it is decided

27. Central Bank, *Annual Report* for 1962, p. 37.
28. The importance of financial intermediaries for development is discussed in A. Basch, *Financing Economic Development* (New York: Macmillan, 1964). For a more modest view of the importance of financial institutions, see Professor Gårdlund's comments in my note 5 to this chapter.

Table 14. *Holders of Federal long-term development securities,*
1962–1964

(£ thousand; December of each year)

	1962		1963		1964	
	Domes-tic	For-eign	Domes-tic	For-eign	Domes-tic	For-eign
Commercial banks	453	—	553	—	542	—
Individuals	179	—	217	6	225	7
Savings institutions	12,560	380	20,815	517	28,205	666
Statutory Board/ Corporations	5,227	—	7,142	—	7,036	—
Other corporations	114	—	845	15	672	—
Local governments (incl. Regions)	159	—	242	5	2,098	—
Insurance companies	227	56	281	122	569	77
Central Bank	—	—	3,595	—	13,860	—
Totals[a]	18,919	436	33,690	665	53,206	750

a. Detail may not add up because of rounding.
SOURCES: Central Bank, *Economic and Financial Review*, December 1964, p. 41; Central Bank, *Annual Report* for 1964, p. 53.

to sell government enterprises to the public. The Lagos Stock Exchange was established in June 1961. Even before that date, the Nigerian Cement Company Ltd. offered for public sale £174,898 worth of £1 shares. During 1962, £7,735,000 worth of new issues were floated, and transactions in government bonds amounted to £2.1 million, in industrials, to £165,300. In 1963, the volume of transactions had increased to £4.9 million and £323,000, respectively. When the Stock Exchange ended its first six months, six government maturities and fourteen other securities were listed. By the end of 1963, thirty-seven had been listed, of which eleven were Federal Stocks.[29]

The smallness of the transactions, inevitable when such a new venture is started, should not detract from the importance the establishment of a stock market has for the mobilization of

29. Data on new issues are found in the *Annual Report* of the Central Bank. Monthly data on stock-market transactions are published in the Bank's *Economic and Financial Review*.

private capital, which is one of the major aims of any development plan. The importance is all the greater when it is recalled that most countries complain of lacking not only entrepreneurs but also capital. Yet there is evidence that small savers will invest in projects that give them a good return and are safe. This in turn means that the role of government could be properly that of a starter and risk taker and that once the risk has paid off, it is possible to roll over government capital for use in new ventures, the old ones being financed by private savers. This is a rational policy for government investments in underdeveloped countries which will in fact give government a substantial role in establishing new industries and, through rollover, give it increasing funds to continue its pioneering operations. Of course, the policy works only if the pioneer enterprises are profitable—but no other enterprises help the economy to grow. The establishment of a market also helps to "Nigerianize" holdings of industries without nationalization, a process that is also of interest to expatriate owners, as is argued further on.

The proof that funds would be available from private investors, if only they would be allowed to invest and if only the machinery were provided, lies in the successes of the placements made so far, even though the Central Bank complained in 1963 of the smallness of public offerings. Table 14 has given data on the holdings of government stock. Although individuals hold only a negligible portion of the total, savings institutions hold half the total, and these are financial intermediaries that do business with the common man.

No systematic data exist on holdings of private stock by type of holder.[30] Some examples can be given, however. The place-

---

30. The only detailed information I have been able to locate relates to the Nigerian Tobacco Company, a subsidiary of British American Tobacco Company, Ltd., and it confirms the possibility of raising funds and simultaneously spreading ownership. The following is from Barclays Bank D.C.O., *Overseas Review*, August 1964, p. 65:

"The main feature during the months was the result of the offer for sale

ment of the shares of the Nigerian Cement Company represented the sale of a public company which was started with Federal funds. The Federal holdings were split 3:1 when first sold. For political reasons, and *not* because there were no private Nigerian takers, a certain amount of shares was reserved for public owner-ship in the Eastern Region where the Cement Company is located. All shares could have been sold to small savers if this had been desired. Similarly, in May 1960, the Nigerian Tobacco Company, a subsidiary of British American Tobacco, offered £100,000 of ordinary shares in one-pound sterling denominations. The factors of the company were among the agents employed to sell the stock in the bush. Within one month, the company had to allocate £200,000 in order to satisfy all individual subscriptions of up to £1,000. On the other hand, a third issue, in August 1960, of 7½ percent Cumulative Preference shares of the new John Holt Investment Company Ltd., with £100,000 of 10/- units offered and £100,000 worth of ordinary shares in 5/- units, was not fully subscribed.

Of particular interest in this context is the issue of the Ni-gerian Sugar Company Ltd. The Federal part of the National Plan allocated £5 million for direct investment in industry, "where lack of funds may seriously delay them."[31] The Federal Government had stood ready to take up £1.5 million of the issue of convertible debenture stock. It turned out that it had to take

---

by British American Tobacco Co. Ltd. of one million ordinary stock units of 5s each at 10s per unit. Over 2,100 applications were received for 1,442,130 units, and in accordance with their policy of encouraging the smaller in-vestor, applications up to and including 2,000 units were accepted in full and the 375 applications for 150,930 units from existing stockholders were also accepted in full. Applications in excess of 2,000 were accepted to the extent of 2,000 units or 55½ per cent, whichever was the greater. The stock at the end of July commanded a price of 10s 3d.

"The Nigerian Tobacco Co. Ltd. now has approximately 3,400 stock-holders, over 1,000 more than any other company currently quoted at the Lagos Stock Exchange and almost certainly the largest in Nigeria."

31. Federation of Nigeria, *National Development Plan, 1962–68* (Lagos: Federal Ministry of Economic Development, 1962), p. 63.

only a little over half a million, and "a part has already been sold to the public through the Lagos Stock Exchange."[32] This success is the more remarkable inasmuch as the company is new and the growing of sugar cane is as yet in the experimental stage!

The successful creation of institutions for the mobilization of private savings indicates that it is by no means necessary for government to provide all the capital for new enterprises. The new institutions actually can be used to help increase government investments and make them more effective. Since it *is* possible to mobilize small and large savings by voluntary means, government tax and fiscal policy must be made to fit into the picture if it is desired to maximize the available resources.

C. PROBLEMS OF TAX POLICY

In all developing countries, deliberate policies aim at stimulating growth. In all of them, government is given the special task of ensuring the growth. It is hardly surprising, therefore, that the national budget assumes central importance whether there is a plan or not. Even when there is a plan, it still has to be translated into administrative procedures which allow the planners to know what is happening in the economy and which allow the government to make its influence on the economy felt. The preceding chapter on investment criteria has given the budget the crucial function of determining the size of the so-called social expenditures and thus the size and composition of the plan. Whatever government does or does not do will be reflected in the plan; whatever efficiency or inefficiency in investment there is will affect government revenues and expenditures.

It is surprising how often the importance of the budget is neglected, how often it is treated as "merely financial" as against economic. Whether a country decides to separate a capital from an ordinary budget is primarily an administrative question.

32. Budget Speech 1963, p. 15.

But even if it has a long-term plan, the need to develop through a timed sequence of expenditures requires that the plan be translated into annual budgetary terms. Similarly, if there is to be any orderly sequence of expenditures, if planned projects are to dovetail in some manner and if the planners are to know whether a project proceeds in a satisfactory manner, proper budgetary procedures are crucial. A plan is no substitute for a capital budget, and it makes a budget (in the widest sense of the term) more, not less, necessary.

The traditional theory of public finance is only moderately helpful. Anglo-Saxon classical theory deals mostly with tax shifting and the incidence of taxation, hence mainly with problems of equity and only secondarily and incidentally with problems of resource allocation. The voluntary-exchange approach to public finance that was developed on the continent of Europe, primarily by Swedish economists from Knut Wicksell to Eric Lindahl, and in the United States by Richard Musgrave and Paul Samuelson, deals indeed extensively with the allocation problem. Its reliance on "revealed preferences" makes it, however, not sufficiently operational in the sense in which the term "operational" is used in this book.[33] The Keynesian aspects of public finance refer primarily to problems of stabilizing the economy. These problems are not the most important ones, and the relevant policies are not the most feasible ones, as I have argued implicitly and explicitly in the context of inflationary policies. In the discussion of the allocative aspects of the budget, only a beginning has been made. Yet these are for developing countries the crucial ones. The great

33. The insistence that road users be made to pay for the roads, or that the cost of education and health might be shifted to local authorities, can be interpreted as a means of forcing people to reveal their preferences. Obviously, as long as customs revenues or export taxes are used for these purposes, no one has an incentive to do so. The urgency to make taxpayers reveal their preferences in the interest of both a better allocation and an increased mobilization of resources is one of the strongest arguments for decentralization and for the policy proposals discussed in this book in various contexts.

scholars in this field have of course not neglected this problem altogether. The American discussion of "performance budgeting" and "program budgeting" is a step in this direction. In any case, in developing countries the stabilization aspects can only be achieved in the context of achieving the allocative aims of public finance. Here, too, the allocation of resources and the amount that can (or should) be raised are intimately related.

Assuming that the administrative problems of the budget are somehow solved—which in no wise belittles their essential importance—the problem from the planning standpoint becomes one of the size and composition of the budget over time. How can the tax and expenditures structure be made to stimulate growth? Who should pay the taxes? How much, and how should they be collected? These are the questions that have somehow to be answered, subject to the limitations of administrative feasibility and general lack of precise data.

In order to answer these and related questions, it is essential to start with the size and phasing of the development plan which the budget is intended to serve. I have argued that there is an optimum-sized plan and that any plan has its own dynamics in the literal sense; i.e., past projects and new projects will affect the time sequence of the growth of national product and the growth of taxable capacity, and will affect the time sequence of changes in recurrent expenditures. The many dangers inherent in too large a plan have a direct relevance to the problems of taxation and of raising resources. It is these dangers that must now be stressed.

In the first place, when attention is diverted from working out in sufficient detail a plan that is based upon reasonably firm expected demands and needs, and that takes account of administrative limitations, what most likely will happen is a kind of numbers game in which ministers and civil servants jockey for position. Every one gets bigger and better visions of the future. The result is, however, not that the nation will be spurred to greater efforts, so that an underfulfilled larger plan would achieve, nevertheless, more than the fulfillment of a less ambitious plan. The result is likely to be twofold: (1) much less will be achieved than could have been, and (2) priorities will be seriously distorted.

The reasons for both should be painfully obvious. A plan, as discussed before, implies a time sequence of projects, a time sequence of cost and revenue streams in the budget, and a time sequence in which domestic and foreign resources become available. The first thing that happens when efforts are diverted from actually working out projects to dreaming up bigger and better ones is that fewer projects are available in a form that can attract foreign aid. For, to attract foreign aid, detailed feasibility studies, economic appraisals, and plans are essential.

The lack of well-prepared projects, in turn, creates undesirable pressures. If feasibility and market studies are not ready, why not buy whole installations ready for operation? There are plenty of governments and firms anxious to oblige. And since cheaper "orthodox" finance is not available for these "turn key" operations, expensive contractor finance takes its place with undesirable repercussions on future budgetary and balance-of-payments charges. Events in Nigeria and elsewhere prove that the fear of these pressures is not groundless. The problem, which is aggravated by the enormously enlarged possibilities of corruption, also makes the control of the Plan even more difficult than it is in any case.

At the same time, projects in the social and administrative sectors are easy to execute, although they are precisely the ones that do not raise taxable capacity and that do build up recurrent expenditures with frightening rapidity. The priorities get distorted in a double way: the social and administrative projects that were planned proceed on or ahead of schedule, while the much more difficult directly productive projects fall behind.

When this happens, the next set of pressures is likely to develop. Because the directly productive projects require less than the funds allocated to them in the capital budget, it appears as if resources were "saved" that could be spent elsewhere. Hence pressure develops to enlarge the social sectors with the money that has been "saved": after all, the money seems available, so why not use it for what frequently are in themselves highly desirable projects?

The result is a pressure on domestic resources much beyond what was planned and to an extent that quickly jeopardizes growth. Here I am concerned primarily with the budgetary effects. Growth and taxable capacity remain smaller, and projected budget surpluses to finance projects in later years become more difficult to achieve as the rise of recurrent cost inherent in the distortion of priorities eats rapidly into the resources that should be available for the later enlargement of the productive apparatus of the nation. Simultaneously, less foreign financing than was expected is available, and domestically controlled assets—if they still exist—are depleted more rapidly than foreseen.

Over the protest of some of the planners, the Nigerian Plan was drawn on the assumption that on balance 50 percent of capital cost would be financed from abroad and with new foreign resources. (The drawing down of previously accumulated foreign assets of Nigeria is not considered to be part of this 50 percent.) As the priorities get distorted, and as fewer productive projects suitable for foreign financing are ready to go ahead, the amount of foreign grants and loans is bound to be substantially less than projected. This then leads to pressures that can hardly be resisted to use increased domestic resources to go ahead—were they not available when the productive projects were put into the capital budget? This in turn inevitably leads to a faster liquidation of domestically controlled foreign assets. And, to make matters worse, it leads to expenditure on projects that will not only absorb resources just to keep them going but will fail to increase taxable capacity or to increase the foreign earning power of the nation or to reduce import requirements. It will make the achievement of the desired ratio of foreign financing at first more difficult and, if allowed to proceed for any length of time, at last impossible.

To make matters still worse, if actual taxes have been raised on the assumption that a certain project mix would be executed, there will be tremendous pressure to spend the money collected in any manner that is possible even if the planned project mix cannot be executed. The taxes that are withdrawn from circulation will reduce private spending on consumption and investment. When government does not spend them, deflationary pressures will appear in the economy: unemployment, reduction of private investment and consumption expenditures, and an increased unwillingness of farmers and other subsistence producers to become a part of the money economy. There may even be attempts to return to subsistence instead of market production, which the reduced demand makes less attractive. In cities, unemployment problems become politically and socially dangerous, and the likely effects on market production, particularly for exports, are no less serious to the economy.

If the taxation resulting in budget surpluses leads to an accumulation of foreign assets, they are at least not permanently lost to the economy but become available when spending finally increases again. But the notion, occasionally found in underdeveloped countries, that an unspent budget surplus of one year represents real resources that can be spent in the next, is of course, fallacious: inflationary pressures will simply follow deflationary ones.

The burden of the argument, however, is that as a rule such a sequence of deflation and inflation will not be allowed to occur. As deflationary pressures mount, the political and economic pressures to spend the tax money on projects which *at the time* are of secondary importance become overwhelming. Since the schools or hospitals or roads are in the plan, why not go ahead with them faster than planned and execute them when resources are available, leaving expenditures on agriculture and industry to the time when those projects are ready?

These problems were all foreseen by the planners in Nigeria. That the fears expressed about the consequences of the size of the Plan are not academic is shown by the record of execution of the first two years.[34]

Control of the Plan

The budgetary problems add to the case for a realistic plan. The budget is the central document of the plan, and the control of spending through budgetary control is essential.

Even the best plan cannot be rigidly adhered to. New data and new ideas are bound to come forward. Introducing flexibility into a plan without making it chaotic is both a budgetary and an economic task. Analysis of new proposals for their growth-inducing and other desired and claimed effects must continue. So must the supervision of existing projects. If, as the result of underspending, resources appear to become available, the question must nevertheless be reopened what to do: whether to undertake projects of secondary priority or whether to shift the composition of the program toward more projects that build up recurrent expenditures very rapidly. Since such projects may jeopardize future budgetary surpluses, it may be preferable not to undertake any new projects at all but to reduce taxes until

34. *Federal Government Development Programme 1962–68: First Progress Report*, Sessional Paper no. 3 of 1964 (Apapa: Federal Ministry of Economic Development); *Eastern Nigeria Development Plan 1962–68: First Progress Report*, Eastern Nigeria Official Document no. 15 of 1964 (Enugu); *Development Plan 1962–1968: First Progress Report* (Kaduna: Ministry of Economic Planning, 1964); *Western Nigeria Development Plan 1962–68: First Progress Report*, Western Nigeria Official Document no. 2 of 1964 (Ibadan, Ministry of Economic Planning and Community Development). The second progress report by the Federal Government was published as Federal Republic of Nigeria, *National Development Plan, Progress Report 1964* (Lagos: Federal Ministry of Economic Development, 1965), which contains a detailed listing of contractor finance.

such time as increased tax revenues can be spent on directly productive projects.

The problem of foreign financing is closely related to the problem of how to prevent the shift of apparently available funds to projects or sectors with lower priority. Once a project is started, foreign financing normally is impossible. At the same time, once a project is started, pressures are overwhelming to finish it—if necessary with the country's own resources. Knowing that the decision in favor of a project is effectively made at the moment when funds for its start are released, its backers naturally press hard to get the camel's nose under the tent. If a country has foreign assets, there will inevitably be a scramble to get one's own project started before these assets are exhausted. Flexibility requires the avoidance of such commitments.

All these problems are inevitable in any case, but a plan that is too big makes them virtually unmanageable. The control procedures that can be adopted include the critical examination of old and new projects by a planning unit and subsequently on the political level by a special cabinet committee, as well as release of funds only by authorization of the ministry of finance or jointly by the ministries of finance and of economic development. This control must be particularly strong over those expenditures which are easy to execute and do not lend themselves to economic calculations, and over those which lend themselves to contractor finance.

A special problem arises in federal countries in which the component parts require subsidies or transfers of funds other than those envisaged by the constitution.[35] In all cases, there

35. The constitutional division of resources envisages some redistribution of revenues through the "distributable pool," i.e., certain taxes, particularly some import duties and oil revenues, that are collected by the Federal Government and then redistributed among the Federal and Regional Governments not according to the principle of origin or destination, as with export duties and some import duties, but according to the presumed need for revenues of the various governments. See Colonial Office, *Nigeria,* Report of the Fiscal Commission ("Raisman Report"), Cmnd 481 (London:

will be a problem of the location of projects in various parts of the country. In Nigeria, the National Plan consists of four co-ordinated governmental capital budgets—the other aspects of the Plan are of only secondary importance in the present con-text—and the problem of the location of Federal projects is complicated by considerations of aiding particular Regions for reasons of national policy and equity.

The Nigerian Plan establishes the principle that each Govern-ment is to finance all of its recurrent and half of its capital cost. Nevertheless, there are two major areas in which intergovern-mental transfers are considered: education and agriculture. The guidelines according to which such intergovernmental transfers ought to be made are therefore quite important. If they are not followed, funds transferred from the Federal to a Regional Gov-ernment for highest-priority expenditures will simply release funds under Regional control for lower-priority projects. This in turn means that the Federal Government must exercise some control over the manner in which Regional funds are spent. Thus again the size and the realism of the Plan and of the budget mean much if this control is to be effective and if priorities are not to be hopelessly distorted.

Distribution of the Tax Burden

In a country such as Nigeria, indirect taxation must account for the bulk of tax revenues because it is administratively difficult

H.M.S.O. 1958); and K. J. Binns, *Report of the Fiscal Review Commission* (Lagos: Federal Ministry of Information, 1965).

The Plan envisages in addition that certain educational expenditures in the Regions will be borne by the Federal Government. Thus the capital allocation for education in the Federal Plan is £28.95 million. This includes £3,117,000 in "Grants Undefined to Northern Region Primary Education," £4 million assistance to Regional universities (in addition to turning over to them buildings of the Nigerian Colleges of Arts, Sciences, and Technology valued at £4,260,000), part of £3,848,000 for an expanded overseas scholarship plan, part of £1,642,000 for postgraduate scholarships, and £135,000 for Sixth Form Development in the Regions. Federation of Nigeria, *National Development Plan, 1962–68*, Part II, sec. G, pp. 43-47 (esp. table XXV).

to collect direct taxes from the majority of the population. Despite the astonishing record of the Eastern Region, which collects comparatively large amounts of income taxes from ordinary citizens, income taxes can usually be collected only from expatriate and other big businesses, expatriate businessmen, and fixed-income receivers such as civil servants whose tax can be (and is being) deducted at the source. The major tax sources are in effect import and export duties.[36]

Nigeria, like any federation, also has the problem of sharing the tax sources among the governmental units. All export and import duties are collected by the Federal Government; all of the export duties and part of the import duties are passed on to the Regions in which the exports originate or to which the imports are presumed to go.[37] Since 1962, petroleum royalties have become an increasingly important source of revenue for the Regions and the Federal Government.

The problem of who should pay can be seen to merge quickly with the problem of raising and allocating resources. It is not merely a problem of equity, for equity and resource mobilization and allocation are by no means inconsistent. I assume without further justification that the poorest should at least not be

36. The Native Authorities of the Northern Region also depend largely on direct taxes for their support, and this is likely to be true for most local taxes. The details are, however, extraordinarily difficult if not impossible to come by. During 1962–63 the Eastern Region collected £3.4 million in income taxes. Total Regional tax revenue was £7.7 million. Federal allocations to the Eastern Region were, by comparison, £14.0 million. These allocations come primarily out of export and import duties. See *Approved Estimates of Eastern Nigeria, 1964–65*, Eastern Nigeria Official Document no. 13 of 1964 (Enugu).

37. See the Raisman Report, cited in my note 35, for the principles underlying the division of revenues. These were adopted several years ago but with some modification with respect to the taxation of expatriate individuals, are still in force. See also the Binns Report, also cited in note 35; this was by a new Fiscal Review Commission on Revenue Allocation appointed in 1964 under the chairmanship of K. J. Binns, Under-Treasurer and State Commissioner of Taxes in the State of Tasmania, Australia. See Federal Ministry of Information, *News from Nigeria*, no. 35/64 (mimeo., June 24, 1964), p. 3, which gives the terms of reference of the commission.

burdened more heavily than the groups better able to pay and that the combined tax-expenditure pattern should at least not be regressive. I also assume without further discussion that the development effort is of such magnitude that the whole nation, including the lowest income group, must of necessity be involved in paying for it through taxes.

The first hurdle that the policy maker has to overcome is the appalling lack of data. Virtually no data on income distribution exist.[38] Nevertheless certain statements can be made: most taxes on agricultural produce are likely to hit the poorer groups; taxes on imports are likely to hit the richer people who can afford the higher-grade imports. From this it follows that import duties could be used in lieu of income taxes to assure against regression in the tax system. Next, though it is not possible to say in general who benefits from budgetary expenditures, it is possible to isolate subsidies and make an intelligent guess as to the recipient's economic status. The very least that can be asked is that subsidies do not obviously make the rich richer.

In Nigeria, a notional road fund and the annual cost of the road system, including maintenance and a 6 percent rate of interest, were calculated. This was compared with the total income

38. Table 15 of the *Annual Abstract of Statistics, 1960*, p. 14, gives the "Distribution of Personal Income Tax by Gross Income Groups: 1956/57, 1957/58, and 1958/59." The figures refer to Federal income tax collections from all expatriates and from Africans "in so far as they receive any income derived from the Federal Territory of Lagos, for whom separate notices were issued by the Income Tax Offices." In 1956–57, 122,697 persons were assessed with a gross income of £30.2 million, paying £1.6 million of Federal income taxes. In 1958–59, the number assessed was 138,104, with gross income of £33.3 million, paying £1.7 million of income taxes. By 1958–59, 157,096 persons with a gross income of £42.2 million paid £2.2 million of income taxes. In 1961–62 the taxes amounted to £2.8 million; they fell to £1.9 million in 1962–63, probably as a result of changes in the law that permitted the Regions to tax expatriates resident in them. Before this, all expatriates regardless of residence were subject to the *Federal* income tax. Similar data are also available for the Western and Eastern Region. The numbers involved and their gross income, as well as the taxes collected are small. No data at all exist for the Northern Region.

derived from road users: import duties, license fees, gasoline taxes, etc. The budget of 1962–63, introduced with the Plan, increased taxes precisely with the purpose of making road users pay a larger share of the running cost of the road system. The road case illustrates also how the Government, by taxing trucks and business vehicles less than cars, can introduce a clear progression while adhering to the general principle that road users as a group should pay for the road system.

The taxation of transport, however, raises a point that cannot be sidestepped: what can be said about the shifting of the tax? The absence of detailed data makes anything one does or says largely guesswork. When an increase of 4d per gallon was announced in the tax on gasoline and diesel fuel, the prices of all goods in the local markets in Lagos rose by 2d regardless of the unit in which they were sold—a beautiful example of market imperfection. When the Ministry of Finance thereupon published a list of the justified cost increases for various goods purchased by the ordinary Nigerian in the local market, prices promptly fell to that level.

There is thus some evidence of forward shifting of the tax from factor of production to final consumer, though none of backward shifting. There may be backward shifting if the producer price at a particular buying station is reduced by the increased cost of transport, but the Marketing Boards could absorb this cost. The alternatives to financing the recurrent cost of the roads would be either to raise import duties other than those of gasoline or to lower producer prices. It seems reasonable to assume that the combination of differential vehicle import duties by size of car and licenses and some forward shifting will in fact place the burden of the cost on the richer segment of the population. Thus there is strong evidence that the achievement of social objectives is quite consistent with the increased mobilization and the more rational allocation of resources.

This point comes out even more clearly in the consideration

of housing policy, particularly as it is intertwined not only with the usual urban problems of slum clearance and low-cost housing but with problems of land ownership and land law and with the problems of city versus rural areas and the capital city versus the rest of the country.

In the former British West African territories non-Africans cannot hold land or can own it only under restrictive conditions; yet quarters must be provided for civil servants from abroad or from diverse ethnic groups. Therefore Government housing becomes a necessity. But it is neither necessary nor desirable to charge a flat portion of income as rent—especially a very low portion—or to make the rent independent of the size of accommodation. Nor is it logical or desirable that mortgages (or car loans) should be given at subsidized interest rates or at rates that involve the Government in actual out-of-pocket expenses. Neither does it make sense to allocate land by lot at low rates regardless of the value of that land, rather than auction it off to the highest bidder—who must be African in any case.

As the Nigerian Plan indicates, when those people who can afford it are charged economic rents and prices, sufficient funds can be raised to provide economic low-cost housing for those who really need it. Similarly, Lagos sewerage, water, and markets can be made to pay for themselves while providing needed and cheap social as well as economic services; and this fact is reflected in the Plan not as a curiosity but as proof that social services can be provided without burdening the taxpayer at large.[39]

The principle that subsidies should be limited to clearly defined social needs and should be deliberate can therefore be shown to go a long way toward making the expenditure and income structure less regressive and perhaps even somewhat progressive.

39. See W. F. Stolper, *Social Aspects in Economic Planning, with Special Reference to Nigeria,* E/CN.14/SPD/3 (Addis Ababa: Economic Commission for Africa, 1963)—reprinted in *East African Economics Review,* II (June 1964).

The principle is all the more important because administrative services cannot be allocated in this manner and because on the tax side there are inevitable erosions in revenues and limitations to tax increases, which are the consequence of policies to stimulate industrialization.

VII

Economic Policies from a Planning Standpoint: Government and Business

SINCE the purpose of economic development is the creation of a more complex economic machine capable of producing increasing amounts of goods and services which people want, it is natural that government should be directly and indirectly concerned with the building and owning of factories. This concern entails a series of more specific policies which, to be meaningful, must be tailored to overcoming the obstacles to the growth of indigenous industries. For a number of reasons governments feel that they are responsible for the direct creation of new producing units and occasionally for taking over previously foreign-owned businesses. The poverty and lack of development of the country is blamed on a lack of entrepreneurs, a shortage which supposedly only government can overcome. The foreign-owned firms are seen as exploiting the country by taking profits out instead of reinvesting them, by preventing citizens from running their own businesses, and, in general, by subordinating the economic welfare of the host country to their own purposes. A colonial relationship adds to the suspicions of exploitation.

It would go beyond the aims of this book to reopen the question of whether colonialism paid and, if so, for whom. Nor is it necessary to do so to understand the pressures and problems which developing countries face. Add to this that Russia, Eastern

Europe, China, and Cuba have become Communist, and the attraction to nationalization and to direct as against indirect government control of production becomes even more understandable. Understandable or not, however, this does not change the fact that the means of achieving control are not always suitable to achieve their ends.

Questions of nationalization and government ownership are, of course, politically and emotionally charged, and controversy cannot be avoided. Yet the performance of government corporations and the effects of government take-overs are matters of record, and it is possible to discuss objectively what this performance was and what pitfalls have to be guarded against in such operations.

A. NATIONALIZATION AND THE PRIVATE SECTOR

If a country has made an irrevocable decision in favor of a fully socialized economy, there is nothing more to be said. The observer may consider it a mistake, but there is nothing that can be done about it, particularly if the country in question is aware of the costs and willing to pay them.

I am convinced, however, that, short of such clear political preference, development will be seriously slowed, at the very least, unless a vigorous private sector can be developed. A mixed economy requires a strong private sector as a partner of an efficient public sector. The desire for extensive government ownership, though easily understandable, springs more from lack of imagination than from ideology; and a fierce nationalism makes exploitation even easier than an attitude of not caring who owns what. The legitimate aim of underdeveloped countries to gain increasing control over their own fate can be easily achieved without bringing on government ownership for its own sake and without centralized control.

It is, of course, easy to overdraw the case against government, simply because government ownership is all too frequently made a shibboleth. There are legitimate reasons why government should set up industries. It is said that in India no one wanted to start fertilizer factories and that Imperial Chemical Industries had been invited and had refused one invitation. It is also said that in India private industry refused to expand steel-making facilities, although in this case there is a question as to what extent governmental price policies contributed to this refusal. In approaching the problem of government's relation to business it therefore seems best not to be sidetracked by spurious ideological issues.

Government also has no monopoly on inefficiency. The wish to let private business invest where possible should not spring from the naive idea that all private business is efficient but that governments inevitably lose money. But at least inefficiency in private business is more visible. Private business can go broke rapidly, whereas in government-owned enterprises the taxpayer can be drawn upon to make up for losses almost indefinitely. Thus in socialized industries the mechanism is lacking which converts a private loss into a public gain, and if heavy losses occur within a framework of government ownership, the economy gets more and more boxed into a situation in which further growth becomes impossible. The case against government ownership would be substantially weakened if socialism were to invent the equivalent to bankruptcy.

The overwhelming desire to gain increasing control over the economy and to correct real or imagined wrongs of the old colonial system undoubtedly accounts for the typical underdeveloped country's inconsistent attitudes toward foreign capital and entrepreneurship and leads to distrust of the private sector. Foreign ownership is everywhere felt to be somehow an infringement of the freedom of action of an economy. The reactions to American ownership of Canadian and Australian businesses, the effects of the Ford Motor Company's decision to repurchase outstanding shares of its English subsidiary, and the discussion of *Ueberfremdung* in the Weimar Republic are sufficient reminders. In many cases such fears are obviously irrational.

Nevertheless it is true that foreign ownership—particularly by nonresident firms with world-wide interests—may mean that business decisions in a particular country are determined not only or not even primarily by conditions in that country but by what is thought to be the best interest of the firms' foreign domicile. In underdeveloped countries which depend not merely on foreign capital but on foreign manpower, the problem is compounded. And to the extent that differences in the social and legal frameworks of the host and guest countries require special treatment, the avoidance of the appearance of special privileges becomes almost impossible.

The lack of entrepreneurs at all levels in a country makes it extremely hard to get modern industry started and, once started, to keep it running efficiently. This helps to explain the temptation to nationalize foreign businesses. Government is under pressure—frequently of its own making—to do *something*, and creating something brand-new may consume too much time. Taking over an existing setup is action. It may even be in some sense justifiable action, but it is not easy to justify as development. The beneficial effects on balance of payments are frequently stressed— after all, profits are now reinvested rather than sent abroad —but this is quantitatively of minor importance, particularly if profits were already reinvested before. Moreover, profits have to be earned before they can be transferred, and they are only part of value added. If the efficiency of the enterprise suffers as the result of nationalization, profits may disappear.

In any case, nationalization of existing enterprise is simply a reshuffling of papers. If the ownership was foreign and compensation is paid, nationalization involves capital exports rather than the desired and needed capital imports. If it was domestically owned and compensation is paid, the change is likely to raise consumption rather than investments. If efficiency suffers and subsidies become necessary, this too raises consumption rather than investment.

This view of nationalization has no ideological bias. The point is simply that nationalization diverts energies from solving the real problem of development: the creation of new and viable economic units. At the same time, the propensity for government ownership cries out for exploitation by equipment salesmen, and by countries (not all capitalist by any means) that specialize in selling so-called "turn key" operations with a minimum of "market research" and no provision for training management and labor.

Moreover, ownership and control are not the same thing, as Americans have had drilled into them for a generation or so. The confusion of the two makes a country susceptible to exploitation by the oldest method known to manipulators of corporate control. The country wishes to start an enterprise for which foreign know-how and capital are essential. It keeps majority control while the foreigner sells the joint company the necessary equipment or brings it in as his part of the equity. Whether or not the valuation of the equipment is excessive is anybody's guess. The foreign partner brings in know-how and management, for which he is paid a fee, which may or may not be reasonable. The company must buy abroad, which lays it open to the old gambit of the minority directors' milking the company by buying from their own subsidiaries at outrageous prices. This can go on for quite a while, because of the widespread distrust of profits as immoral and somehow as "financial" and not "economic." The company's books may be rigged, often by no more subtle methods than subsidized interest rates and unreal depreciation quotas, or by mixing up a cash-flow analysis with a profit-and-loss account. Direct subsidies, or subsidies in the form of excessive prices for the output of the enterprises in which government has a majority share, can be obtained all too easily by reference to infant industries and external economies and, alas, because of plain corruption. When the joint enterprise is milked dry, the minority share is sold back to the government at inflated prices.

It would be invidious to give particular examples or to refer to particular countries, because it is sheer accident when and where information becomes available. In several countries, foreign partners were bought out by governments or their wholly owned corporations without a public accounting. It is one thing to insist that in case of nationalization full and prompt compensation be paid. It is quite a different matter to pay such compensation without having an independent accountant go over the books and ascertain the fair value of the assets.[1]

Such exploitation is by no means confined to private enterprise

1. On a visit to a country that had just repurchased an enterprise at a high price, I raised with a high and extremely able official the question of how the price was fixed and whether independent accountants had gone over the books. His answer was an amused smile at my naiveté. Numerous examples referring to Western Nigeria can be given, but there is every reason to suppose that the same thing has happened also elsewhere inside and outside of Nigeria. For example, the Western Region Finance Corporation purchased the firm of Arab Brothers Motors Limited for £1.1 million, a very substantial sum in any country and certainly an enormous amount for a poor one. "The average profits of the company of the five years ended 31 March 1959, amounted to £15,919," which was considered understated by one accounting firm "by reason of wrong stock valuation figures, excessive provision of depreciation and a high level of director's remuneration." More recently, there were profits for the year ended March 31, 1960, of £19,500; for the next year £1,238; and for the year ended March 31, 1962, losses of £25,848. On that basis a price of £150,000 to £300,000 would have been more than adequate, assuming a capitalization between 5 percent and 10 percent, which is obviously much too low a rate. Of the total purchase price of £1.1 million, £450,000 was deposited in London and is a clear export of capital. Federation of Nigeria, *Report of the Coker Commission of Inquiry into the Affairs of Certain Statutory Corporations in Western Nigeria* (4 vols.; Lagos: Federal Ministry of Information, 1962), II, 51-53.

The irregularities in the transaction are not at issue here, and they have therefore not been stressed. But since I have insisted that nationalism lends itself to an exploitation worse than colonialism, it should be pointed out that the Ministry of Trade did raise the right questions, that an independent valuer put substantially lower valuation on properties than were accepted upon the advice of another accountant, and that only two weeks were permitted for the investigations necessary to arrive at a sound judgment. The Coker Commission has drawn the obvious conclusion.

or capitalist countries. Information on exploitation by the Soviet
Union does not become public except when there is a break in
political relations. The case is illustrated by the debate at the
United Nations and the statement at the time of the Russian-
Yugoslav break, concerning the partnership between Russia and
Yugoslavia in the Yugoslav airlines. Similarly, China has been
warning other "fraternal" countries against Russian exploitation.
It is known that prices of equipment supplied under Russian
loan agreements are sometimes 20 to 30 percent above the prices
of similar equipment purchased in the West, and that Russian
supporting manpower is substantially more numerous and expensive than equivalent American manpower would be—all of
which makes the 2 percent charged on the Russian loans look
quite different and rather high.

As long as the shortage of indigenous managerial talent ne-
cessitates the hiring of expatriates, ownership and control are
even more separated in underdeveloped countries than in advanced countries. It is understandable, therefore, if certain xeno-
phobic tendencies appear in underdeveloped countries, and it
becomes essential to organize matters so as to induce the expatriate expert or capitalist to identify himself with the interests
of the country, its growth and development. This identification
will be difficult to achieve if the enterprise can count on subsidies
and is not expected to show a profit.

In most countries public utilities are publicly owned, though
they are usually run along business principles. Where there is
both a dearth of investment attractive to small savers and a need
to increase the mobilization of domestic resources, there seems
no reason why public utilities should not at least in part be
"privatized." Thus, an electricity undertaking could offer shares
or debentures to the public with a good prospect of paying a
dividend. This is quite consistent with maintaining government
control, which with statutory authorities is only indirect in any
case. The devices of allowing private ownership while keeping

public control are numerous, and there is no limit to the ingenuity that a good lawyer or accountant can exercise. It may be worthwhile to point out that the U.S. Federal Reserve System is owned by the member banks without thereby becoming privately controlled and that the old German Reichsbank had shares in private hands outstanding.

Public utilities are particularly useful because they are burdened with less ideological ballast: public ownership and economic profit in their case are accepted as going hand in hand. The objection to putting into private hands other businesses which government has started stems frequently from the fear that a relatively small group of wealthy persons might acquire ownership of properties that were developed with monies raised from the taxpayer at large. But there are many ways to spread ownership and limit individual holdings. Examples are the (not overly successful) "peoples' shares" of the Volkswagen Werke and the recent allocations of the Communications Satellite Corporation. The issuing of small-denomination stock in the name of the owner should incidentally be a boon to the collection of taxes and presumably would limit the amounts purchased by the very rich for that reason alone. Ownership of the new shares by foreigners could be limited by similar devices. All such schemes are designed to preserve control over the investment in the hands of the government. Since this would be the case it becomes less clear why investments by foreigners should be restricted except to reserve especially profitable investments to citizens.[2] As long as a country needs foreign capital and must increase domestic capital formation, it seems hardly rational to limit both for purely ideological reasons, particularly when there are many methods open to achieve the aim of capital inflow and capital formation without the undesired political side effects.

2. Several internationally known Swiss corporations offer to Swiss citizens special-preference shares which carry a higher rate of interest than the corresponding shares quoted on the international markets.

B. DEVELOPMENT CORPORATIONS

Among the institutions devised to stimulate growth, development banks and corporations have become prominent. Basically the idea of a development corporation is to combine availability of capital with industrial preparatory and supervisory services and to provide a channel for private domestic and foreign funds. Ideological problems are not easily sidestepped, however. As a rule the corporations are found in fields which, unlike public utilities, normally are private. They are usually set up with public funds, although there is no reason why they could not attract private funds from their inception. Once a capital market has been started—as it has been successfully in Nigeria—and once the administration of the development corporation has established itself successfully in the confidence of the people, it should be easy to raise additional money by the issue of government-guaranteed paper even ahead of rolling over the capital by selling all or part of a successful enterprise to the public. This is in fact the purpose of the Nigerian National Development Bank which was established in 1963. However, to the extent to which development corporations finance roads or research, their investments, usually legitimate and economically justifiable, are nevertheless without direct return to them.

If development corporations are to lead to growth, their investments must be profitable. This is also necessary if they are not to run out of funds. For, presumably, taxation cannot continue to be forever the major source of funds which they distribute. It is more normal that they must replenish their resources either by rolling over their investments or by borrowing additional funds. Even if they expect to be allocated further tax revenues, this is a reasonable expectation only if the economy is growing enough to generate these tax resources. If the development corporation is not to become merely a redistribution agency, its own investments must therefore contribute to the growth of taxable capacity.

The basic idea of the development corporation is to use public funds with which to start new enterprises that could not have started without public initiative. Having successfully taken the necessary risks, a corporation should then roll its capital over and start new things with presumably enlarged resources.

All of this presumes successful operations, of course. Successful operations, however, imply careful preparation and supervision of projects. In most countries it is not easy to analyze the actual performance of development corporations or banks. The difficulties of overcoming the limited absorptive capacities of underdeveloped countries and the pressures to do *something* inevitably combine to lead to a less than perfect allocation of investment funds. The examples from West Africa are not unique.

It is no accident that in Nigeria the investments in agriculture have on the whole done better than those in industrial ventures, particularly when the agricultural enterprises involve export commodities. In export agriculture markets and marketing organizations exist and are understood; the returns are in the form of foreign exchange which means *real* goods and services and not some vague non-economic benefits. Agricultural extension services have been successfully started. Agricultural investments involving domestic crops have had harder going, though there too notable successes have been achieved.

Industrial enterprises are a different matter. Failures have often resulted from a lack of know-how in the widest sense, from mixing up economic and technological matters, and from a combination of impatience with the slowness of progress with the view that if only capital were forthcoming the other problems would solve themselves.

Some of the market and economic "feasibility" studies have been little short of shocking: if every man, woman, and child would drink *x* bottles of a particular soft drink, demand would be *y* bottles and the bottling plant profitable. If every Nigerian would buy a cake of soap every so often, the demand for soap would be such-and-such. This would cause a certain demand for oil, which would be most desirable because it would reduce Nigeria's dependence on international markets (a fine non-economic benefit) and would allow Marketing Boards to pay higher prices to farmers, thereby raising Marketing Boards profits (*sic!*). In the case of a fruit-juice canning factory (established in 1952 before self-government) which turned out to be much too big and which is therefore standing idle most of the time, the decision to invest was made on the assumption that if farmers had a guaranteed market, they would grow the necessary citrus fruit.

Considerable detail on the operations of the Western Nigeria Development Corporation has come to light as the result of the voluminous 1962 report of the Coker Commission, headed by Justice G. B. A. Coker of the High Court, Lagos.[3] The Western Nigeria Development Corporation was established in 1959 as one of the two legal successors of the Western Region Production Development Board, which had been established in 1955 as the legal successor of the Western Region Production Board of 1951. (The other legal successor in 1959 was the Western Region Finance Corporation.) Between 1951 and March 31, 1962, the Western Nigeria Development Corporation (and its predecessors) received £17,976,100 for investments and an additional £3,666,-600 to make up for losses. (See Table 15 for the sources of the funds). Of this £17,976,100, some £3.5 million, or 20 percent, was spent on grants; £7.4 million represented fixed assets, i.e.,

3. In addition to its *Report* (cited in my note 1), the commission also published daily transcripts of each of its 92 sittings. The major purpose of the Coker Commission was to enquire into irregularities in the conduct of the Statutory Corporations. In the present context, however, I am interested only in the role of the Western Nigeria Development Corporation in the economic development of the Region and of Nigeria, and the lessons that can be learned.

direct investments; and £5.5 million, or 30 percent, represented "trade investments in industrial companies," i.e., share holdings and industrial loans. (See Table 16 for how the funds were used.)

The details on the £12.9 million of direct investments and trade investments in 1962 are of particular interest in two respects. First, analysis indicates that all direct investments except one did poorly, and as for the trade investments, those in which the Western Nigeria Development Corporation had a majority interest did worse than those in which commercial partners had a substantial share. The second point relates to the discussion of the previous chapters on investment criteria, external economies, and national accounting. We have here some statistical confirmation of why an increasing rate of investment went hand in hand with a reduced rate of growth.

First, of the £5.5 million "trade investments," £4.3 million were unsecured loans and one mortgage debenture (of £420,000), and the rest were shares. The major unsecured loans were given to Nigersol (£1,983,000) and the Nigerian Water Resources Development Ltd. (£989,950)—in addition to equity investment in these two companies—although only £800,000 was actually needed by the companies. In both companies the Western Nigeria Development Corporation held a majority interest of 60 percent, the rest being held by a foreign partner. Both were involved in, or were victims of, a series of transactions which are detailed in the Coker Commission Report, and which involved a transfer of £2.2 million to London for no visible economic reason. Of the fifteen companies in which trade investments were made, only two actually paid dividends by 1962, but a number of others had been founded as recently as 1960, and judgment must therefore be suspended. Thus far only a fraction of these investments has contributed to growth: most of them had the opposite effect.

From the £7.4 million direct investment (after depreciation) cumulatively made by March 31, 1962, total losses of £3,666,600

Table 15. *Sources of Western Nigeria Development Corporation funds*
(£ thousand)

CAPITAL RECEIVED FROM	Cumulative to Mar. 31, 1955	1958–59	1959–60	1960–61	1961–62	Cumulative to Mar. 31, 1962
Nigerian Cocoa Marketing Board	7,551.9	—	—	—	—	7,892.7
Nigerian Oil Palm Produce Marketing Board	2,744.7	373.1	—	—	—	3,467.9
Chillies Marketing Board	18.1	—	—	—	—	18.1
Subtotal	10,314.7	373.1	—	—	—	11,378.6
Western Region Government	—	900.0	2,400.0	1,200.0	1,040.9	5,540.9
Western Region Marketing Board	—	—	2,000.0	1,000.0	—	3,000.0
Revaluation of assets— livestock	3.0	—	—	—	—	—
Revenue for year (— means losses)	7.1	—277.2	—296.8	—679.1	—764.2	—3,666.6
Adjustments relating to previous years	—	14.4	—	—145.3	1.9	782.7
Provision for loss on investments	—	—80.4	6.6	7.3	—	33.6
Interest on loans—unpaid	—	—	7.7	497.7	401.5	906.9
Total	10,324.9	930.0	4,117.4	1,880.6	680.1	17,976.1

Table 15. (Continued)

REPRESENTED IN ACCOUNTS BY	Cumulative to Mar. 31, 1955	1958–59	1959–60	1960–61	1961–62	Cumulative to Mar. 31, 1962
Capital	10,314.7	11,378.6	11,378.6	11,378.6	11,378.6	11,378.6
Capital reserve	3.0	—	—	—	—	—
Revenue account	7.1	—1,000.3	—1,297.2	—2,121.6	—2,883.9	—2,883.9
Loan capital	—	900.0	5,300.0	7,500.0	8,540.9	8,540.9
Provision for interest on loans	—	—	7.7	505.4	906.9	906.9
Provision for loss on investments	—	19.7	26.3	33.6	33.6	33.6

Note: Detail may not add because of rounding. Original figures in £ rather than £ thousand.
SOURCE: Federation of Nigeria, *Report of Coker Commission of Inquiry into the Affairs of Certain Statutory Corporations in Western Nigeria* (Lagos: Federal Ministry of Information, 1962), vol. IV, p. 79, Appendix 27.

Table 16.　Uses of Western Nigeria Development Corporation funds
(£ thousand)

	Cumulative to Mar. 31, 1955	1958–59	1959–60	1960–61	1961–62	Cumulative to Mar. 31, 1962
Grants and nonrecoverable development expenditure	1,756.0	15.7	20.3	31.2	—28.1	3,522.7
Fixed assets—less depreciation	891.2	528.1	1,041.6	1,100.4	773.6	7,417.7
Investment in projects	1,232.9	—	—	—	—	—
Preliminary expenditure on industrial projects	—	—	—	50.1	—5.5	44.6
Trade investments in industrial companies	220.0	68.6	3,338.6	1,855.6	86.5	5,490.0
British Government securities	3,227.6	—640.2	—	—	—	247.5
Long-term deposits	1,010.0	—525.0	—500.0	—	—	—
Short-term deposits	1,852.8	1,750.0	—70.0	—1,530.0	—401.2	—
Increase (decrease) in net current assets	134.4	—267.3	287.0	373.3	254.7	1,253.6
Total	10,324.9	930.0	4,117.4	1,880.6	680.1	17,976.1
Capital commitments	14.7	362.0	767.0	265.0	—	—
CONTINGENT LIABILITIES ON						
Trade investments	—	198.8	177.6	144.5	161.4	—
Undertaking to finance industrial companies	—	1,702.5	1,826.5	561.5	—	—
Guaranteed overdrafts	—	—	—	700.0	—	—

Note: Detail may not add because of rounding. Original figures in £ rather than £ thousand.
SOURCE: *Report of Coker Commission*, vol. IV, p. 81, Appendix 30.

were incurred. Only two direct investments ever made profits and are likely to make profits again.[4] Two Pepsi-Cola factories were approved against the advice of the Permanent Secretary of the Western Region Ministry of Trade and Industry, who quite correctly pointed out: "The first major point is the refusal of the Pepsi-Cola Company to provide any capital or to attract any capital from other resources. They do not appear willing to risk their own money in this venture nor that of their friends. Their profit is, however, secured; they will make a profit on their concentrate, however much or however little Development Corporation may sell."[5] The Permanent Secretary called for substantial foreign participation, careful costing and profitability calculations, written agreements, and the formulation of alternative proposals. Nevertheless, the Western Nigeria Development Corporation invested on its own £672,778, although only £392,000 had been approved, and proceeded to lose £85,020 in 1961 and £117,432 in 1962.

The establishment of the Lafia Canning Factory illustrates the danger of assuming that the "creation" of demand is all that is needed for success. The factory was established in 1952 on the assumption that "once you build a factory here people will start to grow the citrus and supply the factory with the citrus they planted." In a different location the plant might have prospered. At least the supply of raw materials would have been assured. Actual cumulative expenditures on the factory were £576,000, including cumulative losses of approximately £425,000. Its value in 1962, after a decade, was estimated at only £121,896.[6]

Psychologically, there is pressure against selling off government

4. *Report of the Coker Commission,* II, 31 ff. This irregular diversion of funds does not detract from the basic soundness of the two corporations. Details of the investments are given in vol. IV, Appendices 29, 31, 32.

5. *Ibid.,* II, 25.

6. *Ibid.,* II, 22; IV, 32-34. The various estimates of losses do not agree completely, varying between £396,282 (IV, 82), £425,000 (II, 22) and an implicit £454,000 (also II, 22). The quotation (II, 22) in from an official of the Western Nigeria Development Corporation.

enterprises both when the enterprises are profitable and when they are not. Liquidating loss enterprises draws attention to failures, and liquidating profitable enterprises deprives the government of a badge of success. In addition, as the Coker Commission brought out, there are political pressures for increased spending against the sounder advice of the civil servants. These will be felt quite aside from the substantial illegal diversion of funds which is part of reality but not of major interest here.

It can also be stated unequivocally that in Nigeria the goose that laid the golden eggs for years was the farmer who paid taxes in the form of lower producer prices. As of May 31, 1962, the Western Region Marketing Board had cumulatively spent £68,650,000. From this sum, £33,383,000 went in grants to the Western Region Government and "other grants for agricultural purposes." Of the latter, at least £5,541,000 can be identified as having been passed on to the Western Region Development Corporation. Some £10,135,000 was spent in loans and investments to banks, the National Investment and Properties Company (£6,210,000), and a few other enterprises, none of which have recoverable assets, all of which were and are of doubtful economic value, and some of which the Coker Commission indicated were used for purely political purposes. Another £14.2 million was disbursed in short-term loans to the Western Region Government, the Western Region Development Corporation, and the Western Region Finance Corporation, only a small fraction of which seem to have resulted in an addition to the productive capacity of the country.

It would be unfair to single out the Western Region simply because the Coker Commission has given details not available for other Regions. Thus, even though we lack for the Eastern Region the intimate details of the Coker Commission, there can be no doubt that a considerable portion of the investments has been wasted. The Report of the Eastern Nigeria Development Corporation for 1959–60 indicates, however, that attempts are being made to learn from the past: no new loans were made. Pressure and legal action were taken to recoup some loans, and new procedures were instituted:

"Opportunity was taken for a comprehensive review of past policy and administration, with the object of applying the lessons learned from experience and of eliminating or safeguarding against past shortcomings. Concurrent with this programme, a series of conferences of Loans Officers within Nigeria was inaugurated on the suggestion of the Corporation's Credits Manager, and the first conference was held in Lagos in January 1960, under the auspices of the Federal Loans Board. It is planned to hold a series of such conferences in each Regional Headquarters to interchange experience and information, and to study each other's organizations and methods."[7]

Inadequate attention to profitability and pressure to spend regardless of economic rationality have continued to make many investments worthless. Obviously, the spending has had a short-term multiplier effect. Yet reducing the number of unprofitable investments, instead of retarding growth, would have speeded it. The losses have financed essentially consumption of a particularly obnoxious kind. But in all national accounts they are carried as investments!

There can be no doubt that in Nigeria inadequate attention was devoted to investigation before loans, advances, and investments were made and/or that deliberate decisions were made for one reason or another that can only be called unfortunate. The sums involved are substantial. They go a long way to explain the phenomenon of an increasing rate of investments combined

7. *Fifth Annual Report of the Eastern Region Development Corporation, 1959–60, and the Consolidated Accounts Dated 31st March, 1960* (Enugu: Eastern Region Development Corporation, 1960), p. 21. There is some evidence that the Coker Commission hearings have induced the other Regions to reconsider their policies. The Eastern Nigeria Development Corporation's *Seventh Annual Report, 1961/62* (Enugu: Eastern Region Development Corporation, n.d. [1964]) gives further details.

with a decreasing rate of growth. They illustrate the statements made before about the need to discuss the profitability of investments before talking about capital-output ratios. They indicate that creating state agencies to fill the gap caused by the absence of private enterprise does not automatically solve the problem of overcoming the obstacles to sound investments— though it solves the problem of obstacles to spending money.

C. LOW PRODUCTIVITY

The *Report of the Advisory Committee on Aids to African Businessmen* quotes with approval W. A. Lewis' *Report on the Industrialization of the Gold Coast* and a report of the Western Region Finance Corporation to the effect that technical experience, managerial experience, and supervision of industries to be established are more important than money.[8] Investments go bad either because the economics and technology have not been sufficiently prepared or because the plant, once established, has faulty organization and supervision. When a plant is financed by loans, additional difficulties emerge. The difference between a loan and a grant is not always clearly understood, and it is necessary to follow up every loan in order to see that it is spent as agreed. Continuous supervisory aid is necessary. Since there is a shortage of Nigerian entrepreneurs and technicians, the problem cannot be solved by a government take-over, although skilled services can be husbanded through centralization.

Examples of low productivity resulting entirely from inadequate manager and foreman performance or from a lack of understanding of what modern industry involves are all too easy to find. A few will suffice.

The establishment of a factory was decided upon despite

8. *Report of the Advisory Committee on Aids to African Businessmen* (Lagos: Federal Ministry of Commerce and Industry, 1959), para. 171, pp. 34-35.

questionable economic grounds and despite the fact that no
suitable raw material had been found. When the planners pro-
tested, a geologist was sent who found the needed raw material,
and, it was triumphantly added, near the site of production.
Further enquiry revealed that the raw material was not found
in quantities sufficient at any one spot to permit commercial
exploitation. When the planners explained that this ruled out the
economic operation of the factory, it was stated in all seriousness
that there would be no problem. Since it was a policy to use
labor-intensive processes, and since Nigeria had plenty of unskilled labor, the material could therefore be brought to the
plant by headpan. It was not made clear how one could organize
sufficient gangs of workers to supply, by headpan, a modern
automatic machine. The perpetrators of this outrage were foreign
suppliers of machines, abetted by a development corporation and
politicians anxious to industrialize and to create jobs at any cost.

In another region, a modern plant that needed continuous firing
had to be shut down because of lack of fuel. When the plant had
been set up with the help of government loans, the owner's attention had been drawn to this problem. In answer, he just waved
his hand and pointed out that the forest around him as far as the
eye could see was his; there would be no shortage of fuel. He
clearly did not understand the principle of keeping flows of
inputs going.

On the plateau at Jos, tin is mined both with modern methods
by expatriate firms and with traditional methods by Africans on
a much smaller scale. The Federal Minister of Mines and Power
for years tried reasonably and patiently to persuade African tin
miners to organize themselves into a cooperative and accept
technical aid as a condition of getting loans for capital. To this
day he has not succeeded. The African miners are sure they know
what they are doing and need no technical aid since they have
mined tin for centuries; they are sure they are being discriminated
against by their own government and that all they need is capital.

Yet it is clear upon observation that if they had capital and machinery they would only go broke quicker. As examples of waste, I have seen some of them letting diesel pumps use up expensive fuel and precious water for long periods while no washing was being done.

In many cases in which modern enterprises ran into economic difficulties, the managers had no proper accounting, no control systems even of the simplest kind. They had no proper idea what their cost was or how a modern factory, even a small one, must be organized. The flow of raw materials to and inside the enterprise was poorly organized. Work habits dated back to the days when interruption of work meant only loss of income, not continuing capital and other charges. All without exception were sure that their failure was caused by foreign competition and dumping. Goods from Hong Kong and Czechoslovakia undoubtedly were cheap. But the numerous experiences in factories visited made one rather chary of the infant-industry argument. The managers did not want a breathing spell to learn the business. Rather, they were sure that they knew what they were doing, and they wanted permanent protection from "unfair" competition.

There are of course other important reasons for high cost, besides poor organization and managerial inadequacies, and these must be dealt with by devices other than a development corporation. I have already mentioned that electricity is expensive and its supply uncertain. When electricity is used for heating or cooling, its failure for only ten minutes can cause a day's production to be ruined and the machinery to be seriously damaged; the Niger Dam is intended to solve this problem. Also, the distance from the machinery manufacturers requires a costly inventory of spare parts much in excess of what would be needed in advanced countries; the estimates range from nine to eighteen months' supply of spare parts, whereas in England two days to a few weeks would suffice.

It may seem an omission not to mention specific problems of

labor, to say nothing of a backward-sloping supply curve. However, the evidence in Nigeria is strong that the backward-sloping supply curve of labor does not exist over the relevant range, that Nigerian labor is willing and able to learn, and that low productivity, absenteeism, and the like are traceable to a failure of management.

Thus Peter Kilby finds "that the degree of absenteeism and turnover is a fairly accurate measure, not of the acculturation of the African worker, but of the wage paid, conditions of service and the physical surroundings." He presents strong, and to my mind, conclusive evidence "that the African's demand for money is not terminal at an early stage. His demand for goods and services is only limited by his purchasing power, in turn limited by his income possibilities. Having a greater desire for money and a lesser means for earning it, it is not surprising that his willingness to work exceeds that of his European or American counterparts." And Kilby concludes "that the limit on labour productivity is not, in fact, set by the worker's proficiency or skill endowments. Rather, the empirically relevant determinants of labour productivity are various management functions. These . . . include organization of the work process, supervision and production control, planning and coordination, provision of incentives to labour and maintenance of plant and equipment. Thus, in the final reckoning, it is not the African labourer but his employer who must bear the stigma of imperfect performance."[9]

9. Peter Kilby, "African Labour Productivity Reconsidered," *Economic Journal*, LXXI (June 1961), 273-291. See also Kilby's *The Development of Small Industry in Eastern Nigeria* (Ministry of Commerce and USAID, 1964; no place of publication given).

Joyce Cary gives the following description of the African willingness to work: "All this new staff, from Tasuki, chief bridgeman, who six months before was a bush pagan in jail for elephant poaching, to Audu, is young and boundlessly hopeful. Tasuki, who works as only a Negro can work, when he sees the value and purpose of it, who gets up every day before dawn, and can be found at midnight sorting timber by lantern light; Audu, who is responsible not only for supplies but stores, and who spends most nights on the old station bicycle between Fadu and road head, and a dozen

There are fortunately many examples of successful enterprises with African and expatriate managers to offset the examples given. The Nigerian Tobacco Company, the Ports Authority, and tire-retreading and candy and textile factories are among them. It is clear, however, that capital or form of ownership is not so important as technical and managerial advisory services, which must be provided to borrowers and firms in which there are direct government investments. Only when combined with what might be termed industrial extension services does the provision of either government or private capital make sense. It is even probable that any feasible investment whose proponents prove that they can provide the know-how as well as the material will have no difficulty finding finance. To the extent to which expatriate services are needed, the problem is not solved by government's hiring these services. Under a "hiring" system, the services become a charge to government without the interest that equity gives a partner.

D. THE PRIVATE SECTOR AND THE NATIONAL INTEREST

The primary economic purpose of government is the long-run development of its people and its economy. Nationalization of industries is a political decision not an economic one, and it does not come to grips with the immediate problems of raising productivity. There is little doubt that a strong private sector can bolster governmental development policy tremendously and that its growth should therefore have highest priority. Moreover, as long as expatriate advice and expertise in running an economy is needed, it is only reasonable that at least part of the risks should be shifted to the expatriates.

---

more who serve them, obviously believe that some kind of millenium is at hand . . ." Joyce Cary, *Mister Johnson* (New York: Berkeley Publishing Corporation, 1962), p. 87. Mr. Cary was a District Officer in Northern Nigeria.

Development corporations and similar institutions can solve problems associated with the supply of capital, the proper technical and economic preparation of individual investments, and their supervision. They can see to it that capital is available at competitive rates to everyone competent to use it, if their projects promise a reasonable return in the foreseeable future. It is proper to make capital available for government investment when a foreign partner insists upon government participation as a form of risk sharing or as a way of making the profitability of the business sufficiently attractive for him.

Organizing capital, however, is only part of the task of development, and a relatively easy part. A policy of "Nigerianization" (or whatever the nationality may be) is necessary if more is wanted than just to raise income. Training and encouragement of indigenous officials, investors, managers, technicians, and skilled workers should complement monetary and fiscal policies.

"Countrification," if this term be allowed, is comparatively easy when it comes to ownership. Government can require incorporation in the country provided it has enacted a proper corporation law to ensure legal security of operations.[10] It can use tax and other incentives to induce compliance with such a policy; to qualify for a tax holiday in Nigeria, a company must be incorporated there.[11]

Government can insist that shares be made available to local investors. Companies can meet this requirement either by incorporating locally or by issuing special pound-shares in the parent company located abroad. The creation of a capital market is a prerequisite, but government can also hold shares in trust

10. I have been told by businessmen that in some parts of the world the absence of such legislation outweighs, in the opinion of many firms, any tax advantages. They would rather pay any reasonable amount of taxes and know exactly what they can and cannot do than have tax advantages and uncertainty.

11. Federation of Nigeria, *Statement on Industrial Policy,* Sessional Paper no. 6 of 1964 (Lagos: Federal Ministry of Information), p. 3.

for Nigerian private investors until such time as the enterprise is a going concern, as is the case with the Nigerian oil refinery. Tax incentives again can induce compliance; to qualify for a tax holiday, a company must be at least 10 percent Nigerian owned.[12]

The difficulties of such a policy arise from two considerations. The first is that small investors cannot afford to forego dividends and that it is hard for them to understand that on a market the value of shares fluctuates. They should therefore be induced to invest in shares only if there is a reasonable certainty of a stable value and a constant income. Unless the concentration of wealth is of major concern to the government, this difficulty is not insurmountable. The second difficulty arises from expatriates who do not wish to relinquish control. This is a point to be taken seriously, because control and efficiency of an operation are closely linked. Yet it is also to the interest of expatriate business to get out of areas in which African competence makes for keen competition and concentrate on those businesses requiring specialized knowledge.

This brings up another aspect of "countrification": the development of a managerial class and of skills of all kinds. It has been suggested, for example, that certain occupations be reserved for Nigerians. Thus the Federal Minister of Economic Development has proposed to reserve retail and wholesale trade as well as road transport to Africans.[13] Even though this proposal

---

12. *Ibid.*

13. *Ministerial Statement on Nigeria's Economic Planning Policy and Its Relationships with Distributive Trades and Road Transportation,* made in the House of Representatives by Mallam Waziri Ibrahim, Minister of Economic Development (Lagos, 1961). The Minister suggests that "individuals or companies . . . should seriously consider gradual withdrawal from such business. Exception can be allowed in the running of department stores such as Kingsway, UTC stores . . . Exception is also permissible in the sales of technical goods such as tractors, heavy machinery, such as mining machinery . . ."

The *Report of the Advisory Committee on Aids to African Businessmen* made similar suggestions, mentioning specifically Lebanese, Syrians, and Indians. The issue is only partly "racial." Europeans may have higher pro-

has not been made official government policy, there is no doubt that it will come into being voluntarily and automatically as the efficiency of African businessmen improves.

In the case of manufacturing enterprises Nigeria has instituted an "expatriate quota system" to ensure the speedy training of citizens for top management positions.[14] The Advisory Committee on Aids to African Businessmen has complained that "a number of expatriate firms . . . still keep Africans away from the managerial level of their staff. Their favorite excuse is that they cannot find the 'right type' to trust or train."[15] This kind of statement is difficult to prove or disprove but is not likely to contain more than a grain of truth! It is everywhere difficult to find the "right type" to train in a world in which increasing engineering knowledge, legal knowledge, and business acumen are necessary for the top management.[16] Nevertheless, it is also in the interests of expatriate businesses to train Africans for all levels, from foreman up. Expatriates are very expensive. Africans of the same competence may get the same basic salaries, but they are not paid the substantial expatriation allowances, and their housing can be handled differently. Home leaves and family allowances can be dispensed with, and training substituted. If it is legitimate

---

ductivity than Africans, but they are also much more expensive. Provided that they cannot achieve a monopoly position they will therefore withdraw when sufficient Africans can take their place and perform the service cheaper. Indians may also have higher productivity than Africans but are willing to live like Africans. They are therefore felt much more keenly as competitors. Changes are in store, however, as India becomes developed and is capable of both technical assistance and of supplying machinery and manufactured consumer goods other than textiles. The exceptions envisaged by the Minister of Economic Development refer to such goods that require servicing.

14. *Statement on Industrial Policy*, pp. 4-5.

15. *Report of the Advisory Committee on Aids to African Businessmen*, para. 188, p. 37.

16. Kilby, "African Labour Productivity Reconsidered," p. 280, points out that at a sub-management level, "The African is a poor supervisor. This is explained by past patterns of forced dependence on the European and by poor training. The cultural endowment, however, is also negative. A simple technology meant that organization of work was usually unnecessary."

for Africans to demand this training, it is politically expedient and economically profitable for expatriate business to give it.

To the extent that the training of the requisite manpower succeeds, the pressure to nationalize rather than "countrify" will also diminish. As more citizens are competent to run businesses and start them, and as they are helped to do so by expatriate businesses, the grievances will disappear, the group of people interested in developing a private sector will grow, and the weight of ownership and control in the economy will shift towards Nigerians.

Incentives

All developing countries this side of the Iron Curtain compete for foreign capital. In many countries, inducements to foreign capital include free land and factories. Countries offering such inducements must have developed a substantial tax base to be able to afford such generosity to particular areas within their boundaries. Unless such a substantial contribution is viewed as a form unemployment compensation or of public works to create employment, it is justifiable only if the enterprise so attracted will be able to stand on its own feet and not require further subsidies and if it will eventually directly and indirectly contribute to the economy as much as, or more than, it costs.

Most discussions of such concessions are in terms of *foreign* capital mainly because countries need not only the capital but also the know-how and sometimes the markets that come with it. There is, however, no inherent reason why the same rules should not apply also to indigenous enterprise. The major difference is likely to be that foreign enterprise needs more of everything *except* know-how and capital.

Governments everywhere have a whole range of tax policies that are designed to stimulate industries and particularly to attract foreign industries. Nigeria's so-called "Pioneer Certificates" exempt firms declared to be "pioneer" from payment of income taxes for a number of years, depending on the amount of investment.[17] Since this relief will benefit a firm only if it makes profits, at least there is assurance that no aid is given to otherwise inefficient enterprises. "A pioneer industry is one which is either not carried on in Nigeria at present, or one which is not being conducted on a commercial scale suitable to the economic requirements or the development of Nigeria. In order to qualify as a pioneer enterprise, a company must, in addition to [minimum investment] be incorporated in Nigeria and be a public company with at least 10 per cent of Nigerian share in the equity capital and up to 45 per cent Nigerian components."[18]

The incentives are generous, perhaps even unnecessarily so. At the same time, the administration of the incentives is cumbersome and may even be restrictive. The Nigerian provisions are fairly typical. First, whoever wishes to get income-tax relief must convince the government that he in particular should get it. Second, someone must decide that an industry is not already being conducted on a suitable scale. Third, someone must decide that an applicant's production is in the public interest.

The first condition is understandable. Public funds must not be given away for no purpose. But the second and third conditions are dangerous to industrial development. It seems slightly absurd that in an underdeveloped country one should have to worry about overproduction; yet this is what seems to be involved. Apparently a government committee can deny pioneer status on the grounds that enough is already being produced or that a firm that has already been granted pioneer status must be

17. Federation of Nigeria, "An Ordinance To Make Further Provision Whereby the Establishment and Development in Nigeria of Commercial Enterprises May Be Encouraged by Way of Relief from Income Tax and for Purposes Connected Therewith" (no. 8 of 1958). A brief account of "Incentives for Industrial Development" is found in Federation of Nigeria, *1964 Supplement to the Handbook of Commerce and Industry (5th ed.),* Federal Ministry of Information, Lagos (1964), pp. 51-55. Incentives are also mentioned in *Statement on Industrial Policy.*
18. *Statement on Industrial Policy,* pp. 2-3.

protected from further competition. Thus administrative delays and restrictive practices, the opposite of what was intended, are possible.[19] In connection with the "public interest," it may very well be that the manufacture of hairpins or cosmetics adds less flexibility to the economy than the manufacture of steel rods and angle irons. Yet it is not clear why only the latter should qualify for pioneer status. After all, hairpin production too adds to capital formation and employment and possibly even to the saving of foreign exchange.

The general policy of stimulating industrialization is so obviously sensible as to require no further defense. This being the case, it seems desirable to make it as automatic and as expansionary as possible. It has been suggested that lists of industries be prepared that are considered "pioneer" and for which pioneer certificates will be granted automatically to any acceptable comer. This would reduce administrative decisions—a desirable thing in view of the shortage of competent staff.[20] It seems further desirable to specify on the certificate a time limit within which operations must start. If a firm must be attracted through an assurance that no other firm will get the same tax privileges, the least that could be asked in return is that pioneer status not be used to prevent or delay the establishment of production indefinitely.

Protective tariffs and relief from import duties may also be used to stimulate industrialization.[21] Both are everywhere time-

19. Between 1956 and 1963, 52 enterprises were declared to be "pioneer," with the number per year generally decreasing. *1964 Supplement to the Handbook of Commerce and Industry (5th ed.)*, pp. 320-324, gives details on industry and product for 1955–1962.

20. I should like to stress that the Nigerian civil service is competent and honest. It is also overworked, and it would like to see as many decisions as possible made automatically.

21. For Nigeria, see *Statement of Policy Proposed by the Federal Government on the Report by a Committee Appointed to Advise on the Stimulation of Industrial Development by Affording Relief from Import Duties and Protection to Nigerian Industry*, Sessional Paper no. 10 of 1956 (Lagos); Industrial Development (Import Duty Relief) Act (no. 27 of 1957);

honored methods of doing this. The particular difficulties in underdeveloped countries arise from the fact that import duties are also the major revenue source. In Nigeria, import-duty relief is given only up to ten years and only if an enterprise is expected eventually to stand on its own feet. This is a sound principle. Yet administrative delays again counteract the benefits, and it would be better to make the import-duty relief automatic in two respects. First, it seems much more logical to revamp the tariff structure so as to make the imports of raw materials and intermediate goods duty-free and to put the duties needed for tax purposes upon final goods (the new Malta tariff follows this principle). Second, it is costly to both government and private business to collect duties first and then refund them. In particular, the existing system means for private business a much larger working capital than should be necessary. If it is not possible or desired in a particular instance to make imports generally and automatically duty-free, a certificate system—whereby imports of firms getting import-duty relief would for specified amounts and a specified period of years be cleared without payment of duty—can at least mitigate the situation.[22] Such a system would also simplify administrative procedures.

Land as an Obstacle

There is a whole complex of problems that stems from African land law and from the fact that in West Africa under British rule alienation of land was allowed only under stringent conditions. Conditions, of course, vary from place to place. Only in Lagos and the old Colony Province of the Western Region can non-Africans hold land as freehold. In the Northern Region, land has as a rule passed from the Crown to the Region since Nigeria

Customs (Drawback Regulation of 1958); Customs Duties (Dumped and Subsidized Goods) Act (no. 9 of 1958); *Statement on Industrial Policy* (my note 11), p. 3.

22. *Statement on Industrial Policy*, p. 3, explains the licensing system in Nigeria for "approved users."

has become a Republic; foreigners and most Africans can get titles though not freehold. Foreigners must reside in the sections of town set aside for them, and that includes non-Moslem Nigerians from other parts of the Federation. Land is frequently not owned by individuals though individual rights of usage exist. Even wild palm trees belong to someone who has the right to the fruit—the Latin *usufructus* is literally applicable.[23]

The complexities of land law and the problems arising from them require discussions that go far beyond my competence. Although freehold is limited, it is said to be increasing, even in the North where it continues to be illegal. In many countries it is generally assumed that the existing traditional systems of land tenure are an impediment to development. Just how and why this should be is not certain, however. Investigation of specific cases suggests that it is the uncertainty of titles rather than their inherent nature that causes the trouble. Thus in the Western Region one can see an astonishing number of cement houses left uncompleted, not for lack of money, but because ownership cannot be clearly established in the welter of conflicting claims and litigations. Slum clearance in Lagos has run into similar trouble. In such cases it appears that uncertainties could be eliminated by a system of registering traditional titles without the necessity of supplanting the traditional system of land-holding with a European one. Investigations on how to go about such registration are indeed under way. Creating legal certainty seems the primary prerequisite for development. Certainly the indigenous system of landholdings has not prevented Ghanaian farmers from acquiring cocoa lands by purchase.[24]

23. A summary on land-tenure provisions in Nigeria is found in *Handbook of Commerce and Industry* (5th ed.; Lagos, 1962), pp. 318-319.
24. See Polly Hill, *Migrant Cocoa Farmers of Southern Ghana* (Cambridge: Cambridge University Press, 1963), for documentation. Problems seem to be very different in East Africa, probably because of racial policies. See Montague Yudelman, *Africans on the Land* (Cambridge, Mass.: Harvard University Press, 1964).

It may well be that a radical remedy is needed, such as the establishment of freehold titles. But the consequences of a complete change from an indigenous to a European system are difficult to foresee unless one is really expert in law and social customs. Land provides social security which cannot be achieved by any other means in the foreseeable future for more than a small fraction of the people. Land may or may not have the mystical quality for the African it is frequently claimed to have. New countries, however, have enough birth pangs of nationhood without adding a landless proletariat, and large numbers of people would become uprooted as the result of such radical change.

Yet the present situation also has led to substantial abuse and concentration of wealth. Examples of exploitation of Nigerians in Lagos by Syrians, Lebanese, and Indians are found in the *Report of the Advisory Committee on Aids to African Businessmen* (p. 51). Exploitation of expatriates by Africans can be as easily documented. To give an example: a piece of land is allocated, by lot or otherwise, for a nominal sum, say £100. If the property is desirable, a house can be built upon it for, say, £6,000. That house can be leased for £1,500 a year, five years in advance, to an expatriate firm or foreign embassy. In these circumstances it is easy to get a loan from a bank for the full value—all one needs is a piece of developable property and perhaps a lease agreement—and the operation can be repeated as often as it is possible to get hold of a parcel of land. That this has happened in urban centers is well known. When it comes to exploitation, all men are brothers under the skin, and original sin is neither a national nor a racial characteristic.

Overbuilding will remedy the situation. Rents payable in advance appear to have "shortened" to three years, and the Federal Minister of Finance has said that "fortunately, there are signs that this type of speculative investment in real estate is becoming less remunerative," at least in some parts of the country.[25] But it would help even more if land could be auctioned off instead of being allocated and if a market could be established for land which would make such round-about processes unnecessary.

For industrial development, the land problem takes on additional and somewhat different dimensions. The establishment of industrial estates cuts through many of these problems and gives impetus to the establishment of both domestic and expatriate businesses. Such estates minimize the necessary ancillary cost. Roads, electricity, water supplies, and so forth can be planned with a market assured by a concentration of industries. The temptation is to establish too many "growing points" too early, to disperse industries before there is anything to disperse. If the industrial estates are no more than areas zoned for industrial use in which clear titles can be obtained, the cost is low but the attraction to industries limited. If services have to be supplied, the cost quickly soars, and advantages of concentration appear which are at times politically difficult to accept.

The cost of industrial estates is very high. Since they are designed to attract foreign entrepreneurs and stimulate industrialization by both foreigners and citizens, they are not intended to be profit-making institutions. For most foreign firms the problem is likely to be whether they can get enough land and ancillary services at reasonable cost. Whether they pay for the cost in a lump sum or with an annual economic rent is secondary. The estates need not cause loss, however. It seems reasonable to expect that governments will eventually recoup the cost of development. Certainly without government help to make land available and provide services, industrialization will proceed very slowly or not at all in many parts of the world.

25. Budget Speech 1962, p. 15. Full citation: "The Mobilization Budget," Budget Speech by Chief Festus Sam Okotie-Eboh, Federal Minister of Finance (Lagos: Federal Ministry of Information, 1962).

VIII

Politics and Economics[1]

The spirit of a people, its cultural level, its social structure, the deeds its policy may prepare—all this and more is written in its fiscal history, stripped of all its phrases. He who knows how to listen to its message here discerns the thunder of world history more clearly than anywhere else.—J. A. Schumpeter, "The Crisis of the Tax State," *International Economic Papers*, IV (1954), 7.

IT is obvious that one cannot make policy without politics. Nor is this at all deplorable. Experts must of necessity look at narrow issues and trace through consequences of specific acts and assumptions. Politicians must mediate among conflicting ends, have a broader view, and are indispensable.

The decision to develop is itself a political decision. Once it is made, certain conclusions follow inescapably, and politicians find that their area of action is necessarily restricted by the economic implications of their political decisions. Every political decision made without due regard to its economic implications has a cost in terms of political or economic opportunities foregone. Backwardness may continue in the form of illiteracy, ill health, and political weakness; or the rate of growth achieved may be lower than was possible; or unnecessary sacrifices may have been imposed upon the population, "unnecessary" being defined in terms of the goal to be achieved.

1. An earlier, longer version of this chapter appeared in *Revista di Politica Economica*, no. 6 (1963), under the title "Politics and Economics in Economic Development."

In the new nations the economic aspects of political decisions and aspirations have gained even greater importance than in the past. Economic growth plays, at least officially, a major role in their ideologies. Yet their actions suggest that its greatest importance may be as an ancillary to nation building and the creation of political and possibly military power. Thus, Indonesia has rushed with indecent haste from becoming independent to becoming a colonial power. In all cases, political and social tensions are created by the conflict between an overwhelming desire for change and a feeling that the costs involved are close to being unbearable and the obstacles overpowering.

These tensions are aggravated by the fact that economic development means change in a manner and toward an ultimate destination which no economist or anthropologist or sociologist or politician can really foresee. The old societies have worked after a fashion, and people have understood their working. The "winds of change" bring ideas that have not arisen in these societies; and these ideas are even less likely to be properly appreciated than in the West whence they have come. And it is by no means so sure that the West (or, for that matter, Russia) knows where change is taking the world.

If these tensions are to remain within bearable bounds, manageable and realistic economic development programs and policies become essential. Plans made must really achieve their ends and do so without imposing unnecessary sacrifices. The sacrifices that must inevitably be made in terms of taxes, dislocation, and disruption of traditional patterns are sufficiently frightening to make the economist conscious of his responsibilities. Changes are inevitable, and the economist must help to allow the changes to work themselves out with as little political irritation as possible. Old loyalties and institutions break up, and new ones arise. Status patterns change. The role of traditional rulers is transformed. New disciplines become necessary. The economist's plans had better be good.

There is danger in the expectations that have been aroused during the struggle for independence. Independence is expected to bring not only self-rule but also accelerated development. For better or for worse, colonialism has meant rule by aliens. It is irrelevant to argue that this has frequently been beneficial to the indigenous population; that law and order were introduced where tribal warfare and arbitrariness ruled; that slavery was abolished, hunger and disease effectively fought, and standards of living raised. All of this is true enough, and the desire for modernization is proof that the new ideas are welcome. But it is also true that the former colonial subject has certain strong feelings: that he has been kept in subordinate jobs longer than necessary; that the foreigner was not really so superior and created the impression of superior ability to keep himself indispensable; that, in short, economic and personal development has been held back by alien rule and that standards of living will rise more rapidly with self-rule.

Nigerians are full of hope and high expectations, energetic and willing to work and experiment as well as to follow the example of others. They are alive to progress and anxious for self-improvement. Examples of successes abound: farming in Bornu, fishing in Lake Chad, cocoa cultivation and tire retreading in the Western Region, self-help schools and community markets and roads in the East, and many more examples everywhere. But there are limitations to the speed with which progress can be achieved, because development has its inner logic and is difficult to speed up. Planners and economists must be aware of a country's tensions and hopes, as well as of their own limitations, and must listen to the politicians. But they cannot abdicate at this stage. The politician must be able to get honest advice, and the economist responsible for a plan (including economic policies), must insist on a realistic one. For not only is an unrealistic plan wasteful, but when expectations are disappointed, as they inescapably will be with an oversized and poorly thought-out plan, new and worse political tensions are set up. They are worse because they are now directed not against the foreigners but against one's own kin. Seven new demons take the place of the one that has been ejected. In some countries, older statesmen, caught up by the expectations they have raised and counseling a more gradual development, are challenged by the younger and more impatient generation. Far from leading, they are pushed by forces they cannot control. One wonders how often "neocolonialism," African or Arab "socialism," and similar battle cries are symptoms of disillusionment. The older generation that has achieved independence finds itself suddenly exposed to very much the same pressures which it had itself put upon the metropolitan power, pressures now from a younger generation impatient for the fruits of independence. The techniques and approaches which will achieve independence are not necessarily the same as those suitable to achieve stability and development once independence is won.

There is thus a difficult task ahead, in which development planning plays a major role. A well-conducted, realistic plan can provide a focus for the efforts of a new nation; it can give buoyancy to the hopes of the people and politicians. Bad planning and policies, too many sacrifices for intangible and uncertain aims, are bound to compound the already enormous difficulties of new nations; they are bound to aggravate internal tensions and make the achievement of *both* idealistic and material aims difficult and perhaps even impossible.

Nigeria, like Ghana, is a modern creation. Both have resources to be developed, and both have centuries-old political traditions that have transcended the tribal level. Undoubtedly there exists a national Nigerian political consciousness. But tribal feelings and loyalties and antagonisms are strong. The desire to create a nation that is viable and independent of the outside world in general (and of the former metropolitan power in particular) is one thing. Overcoming inner distrust is another. There is in

Africa as elsewhere some sense of what is equitable in the imposition of burdens; and there is a desire to improve the lot of the ordinary farmers and workers. What is true in Nigeria and Ghana is true everywhere. For all countries are plural societies, even if centralized one-party states or dictatorships try to pretend that it is not so.

The slogan that "political independence means nothing without economic independence" is not particularly illuminating. Yet it is symptomatic of the incipient frustrations that can break out on short notice. Why become independent after all if the end result is that you are worse off than before? Why exchange one master for a worse one simply because the color of his skin is the same as your own?

This is not an outsider's view. Many ordinary people freely express their dissatisfaction with their new superiors, complaining that jobs or contracts go to friends and relatives, or that the new superior shows as much or more insensitivity as the old colonial master or that nothing has changed except the person who receives all the perquisites. Such situations are revolutionary, and they have produced revolutions without always thereby being solved.

There is thus enormous pressure upon young nations to perform. Expectations have been built up to a high pitch. A few people may be content just with self-rule. For most people, I should think, self-rule means that government is not merely of the people but also by and for the people. All emergent countries are thus under a pressure to accelerate the development which they are tempted to believe was withheld from them or deliberately retarded before independence. For if it had proceeded sufficiently, would they still be underdeveloped?

In such a situation, to create a stable nation and a viable economy taxes the statesmanship of the best the new nations have to offer. Good planning can ease the task, and bad planning can immeasurably hamper a country. In Nigeria, federalization has helped to hold the country together by giving the major tribes individual *lebensraum* to make living together possible. At the same time, there are costs in a federal setup to be offset against benefits: for example, five administrations in a country in which skilled manpower is scarce.[2]

The new countries have the desire to create a nation and the will to make sacrifices to achieve their desires. They are faced with poverty and disease, lack of sufficient modern education, of modern technical know-how, of executive capacity, of absorptive capacity. In this situation, good economic policy, including good planning, becomes politically essential. Resources must be allocated in the best possible manner—not the perfect, just the best possible. The amount of sacrifices that can be asked of the people and that they will willingly undertake depends on the purposes for which the sacrifices are asked.

When we as economic theorists build models, we make, legitimately, some simplifying assumptions. One of them is that savings depend upon the level of income. If we want to be sophisticated, we add other determinants: relative prices and the income distribution and perhaps some demographic variables. This is a useful approach. Yet I would suggest that the funda-

2. See Arthur Hazlewood, "The Finances of Nigerian Federation," *West Africa,* August 27, 1955—reprinted in Oxford University Institute of Colonial Studies, Reprint Series, no. 14. See also John R. Hicks, "A Chapter in Federal Finance: The Case of Nigeria," in *Essays in World Economics* (Oxford: Clarendon Press, 1959), pp. 216-236, for an excellent discussion of the fiscal problems of federalism. In 1963, the Mid-West State was created, causing a further demand for administrative talent and for economic resources. According to the Western Nigeria Government: "During 1962–63, staff problems were very small both in the executive Ministries and in the Ministry of Economic Planning and Community Development. With the mass transfer of officers of Midwest origin in mid-1963, however, the problems of staff have become rather acute. The Region has lost not only in numbers but also in experience some of its best officers. In the short run, therefore, the effective execution and coordination of the Plan cannot but be affected." *Western Nigeria Development Plan 1962–63, First Progress Report,* Western Nigeria Official Document no. 2 of 1964 (Ibadan), p. 5.

mental development problem is not primarily to find resources but is to find profitable outlets for them and to find competent people who can execute the programs. Savings do depend on what economists usually assume. But they also depend to a considerable extent on the uses to which they are to be put.

This requires a good flow of information between the government and the people—between the planners and the citizens—which is not easy to organize. It requires a sensitivity to the need for incentive goods, be they public or private. But it also requires a realistic plan. I have argued that there is an optimum-sized program. Simply to tax for bigger "investments" which in turn will not bring results will inevitably cause trouble. The large programs that look so impressive on paper necessarily contain projects that will not pay off either in terms of growth or in terms of satisfactions. African peasants may be illiterate, but they are not stupid. They are not impressed by the length of the cars of politicians. They know that public buildings and officials' houses cost a lot and that subsidies to unprofitable prestige projects cost a lot too. They couldn't care less about the prestige supposedly derived from jets criss-crossing continents without paying passengers. To impose larger sacrifices in order to achieve smaller gains is bad economics. It is also asking for political trouble.

Thus it becomes important in nation building not to put excessive stresses into the inherently difficult and disturbing process of growth. How often we can see a sequence approximately as follows. We are poor, say the leaders of a new nation; we must become rich by sacrifices. We were unfree, we must be free. We must accelerate growth. That means more sacrifices. Sacrifices (in the form of taxes, import restrictions, detailed regulation, compulsory labor, and so forth) are then imposed in order to build up projects that do not pay. The expected results do not materialize. The projects require subsidies, which means more taxes. The sacrifices required are thus used to go backward, since losses mean that as the end result of your "development" you come out with less resources than you had. People know when they get nothing for something, and they become restless. They object to paying taxes. They are told by their political leaders that they should not be immature. When they continue to object, they are told that in the interest of the nation they must forego their personal freedoms. They and we are told that democracy doesn't work. This is usually accompanied by such obviously true and, in my view, equally uninformative statements as that one can't export the forms of Westminster and Washington to different environments. We are told that the necessary sacrifices can be extracted only by a dictatorial leader who, to add insult to injury, is represented as "truly" democratic, whatever "truly" is supposed to mean. Yet the question of whether the sacrifices were either necessary or capable of achieving their intended ends is not asked.[3]

Strong leadership is necessary also in a democracy. The consent of the led is essential, however, and it could be achieved for any sensible economic program. Bad economics create unnecessary political difficulties, and good, or at least better, economics can substantially help in the process of nation building and political development. Man does not live by bread alone, but the Bible nowhere says that man can live without bread. The aims of development are non-economic. But the fuller life—whether it entails a comfortable home or better nutrition or the reduction of infant mortality, or a powerful army, or the provision of beautiful museums and fostering of the arts—requires real resources. No political ends, no non-economic ends can be achieved without the creation of a viable economy. This,

3. Obviously, bad economics is neither the only nor the major reason for the establishment of dictatorships. The reason can be more adequately traced to original sin. I am discussing here the specific assumption that political immaturity in the people and/or an entrenched power group which resists progress justifies abridging personal liberties in the name of development.

perhaps, is the real meaning of the desire to get rid of "economic colonialism."

To achieve this, economists must not abdicate too early, as they tend to do. The contribution that economics, and particularly economic theory, can make is substantial. I believe that all too frequently such statements as "this is really a political decision" or "you must take non-economic factors into consideration" and the like are as trivial as they are true; that they hide incompetence or unwillingness to analyze; and they are all too often excuses for arbitrary actions.

There are in fact fairly narrow limits to political decisions in economic matters, limits that spring not only from the poverty of a country but also from the difficulties inherent in the attempts to push out the limits of absorptive capacity. Development undoubtedly requires that more of the total product should be saved and invested. But, as has been argued throughout this book, a rational allocation of increasing resources is not at all easy to achieve.

An uneconomic allocation of resources quickly becomes untenable, and stringent measures of import control, high taxation, and forced savings that have resulted from past neglect of economic considerations have led to bloody uprisings of the very people for whose benefit the austerity was supposedly introduced. It seems obvious that in a young and politically as yet untried country it is extremely dangerous to start off by making the ordinary man in the street worse off than he was before independence. It is necessary that his standard of living should rise more slowly than the anticipated rate of growth of the economy, so that the country may as quickly as possible reach what it has become fashionable to call the takeoff stage. But if the standard of living does not rise at all, or if it deteriorates, there had better be a very good and plausible reason why this must be so, such as a catastrophic deterioration in the terms of trade or a really powerful investment program with a large economic payoff in the reasonably foreseeable future.

In fact, limited absorptive capacity means that the amount of income-raising investments can be increased only slowly. Whether one likes it or not, the economies for which decisions have to be made are part of the world economy. The causal connection between balance-of-payments troubles and import substitution does not appear to be one-way only. The import substitutions themselves appear to have led to import needs which the policy makers hope are only temporary.

All of this means that the political variations in economic decisions are limited. If past investment ratios were, say 10 percent, they cannot be raised to 15 percent very quickly with any hope of making this 15 percent self-sustaining in the foreseeable future. Savings ratios cannot be doubled quickly. Politicians may quarrel over whether a school should be located in this or that village and whether there should be 10 percent more or fewer schools. But they cannot ignore the limitations arising from lack of teachers or, at higher levels, from the lack of students trained at lower levels.

At the level of economic investments—as distinct from the investments for which it is repugnant to make payoff calculations— the appeal to non-economic benefits becomes doubly dubious when these investments do not lead to an increase in available resources. There is no virtue in "modern" agriculture if it does not pay. Loss industries are toys, and very expensive ones to boot. To insist on high taxation—on austerity—in order to transfer resources which might have been consumed to projects that lose money and slow down the rate of growth is economically irresponsible and politically explosive. Permitting a higher level of consumption would, at the very least, have been neutral as far as growth is concerned, and it might have had a positive effect through creating markets and incentives. Loss investments reduce the rate of growth. The austerity imposed has been austerity not to achieve growth but to hide mistakes.

The point of the argument, then, is that the size of sacrifices required and the size of the program must depend to a larger extent than is commonly realized on the profitability and rationality of this program. No one denies that the size of a program is *also* politically determined. It is, however, irresponsible for any economist to take the size of any program as purely politically determined and then busy himself with methods of raising the required resources.

The economist must see the resource-raising side and the resource-using side as a unit. It is, after all, by now accepted that the taxing and spending sides of public finance should be considered together. Similarly, the size of the program, the sacrifices required, the political benefits and cost must be jointly considered. The insistence by the economist on economic rationality and on a rational size and composition of a development program is of prime political importance. The idea, all too frequently found, that a program is better if it is bigger, and that objections to bigness come from egotism, neocolonialism, and similar despicable emotions, is playing a politically dangerous numbers game.

It is difficult to believe that as a general rule dictatorships must be established and opposition must be suppressed if development is to take place. Undoubtedly there are many instances where, say, overdue land reforms cannot be achieved with the consent of the landlords. Undoubtedly there are cases where the centrifugal forces of tribalism are too strong to be overcome by the new kind of democracy. Yet one may be permitted to wonder whether a federal constitution might not frequently suffice to harness these forces to a common goal. And it is equally true that people will quite rationally resist austerity if they can feel in their bones that this austerity will benefit a very few who will be subsidized. One wonders how often the cry for central control or for increased sacrifices stems from a desire to hide the unpalatable fact that resources have been wasted and the sacrifices have been in vain.

Economists are accused of having a narrow economic view and of neglecting the non-economic benefits to be derived from what looks to them a wasteful expenditure of time, labor, and resources. Now obviously there are non-economic benefits. No one would deny that health or education should not be looked at only, or even primarily, in terms of improved productivity and added income. Nevertheless, non-economic benefits can be achieved in a more or less economic manner; they do cost economic resources that have alternative uses, and they are frequently illusory. And, of course, they must not be offset by non-economic costs whose existence seems frequently to be forgotten.

As John R. Hicks has put it in another context: "The high value which people set upon security and equality has been shown by experience; but experience has also shown that any large movement towards fulfilling these aims at once encounters the obstacle of deficient productivity."[4] What is true for security and equality is equally true for other aims of society: to achieve a healthy people, to have general education, to have leisure, and so forth.

Take the argument that people have to learn their business and that, while they are learning it, it is only natural that they will make losses. This is true. But the learning process has something in common with research and education. One does not allocate such a large amount of resources to education that nothing is left over for the employment of the educated, nor is it reasonable to allocate such large amounts to deficit enterprises that growth in the economy is slowed—on the grounds that eventually people will learn their business. By the time they have

4. John R. Hicks, *Essays in World Economics* (Oxford: Clarendon Press, 1959), p. 43.

learned it, there are no resources left with which to practice the newly-gained knowledge!

Moreover, non-economic benefits can be had as easily from enterprises which yield economic returns as from those which do not. The economists must ask why an enterprise which possibly could be profitable in fact needs subsidies. This will reveal current obstacles, and it will suggest the proper remedies for them. It will also reveal whether there is any chance that the enterprise will become profitable and when. An enterprise that has no chance to become profitable any time soon is not likely to confer the economic benefit of learning the business or of modernizing the economy. Only profitable enterprises can do this.

Obviously excessively high cost and other shortcomings are not necessarily inherent in any particular program. At the least, therefore, analysis would show whether in fact particular non-economic benefits can be achieved and what the economic costs of achieving non-economic benefits are. Even if everyone agrees on the desirability of non-economic benefits, and even if they can be clearly formulated instead of being merely vaguely postulated, it is precisely the lack of economic justification which makes the non-economic ends unobtainable.

Good economic policy and careful planning are essential to political stability, and austerity is an explosive idea. There is every evidence that people will undergo hardships to achieve ends where they see the results, but they are justifiably suspicious of general phrases and promises. It would be good if economists and politicians were also.

APPENDIX

An Input-Output Analysis of the Nigerian Economy, 1959-60[1]

By Nicholas G. Carter

The Federal Republic of Nigeria is now executing her first National Development Plan. This will be followed by her second one and within a few years a third one. At some point in this continuing planning process she will be likely to embrace some of the more highly sophisticated planning techniques that are now being refined. When this time comes, Nigeria will need, among other things, an input-output table.

The tables gathered here are the first for Nigeria. They have been constructed in order to portray the structure of the Nigerian economy in the period just prior to independence. Their purpose is thus both historical and analytical; more than this, they are intended to be the basis for a considerable amount of further work in the area of Nigerian national accounts.

The limits of the tables are limits of data. This holds for both availability and reliability. The foundations are the accounts of Okigbo, which are the best data about the Nigerian economy.[2] In addition, the tables rely on various published works of the Federal Office of Statistics, the estimates of the Economic Planning Unit, the

1. This brief discussion has been extracted from my *An Input-Output Analysis of the Nigerian Economy, 1959/60*, Working Paper no. 29-63, M.I.T. School of Industrial Management, Cambridge, Mass., mimeo., 1963. The longer version contains a complete description of all the data, methods of analysis, and individual sector-flow accounts.
2. P. N. C. Okigbo, *Nigerian National Accounts 1950–57*, published [December 1961] by the Federal Ministry of Economic Development, printed by the Government Printer, Enugu, Eastern Nigeria.

work of Peter Kilby on small industry, some unpublished reports on manufacturing, and personal observations.

The information presented by Okigbo ends with the fiscal year 1957–58; the tables here refer to the fiscal year 1959–60. Thus a major amount of estimation was done by extrapolation of trends. Other available data, while often pertaining to the correct year (or later), were invariably incomplete; thus another important technique was ratio projection. Finally, in many cases the desired figure could be obtained as a residual; this was especially true of distributive margins.

The choice of sectors reflects a definite bias in favor of manufacturing. Agriculture, for example, has been split into two sectors, the division being where mechanical processing enters. On the other hand all services, including rents, banking, church missions, entertainment, and so on, are placed in a single sector. This bias, however, shows the extent of industrialization in Nigeria and will allow the tables to be used as a bench mark as the country grows over the next decades. Because of this bias, the blank "boxes" in the input-output calculation proper amount to 49 percent of the total. In spite of this, the matrix remains both nonsingular and nontriangular.

The estimates used here are valued in 1959–60 producer prices. These prices were chosen because the manufacturing sections were taken from as yet unpublished statistical returns for that year. Every attempt was made to put all figures in these prices. Problems arose, however, with the data projected from Okigbo. Although estimates were made on current-price series, they depend on general constancy in the rate of price rise. Recent data show that this was not in fact so, and consequently the tables slightly understate the value added in current prices for Nigeria in 1959–60.

Imports were treated as though they were all noncompetitive, and they appear in a row vector beneath the main matrix. The major reason for this treatment was computational convenience. This means that using the matrix in growth models entails the assignment of competitive imports to a column vector. However, in dealing with a less developed economy this is essentially a dynamic choice based on the time span of the particular model. Therefore all imports have been left in the noncompetitive vector.

Some of the industry names in Tables 18, 19, and 20 are abbreviated; see Table 17 for the full names.

Table 17 presents the national accounts on a product basis. These accounts are a companion piece to Table 18, the input-output transactions matrix. Tables 19 and 20 are the technology matrix ($[A] \times 10^4$) and the inverse matrix ($[I - A]^{-1}$). Table 21 is a breakdown of investment for 1959–60 according to the nature of the asset. Table 22 shows the import structure of the economy, and, finally, Table 23 shows the degree of interdependence of the various sectors of the economy. Tables 21 through 23 have been calculated from the input-output matrices.

It is obvious that this input-output analysis is only a beginning, designed to be a guide for the more complete analyses that will undoubtedly be undertaken when Nigerian statistics have been developed further.

(The tables begin on the next page.)

Table 17. Nigerian Gross Domestic Product, 1959–60
(£ thousand)

SECTOR 1. *Agriculture*

Groundnuts	25,564.0
Cocoa	19,579.7
Palm fruit	10,725.0
Cotton	5,488.1
Rubber	7,631.1
Benniseed	829.1
Soyas	74.1
Shea nuts	176.2
Palm wine	5,000.0
Coffee, copra, ginger	1,097.6
Tobacco	357.0
Kola nuts	5,308.3
Miscellaneous (non-edible)	32.6
Roots	202,000.0
Beans, etc.	28,800.0
Cereals	136,800.0
Bananas and plantains	7,313.8
Miscellaneous vegetables	576.3
Subtotal	457,350.9
Less general inputs	1,903.2
Total, Sector 1	455,447.7

SECTOR 2. *Livestock, fishing, forestry*

Cattle	9,957.4
Sheep and goats	9,383.6
Goats' milk	6,600.0
Cows' milk	12,023.1
Poultry and eggs	10,180.0
Pigs	341.4
Miscellaneous animal products	246.1
Fishing	14,349.1
Forestry	30,263.8
Total, Sector 2	93,344.5

SECTOR 3. *Agricultural processing*

Sawmills	1,869.4
Hand sawyers	1,671.3
Rice mills	13.3
Corn mills	345.7
Tanning	341.1
Groundnut processing	1,593.2
Cotton ginning	418.7
Rubber processing	3,281.6
Palm products	18,628.2
Total, Sector 3	28,162.5

SECTOR 4. *Textiles*

Large textiles	597.9
Weaving and dyeing	650.6
Domestic weaving	1,928.6
Total, Sector 4	3,177.1

SECTOR 5. *Clothing*

Domestic tailoring	6,836.5
Tailors and seamstresses	10,045.1
Singlets	118.6
Footwear	38.1
Rubber shoes	486.9
Shoes (repair)	483.8
Total, Sector 5	18,009.0

SECTOR 6. *Drink and tobacco*

Beer and soft drinks	2,514.3
Tobacco manufacturing	6,189.4
Total, Sector 6	8,703.7

SECTOR 7. *Food*

Butter	156.8
Meat and dried milk	9.4
Miscellaneous foods	89.7
Margarine, tea blending, and fruit canning	54.1
Pork	(134.1)
Baking	2,095.1
Small food	4,522.8
Total, Sector 7	6,793.8

SECTOR 8. *Metal mining* 5,046.5

SECTOR 9. *Non-metal mining*

Petroleum extraction	(93.9)
Sand, stone, and gravel	4,595.0
Coal	1,343.3
Total, Sector 9	5,844.4

Table 17. (Continued)

SECTOR 10. *Chemicals*	
Industrial gases	5.5
Carbon dioxide and dry ice	23.2
Bitumen	84.6
Soap (large)	1,194.1
Soap (small)	25.6
Lime	3.0
Vaccine	(24.7)
Total, Sector 10	1,311.3
SECTOR 11. *Transport*	80,501.6
SECTOR 12. *Utilities*	
Electricity	2,866.9
Water	336.1
Total, Sector 12	3,203.0
SECTOR 13. *Trade*	68,457.8
SECTOR 14. *Construction*	38,154.0
SECTOR 15. *Service*	
Domestic service	5,500.0
Entertainment	1,086.7
Intrahousehold service	10,000.0
Ownership of buildings	10,300.0
Scrap	288.1
Other services	82,724.6
Total, Sector 15	109,899.4
SECTOR 16. *Transport equipment*	
Vehicle assembly	121.7
Transport repair (large)	2,772.0
Transport repair (small)	1,956.1
Boats	82.2
Total, Sector 16	4,932.0
SECTOR 17. *Non-metallic mineral products*	
Tiles and concrete products	136.7
Cement and ceramics	663.5
Drilling mud	30.3
Total, Sector 17	830.5

SECTOR 18. *Metal manufacturing*	
Large metallic mfg.	1,009.5
Small metallic mfg.	2,679.7
Bicycle assembly	20.2
Total, Sector 18	3,709.4
SECTOR 19. *Products of wood, leather, paper, rubber, plastic*	
Large furniture	324.6
Small furniture, carpentry	5,684.3
Plastics and foam rubber	107.8
Tire retreading	237.5
Printing, publishing, and stationery	1,951.2
Miscellaneous	989.1
Total, Sector 19	9,294.5
SECTOR 20. *Miscellaneous manufacturing*	
Perfumes	215.9
Miscellaneous textiles	9.2
Umbrellas	21.6
Tarpaulins	58.0
Maps	2.6
Mattress making	75.1
Miscellaneous (small)	730.2
Total, Sector 20	1,112.6
TOTAL, ALL SECTORS	945,935.2
Plus:	
Marketing Boards	13,481.3
Government	44,500.0
Non-intermediate value added	17,237.9
GDP at factor cost	1,021,154.4
Indirect taxes[a]	42,700.0
GDP at market prices	1,063,854.4
Income from abroad	(1,700.0)
GNP at current prices	1,062,154.5

a. In the absence of definite information, I have assumed subsidies to be equal to zero.

Table 18. Transactions matrix, showing direct purchases from industries named at the left by industries whose code numbers appear across the top (transfers in £ thousand)

	1	2	3	4	5	6	7	8	9	10
1. Agriculture	0.0	0.0	27,730.7	2,060.0	0.0	282.6	2,142.0	0.0	0.0	7.6
2. Livest'ck, fish'g, forestry	10.0	0.0	5,629.4	0.0	0.0	0.0	6,729.2	35.7	55.0	8.2
3. Agric. processing	94.9	583.6	0.0	363.4	241.4	0.0	100.9	0.0	0.0	601.4
4. Textiles	0.0	0.0	0.0	0.0	6,491.8	0.0	0.0	0.0	0.0	0.0
5. Clothing	0.0	0.0	0.0	0.0	0.0	0.0	0.0	0.0	0.0	0.0
6. Drink and tobacco	0.0	0.0	0.0	0.0	0.0	0.0	0.0	0.0	0.0	0.0
7. Food	0.0	0.0	0.0	0.0	0.0	0.0	0.0	0.0	0.0	0.0
8. Metal mining	0.0	0.0	0.0	0.0	0.0	0.0	0.0	0.0	0.0	0.0
9. Non-metal mining	0.0	0.0	22.0	5.2	0.0	0.6	1.6	19.4	0.0	24.9
10. Chemicals	0.0	35.3	0.0	0.0	0.0	29.1	0.0	0.0	0.0	0.0
11. Transport	283.2	536.9	6,221.6	35.0	1,273.2	182.7	1,008.1	51.6	231.6	81.7
12. Utilities	1.5	0.2	597.7	76.8	21.7	71.6	42.2	236.2	74.0	42.9
13. Trade	189.3	30.4	304.6	72.6	1,456.0	60.1	630.7	62.4	128.2	31.8
14. Construction	0.0	0.4	69.5	9.8	0.5	8.3	17.8	19.2	91.0	16.9
15. Service	421.3	68.0	1,557.6	92.4	772.0	341.6	1,056.3	126.7	58.4	214.5
16. Transport equipment	0.0	0.5	128.8	1.2	0.4	9.3	19.7	19.3	16.0	9.8
17. Non-metallic mineral	0.0	0.0	0.0	0.0	0.0	0.0	0.0	0.0	50.0	0.0
18. Metal mfg.	0.0	0.0	142.8	45.9	741.8	57.8	79.8	27.1	22.0	181.5
19. Wood, leather, etc.	0.0	0.0	50.3	6.4	4.7	47.1	168.3	15.6	26.0	37.2
20. Miscellaneous mfg.	0.0	0.0	25.1	3.2	2.4	23.5	65.4	7.8	13.0	15.2
Total intermediate inputs	1,000.2	1,255.3	42,480.1	2,771.6	11,005.9	1,114.3	12,062.0	621.0	765.2	1,273.6
Imports	2,070.6	4,843.5	2,135.3	619.7	4,567.9	3,780.7	3,477.3	397.8	3,114.2	826.7
Total inputs	3,070.8	6,098.8	44,615.4	3,391.3	15,573.8	4,895.0	15,539.3	1,018.8	3,879.4	2,100.3
Total outputs	458,518.5	99,443.3	72,777.8	6,568.4	33,582.8	13,598.7	22,333.1	6,065.3	9,723.8	3,411.6
Value added	455,447.7	93,344.5	28,162.4	3,177.1	18,009.0	8,703.7	6,793.8	5,046.5	5,844.4	1,311.3

Table 18. (Continued)

	11	12	13	14	15	16	17	18	19	20
1. Agriculture	0.0	0.0	0.0	0.0	0.0	0.0	0.0	0.0	0.0	14.3
2. Livest'ck, fish'g, forestry	0.0	0.0	0.0	1,700.8	0.0	5.2	0.4	174.6	211.3	101.4
3. Agric. processing	0.0	205.0	0.0	6,574.3	0.0	209.3	0.0	0.0	5,182.0	0.0
4. Textiles	0.0	0.0	0.0	0.0	0.0	0.0	0.0	0.0	0.0	14.3
5. Clothing	0.0	0.0	100.0	0.0	100.0	0.0	0.0	0.0	0.0	0.0
6. Drink and tobacco	0.0	0.0	0.0	0.0	0.0	0.0	0.0	0.0	0.0	0.0
7. Food	0.0	0.0	0.0	0.0	0.0	0.0	0.0	0.0	0.0	0.0
8. Metal mining	0.0	0.0	0.0	0.0	0.0	0.0	225.7	12.0	0.0	0.0
9. Non-metal mining	813.9	430.0	0.0	4,568.0	27.6	9.3	0.0	30.7	0.0	0.0
10. Chemicals	4.3	0.0	0.0	740.1	0.0	0.0	0.0	17.7	0.0	0.0
11. Transport	0.0	296.7	1,699.7	7,181.0	1,341.4	245.3	59.4	356.3	652.9	107.7
12. Utilities	0.0	0.0	0.0	121.0	715.9	107.2	134.5	88.0	111.1	6.8
13. Trade	1,647.2	104.7	0.0	6,072.0	2,863.5	237.4	10.1	441.4	418.3	35.7
14. Construction	0.0	19.2	317.4	0.0	1,961.3	20.0	1.2	16.0	13.0	1.1
15. Service	2,958.7	99.6	2,198.8	934.0	0.0	355.3	48.0	607.6	695.9	88.9
16. Transport equipment	6,158.8	0.0	0.0	217.0	0.0	0.0	2.1	3.7	7.2	4.7
17. Non-metallic mineral	0.0	0.0	0.0	1,372.9	0.0	0.0	0.0	0.0	0.0	0.0
18. Metal mfg.	109.2	363.0	160.4	235.0	180.3	3.4	9.7	0.0	103.5	10.0
19. Wood, leather, etc.	748.8	12.7	320.8	1,956.9	1,129.2	5.7	7.1	11.4	0.0	2.3
20. Miscellaneous mfg.	109.1	6.4	309.0	0.0	795.2	2.8	3.5	5.7	8.0	0.0
Total intermediate inputs	12,550.0	1,537.3	5,106.1	31,673.0	9,114.4	1,200.9	501.7	1,765.1	7,403.2	387.2
Imports	11,867.8	738.9	820.0	20,673.0	3,211.6	2,559.5	123.7	4,507.0	3,477.1	736.9
Total inputs	24,417.8	2,276.2	5,926.1	52,346.0	12,326.0	3,760.4	625.4	6,272.1	10,880.3	1,124.1
Total outputs	104,919.4	5,479.2	74,383.9	90,500.0	122,225.4	8,692.4	1,455.9	9,981.5	20,174.8	2,236.7
Value added	80,501.6	3,203.0	68,457.8	38,154.0	109,899.4	4,932.0	830.5	3,709.4	9,294.5	1,112.6

Table 18. (Continued)

	I Total intermediate demand	II Final demand Investment	III Final demand Exports	IV Final demand Consumption	V = I+II+III+IV Total demand
1. Agriculture	33,237.2	0.0	40,476.8	385,804.5	458,518.5
2. Livestock, fishing, forestry	14,661.2	0.0	6,190.9	78,591.2	99,443.3
3. Agricultural processing	14,156.2	0.0	46,640.0	11,981.6	72,777.8
4. Textiles	6,506.1	0.0	62.3	0.0	6,568.4
5. Clothing	200.1	0.0	0.0	33,382.8	33,582.8
6. Drink and tobacco	0.0	0.0	89.5	13,509.2	13,598.7
7. Food	0.0	0.0	139.7	22,193.4	22,333.1
8. Metal mining	12.0	0.0	6,053.3	0.0	6,065.3
9. Non-metal mining	6,178.9	0.0	3,519.6	25.3	9,723.8
10. Chemicals	826.5	0.0	151.5	2,433.6	3,411.6
11. Transport	21,846.0	4,273.9	11,211.3	67,588.2	104,919.4
12. Utilities	2,449.3	0.0	0.0	3,029.9	5,479.2
13. Trade	14,796.1	3,029.8	1,197.6	55,360.4	74,383.9
14. Construction	2,582.6	85,000.0	0.0	2,917.4	90,500.0
15. Service	12,695.6	4,977.7	8,715.0	95,837.1	122,225.4
16. Transport equipment	6,598.5	1,293.9	0.0	800.0	8,692.4
17. Non-metallic mineral products	1,422.9	0.0	17.4	15.6	1,455.9
18. Metal manufacturing	2,473.2	1,737.2	7.5	5,763.6	9,981.5
19. Wood, leather, paper, rubber, plastic	4,550.5	0.0	0.0	15,624.3	20,174.8
20. Miscellaneous manufacturing	1,395.3	0.0	6.5	834.9	2,236.7
Total outputs (sum of 1–20)	145,588.1	100,312.5	124,478.9	795,693.0	1,166,072.5

(Continued on next page)

Table 18. (Concluded)

Consumption of intermediate goods	795,693.0
Consumption of imports	119,859.4
Investment in intermediate goods	100,312.5
Investment in imports	30,338.0
Investment value added—Final	17,237.9
Trade balance (exports-imports)	27,648.1
Indirect taxes[a]	24,711.7
Income from abroad	1,700.0
GNP at current prices	1,062,154.4

a. Except import duty on final consumption and investment.

Table 19. *Technology matrix ([A] × 10⁴), showing the relation of inputs to outputs for industries whose code numbers appear across the top**

	1	2	3	4	5	6	7	8	9	10
1. Agriculture	+	—	3,810	3,136	—	208	959	—	—	22
2. Livestock, fishing, forestry	2	59	774	—	—	—	3,013	59	57	24
3. Agricultural processing	—	—	—	553	72	—	45	—	—	1,763
4. Textiles	—	—	—	—	1,933	—	—	—	—	—
5. Clothing	—	—	—	—	—	—	—	—	—	—
6. Drink and tobacco	—	—	—	—	—	—	—	—	—	—
7. Food	—	—	—	—	—	—	—	—	—	—
8. Metal mining	—	—	—	8	—	+	+	32	—	—
9. Non-metal mining	—	—	3	8	—	21	+	32	—	73
10. Chemicals	—	4	—	—	—	—	—	—	—	—
11. Transport	6	54	855	53	379	134	451	85	238	239
12. Utilities	+	+	82	117	6	53	19	389	76	126
13. Trade	4	3	42	111	434	44	282	103	132	93
14. Construction	—	+	10	15	+	6	8	32	94	50
15. Service	9	7	214	141	230	251	473	209	60	629
16. Transport equipment	—	+	18	2	+	7	9	32	16	29
17. Non-metallic mineral products	—	—	—	—	—	—	—	—	51	—
18. Metal manufacturing	—	—	20	70	221	43	36	45	23	32
19. Wood, leather, paper, etc.	—	—	7	10	1	35	75	26	27	109
20. Miscellaneous manufacturing	—	—	3	5	+	17	29	13	13	45

Table 19. (Concluded)

	11	12	13	14	15	16	17	18	19	20
1. Agriculture	—	—	—	—	—	—	—	—	—	64
2. Livestock, fishing, forestry	—	—	—	188	—	6	3	175	105	453
3. Agricultural processing	—	374	—	726	—	241	—	2,569	—	—
4. Textiles	—	—	—	—	—	—	—	—	—	64
5. Clothing	—	—	13	—	8	—	—	—	—	—
6. Drink and tobacco	—	—	—	—	—	—	—	—	—	—
7. Food	—	—	—	—	—	—	—	—	—	—
8. Metal mining	—	—	—	—	—	—	—	12	—	—
9. Non-metal mining	78	785	—	505	2	11	1,550	31	—	—
10. Chemicals	+	—	—	82	—	—	—	18	—	—
11. Transport	—	542	229	793	110	282	408	357	324	482
12. Utilities	—	191	—	13	59	123	924	88	55	30
13. Trade	157	35	43	671	234	273	69	442	207	160
14. Construction	—	182	296	—	160	23	8	16	6	5
15. Service	282	—	—	103	—	409	330	609	345	397
16. Transport equipment	587	—	—	24	—	—	14	4	4	21
17. Non-metallic mineral products	—	663	—	152	—	4	67	—	—	—
18. Metal manufacturing	10	663	22	26	15	4	67	—	51	45
19. Wood, leather, paper, etc.	71	23	43	216	92	7	49	11	—	10
20. Miscellaneous manufacturing	10	12	42	—	65	3	24	6	4	—

* To illustrate: the figure 3,810 in the top row, column 3, means that for each £10,000 of sales by the agricultural processing industry (Industry 3), this industry made £3,810 of direct purchases from agriculture. The figure 22 in column 10 means that for each £10,000 of sales by the chemicals industry (Industry 10), this industry made £22 of direct purchases from agriculture.
+ = small positive transaction, $a_{ij} < 10^{-4}$.

Table 20. Inverse matrix $([I - A]^{-1})$, showing the relation of inputs to outputs for industries whose code numbers appear across the top*

	1	2	3	4	5	6	7	8	9	10
1. Agriculture	1.0001	.0023	.3816	.3351	.0677	.0215	.0993	.0010	.0008	.0712
2. Livest'ck, fish'g, forestry	.0000	1.0005	.0776	.0046	.0019	.0004	.3024	.0064	.0062	.0179
3. Agricultural processing	.0002	.0060	1.0016	.0564	.0185	.0017	.0089	.0027	.0020	.1808
4. Textiles	.0000	.0000	.0000	1.0000	.1933	.0000	.0000	.0000	.0000	.0000
5. Clothing	.0000	.0000	.0000	.0000	1.0001	.0000	.0000	.0000	.0000	.0000
6. Drink and tobacco	.0000	.0000	.0000	.0000	.0000	1.0000	.0000	.0000	.0000	.0000
7. Food	.0000	.0000	.0000	.0000	.0000	.0000	1.0000	.0000	.0000	.0000
8. Metal mining	.0000	.0000	.0000	.0000	.0000	.0000	.0000	1.0000	.0000	.0000
9. Non-metal mining	.0000	.0000	.0018	.0020	.0009	.0007	.0008	.0066	1.0022	.0094
10. Chemicals	.0000	.0004	.0000	.0000	.0000	.0022	.0001	.0000	.0000	1.0002
11. Transport	.0007	.0060	.0877	.0121	.0433	.0149	.0499	.0125	.0263	.0451
12. Utilities	.0000	.0000	.0085	.0124	.0035	.0056	.0024	.0393	.0083	.0152
13. Trade	.0004	.0005	.0070	.0128	.0483	.0059	.0311	.0127	.0150	.0163
14. Construction	.0000	.0000	.0015	.0020	.0011	.0011	.0018	.0038	.0096	.0066
15. Service	.0010	.0010	.0252	.0172	.0305	.0266	.0510	.0232	.0082	.0732
16. Transport equipment	.0000	.0004	.0069	.0010	.0026	.0016	.0038	.0039	.0032	.0059
17. Non-metallic mineral	.0000	.0000	.0000	.0000	.0000	.0000	.0000	.0000	.0053	.0001
18. Metal mfg.	.0000	.0000	.0027	.0080	.0239	.0048	.0040	.0072	.0030	.0549
19. Wood, leather, paper, etc.	.0000	.0000	.0016	.0014	.0012	.0039	.0086	.0031	.0033	.0124
20. Miscellaneous mfg.	.0000	.0000	.0006	.0007	.0006	.0020	.0035	.0016	.0015	.0052

Table 20. (Concluded)

	11	12	13	14	15	16	17	18	19	20
1. Agriculture	.0013	.0148	.0008	.0308	.0016	.0096	.0021	.0007	.0983	.0090
2. Livest'k, fish'g, forestry	.0005	.0048	.0005	.0257	.0011	.9927	.0021	.0178	.0306	.0456
3. Agricultural processing	.0035	.0389	.0017	.0807	.0040	.0253	.0056	.0017	.2579	.0015
4. Textiles	.0000	.0000	.0003	.0000	.0002	.0000	.0000	.0000	.0000	.0064
5. Clothing	.0000	.0000	.0014	.0001	.0009	.0000	.0000	.0001	.0000	.0000
6. Drink and tobacco	.0000	.0000	.0000	.0000	.0000	.0000	.0000	.0000	.0000	.0000
7. Food	.0000	.0000	.0000	.0000	.0000	.0000	.0000	.0000	.0000	.0000
8. Metal mining	.0000	.0000	.0000	.0000	.0000	.0000	.0000	.0012	.0000	.0000
9. Non-metal mining	.0080	.0797	.0005	.0541	.0017	.0025	.1632	.0043	.0013	.0008
10. Chemicals	.0000	.0002	.0000	.0082	.0001	.0000	.0000	.0018	.0000	.0000
11. Transport	1.0034	.0635	.0243	.0919	.0144	.0328	.0523	.0389	.0567	.0502
12. Utilities	.0011	1.0018	.0003	.0043	.0061	.0129	.0942	.0094	.0080	.0035
13. Trade	.0185	.0255	1.0018	.0713	.0254	.0296	.0138	.0470	.0245	.0184
14. Construction	.0008	.0049	.0048	1.0013	.0162	.0032	.0034	.0029	.0018	.0013
15. Service	.0318	.0266	.0310	.0196	1.0023	.0438	.0391	.0641	.0433	.0425
16. Transport equipment	.0589	.0040	.0015	.0081	.0009	1.0020	.0048	.0027	.0042	.0051
17. Non-metallic mineral	.0000	.0005	.0000	.0155	.0003	.0000	1.0009	.0000	.0000	.0000
18. Metal mfg.	.0013	.0668	.0023	.0041	.0021	.0015	.0135	1.0010	.0064	.0049
19. Wood, leather, etc.	.0076	.0036	.0049	.0232	.0099	.0016	.0064	.0023	1.0012	.0019
20. Miscellaneous mfg.	.0014	.0017	.0044	.0007	.0067	.0008	.0031	.0013	.0009	1.0004

* This table shows both direct and indirect purchases per £1 of sales. To illustrate: the figure .3816 in the top row, column 3, means that for £1 of sales by the agricultural processing industry (Industry 3), this industry made a total of £0.3816 of direct and indirect purchases from agriculture. (Of this, £0.3810 represents direct purchases—see Table 19—and £0.0006 represents indirect purchases.)

Table 21. Investments in Nigerian economy, by nature of investment, 1959–60
(£ thousand)

Civil engineering	18,000.0	
Non-concrete buildings	18,100.0	
Concrete buildings	48,900.0	
Vehicles (local)	1,293.9	
Metal fabrication	1,737.2	
Distribution	12,281.4	
Domestic purchases, total	100,312.5	100,312.5
Imports of plant and machinery	18,384.3	
Commercial vehicle imports	11,209.6	
Less exports	937.3	
Plus duty	1,681.4	
Foreign purchases, total	30,338.0	30,338.0
Clearance of land by farmers		8,200.0
Investments in mines and plantations		9,037.9
Total investment		147,888.4

Note: Figures were derived following the method of Okigbo (his table B.15), using data from the trade summaries, the statistical returns of companies, and from my input-output analysis of the Nigerian economy. Changes in Marketing Board Stocks are not included above.

Table 22. Import composition of Nigerian output, 1959–60
(percentage)

Sector	Direct imports	Direct and indirect imports	Sector	Direct imports	Direct and indirect imports
1	.45	.47	11	11.31	13.73
2	4.87	4.99	12	13.49	20.40
3	2.93	5.14	13	1.10	2.00
4	9.43	10.69	14	22.84	27.39
5	13.60	17.45	15	2.63	3.88
6	27.80	28.64	16	29.45	30.56
7	15.57	18.51	17	8.50	16.78
8	6.56	8.19	18	45.15	46.50
9	32.03	33.18	19	17.23	19.62
10	24.23	29.31	20	32.95	34.46

Import composition of final demand

Consumption	17.75
Exports	4.21
Investment	17.12

Table 23. *Degree of interdependence in Nigerian economy, 1959–60*
(percentage)

Sector	Backward linkage[a]	Forward linkage[a]	Sector	Backward linkage[a]	Forward linkage[a]
1	0	7	11	12	21
2	1	14	12	28	45
3	58	19	13	7	20
4	42	99	14	35	3
5	33	1	15	7	10
6	8	0	16	14	76
7	54	0	17	34	98
8	10	2	18	18	25
9	8	64	19	37	23
10	37	24	20	17	63

a. Backward linkage is defined as the ratio of inputs from other industries to total output of the sector. Forward linkage is the ratio of sales to other industries to total sales.

Index

339

PUBLICATIONS WRITTEN UNDER THE AUSPICES OF THE
CENTER FOR INTERNATIONAL AFFAIRS
HARVARD UNIVERSITY

BOOKS

The Soviet Bloc, by Zbigniew K. Brzezinski (jointly with the Russian Research Center), 1960. Harvard University Press.

The Necessity for Choice, by Henry A. Kissinger, 1961. Harper & Bros.

Strategy and Arms Control, by Thomas C. Schelling and Morton H. Halperin, 1961. Twentieth Century Fund.

Rift and Revolt in Hungary, by Ferenc A. Váli, 1961. Harvard University Press.

United States Manufacturing Investment in Brazil, by Lincoln Gordon and Engelbert L. Grommers, 1962. Harvard Business School.

The Economy of Cyprus, by A. J. Meyer, with Simos Vassiliou (jointly with the Center for Middle Eastern Studies), 1962. Harvard University Press.

Entrepreneurs of Lebanon, by Yusif A. Sayigh (jointly with the Center for Middle Eastern Studies), 1962. Harvard University Press.

Communist China 1955-1959: Policy Documents with Analysis, with a Foreword by Robert R. Bowie and John K. Fairbank (jointly with the East Asian Research Center), 1962. Harvard University Press.

In Search of France, by Stanley Hoffmann, Charles P. Kindleberger, Laurence Wylie, Jesse R. Pitts, Jean-Baptiste Duroselle, and François Goguel, 1963. Harvard University Press.

Somali Nationalism, by Saadia Touval, 1963. Harvard University Press.

The Dilemma of Mexico's Development, by Raymond Vernon, 1963. Harvard University Press.

Limited War in the Nuclear Age, by Morton H. Halperin, 1963. John Wiley & Sons.

The Arms Debate, by Robert A. Levine, 1963. Harvard University Press.

Africans on the Land, by Montague Yudelman, 1964. Harvard University Press.

Counterinsurgency Warfare, by David Galula, 1964. Frederick A. Praeger, Inc.

People and Policy in the Middle East, by Max Weston Thornburg, 1964. W. W. Norton & Co.

Shaping the Future, by Robert R. Bowie, 1964. Columbia University Press.

Foreign Aid and Foreign Policy, by Edward S. Mason (jointly with the Council on Foreign Relations), 1964. Harper & Row.

Public Policy and Private Enterprise in Mexico, by M. S. Wionczek, D. H. Shelton, C. P. Blair, and R. Izquierdo, ed. Raymond Vernon, 1964. Harvard University Press.

How Nations Negotiate, by Fred C. Iklé, 1964. Harper & Row.

China and the Bomb, by Morton H. Halperin (jointly with the East Asian Research Center), 1965. Frederick A. Praeger, Inc.

Democracy in Germany, by Fritz Erler (Jodidi Lectures), 1965. Harvard University Press.

The Troubled Partnership, by Henry A. Kissinger (jointly with the Council on Foreign Relations), 1965. McGraw-Hill Book Co.

The Rise of Nationalism in Central Africa, by Robert I. Rotberg, 1965. Harvard University Press.

Pan-Africanism and East African Integration, by Joseph S. Nye, Jr., 1965. Harvard University Press.

Communist China and Arms Control, by Morton H. Halperin and Dwight H. Perkins (jointly with the East Asian Research Center), 1965. Frederick A. Praeger, Inc.

Problems of National Strategy, ed. Henry Kissinger, 1965. Frederick A. Praeger, Inc.

Deterrence before Hiroshima: The Airpower Background of Modern Strategy, by George H. Quester, 1966. John Wiley & Sons.

Containing the Arms Race, by Jeremy J. Stone, 1966. M.I.T. Press.

Germany and the Atlantic Alliance: The Interaction of Strategy and Politics, by James L. Richardson, 1966. Harvard University Press.

Arms and Influence, by Thomas C. Schelling, 1966. Yale University Press.

Export Instability and Economic Development, by Alasdair MacBean, 1966. Harvard University Press.

Political Change in a West African State, by Martin L. Kilson, 1966. Harvard University Press.

Planning without Facts, by Wolfgang Stolper, 1966. Harvard University Press.

OCCASIONAL PAPERS, PUBLISHED BY THE CENTER FOR INTERNATIONAL AFFAIRS

1. *A Plan for Planning: The Need for a Better Method of Assisting Underdeveloped Countries on Their Economic Policies,* by Gustav F. Papanek, 1961.
2. *The Flow of Resources from Rich to Poor,* by Alan D. Neale, 1961.
3. *Limited War: An Essay on the Development of the Theory and an Annotated Bibliography,* by Morton H. Halperin, 1962.
4. *Reflections on the Failure of the First West Indian Federation,* by Hugh W. Springer, 1962.
5. *On the Interaction of Opposing Forces under Possible Arms Agreements,* by Glenn A. Kent, 1963.
6. *Europe's Northern Cap and the Soviet Union,* by Nils Örvik, 1963.
7. *Civil Administration in the Punjab: An Analysis of a State Government in India,* by E. N. Mangat Rai, 1963.
8. *On the Appropriate Size of a Development Program,* by Edward S. Mason, 1964.
9. *Self-Determination Revisited in the Era of Decolonization,* by Rupert Emerson, 1964.
10. *The Planning and Execution of Economic Development in Southeast Asia,* by Clair Wilcox, 1965.
11. *Pan-Africanism in Action,* by Albert Tevoedjre, 1965.
12. *Is China Turning In?* by Morton H. Halperin, 1965.
13. *Economic Development in India and Pakistan,* by Edward S. Mason, 1966.